Hellenic Studies 5

PRIENE
Second Edition

Kindly supported by
VIVODI TELECOM
http://www.vivodi.gr/

PRIENE

Second Edition

Published by

Foundation of the Hellenic World
Athens, Greece

and

Center for Hellenic Studies
Trustees for Harvard University
Washington, D.C.

Distributed by Harvard University Press,
Cambridge, Massachusetts, and London, England

2005

PRIENE: Second Edition

Copyright © Foundation of the Hellenic World.
All rights reserved.
Published by the Foundation of the Hellenic World, Athens, Greece
and the Center for Hellenic Studies, Trustees for Harvard University, Washington, D.C.
Distributed by Harvard University Press, Cambridge, Massachusetts, and London, England

Printed in Athens, Greece.

Technical Production: FHW Publications Department
First Edition Coordinator: Yiannis G. Houtopoulos
Second Edition: Kleopatra Ferla (FHW), Maria-Zoie Lafis (CHS)
Publishing Editor: Athanasios Konstantopoulos
Publishing Consultant for Architectural Drawings: Maria Lafazani (FHW)
Electronic Design: FHW Publications Department, Athanasios Konstantopoulos, Head of the Department, Asimina Pothou, Katerina Mavroidi
Translation: Foteini Stefani
English Text Editing: George Hatziandreou, George Sioris, Alexander Hollman, Elizabeth Stone

CHS Editorial Board: Gregory Nagy (Chair), Christopher Blackwell, Christopher Dadian, Casey Dué, Mary Ebbott, Anne Mahoney, Leonard Muellner, Ross Scaife

Phototypesetting – Production: BIBLIOSYNERGATIKI
Pictorial Sources: Bildarchiv Preussischer Kulturbesitz, Berlin
Published photographs from the following publications were photographed by the Photographic Archives of the American School of Classical Studies, Athens Greece:
Wiegand, Th., Priene – Ergebnisse der Ausgrabungen und Untersuchungen in den Jahren 1895-98 I & II, Koenigliche Museen zu Berlin, 1904, Text & Tafeln.
Schede, M., Die Ruinen von Priene, Archaeologisches Institut des Deutschen Reiches – Abteilung Istanbul, Berlin 1934.
Raeder, J., Priene – Funde einer griechischen Stadt im Berliner Antikenmuseum, Staatliche: Museen/Preussischer Kulturbesitz Berlin: Gebr Mann Verlag, 1984.
FHW wishes to thank the Deutsches Archaeologisches Institut, Abteilung Istanbul and the Society of Antiquaries of London for their kind permission to publish the photographs.

ISBN: 0-674-01272-0

FOUNDATION OF THE HELLENIC WORLD
38 POULOPOULOU St., ATHENS 118 51
Tel: +3021 254 03800 Fax: +3021 254 03838
http://www.fhw.gr/   E-mail: info@fhw.gr

First Edition (published by FHW)

Author, Academic Editor, Project Coordinator, First Edition Editor: Nikos A. Dontas, Architect

Academic Consultants: Kleopatra Ferla, Historian
　　　　　　　　　　　Ioannis Svolos, Architect

Research – Documentation: Dimitra Agoropoulou, Architect
　　　　　　　　　　　　　Athanasia Sofou, Historian-Archaeologist

Contributors: Ioannis Svolos, Wolfram Hoepfner (University of Berlin),
　　　　　　　Ioannis Arvanitis, Eleni Zymi

Architectural Drawings: Dimitra Agoropoulou, Sophia Mikropoulou, Architects
　　　　　　　　　　　　Christina Yannou, Maria Mazaraki, Draughtspersons

Perspective Drawings of Theatre, Processing of Architectural Drawings: Maria Mazaraki, Draughtsperson

Graphics Processing: Irene Koïmtzi, Graphic Artist

Digital Ground Model: George Sidiropoulos, Planner-Surveyor
　　　　　　　　　　　Nikos Mostratos, Technologist-Topographer Engineer

Photography of Priene's Archaeological Site: Ioannis Svolos, Giorgos Pilichos (external collaborator)

Art Director – Cover Design: Fotini Georgakopoulou, Architect

Second Edition (co-published by FHW and CHS)

Second Edition Editor: Kleopatra Ferla, Historian, *FHW*

Academic Consultant: Alexander Hollmann, Classical Philologist

Contributors: Fritz Graf, University of Ohio
　　　　　　　Athanasios Sideris, *FHW*

It was the summer of 1991. As Vice-President of the Council of Europe and Head of the Greek Delegation I was travelling from the coast to the interior of Asia Minor, when suddenly, out of the pine trees, an ancient city and the outlines of a huge, ruined temple came into view. But there were no relevant map references for this city and no mentions in any guide book, and when I subsequently looked into the matter in order to discover the name of this forgotten city, I was astounded: it was called Euromos.

This incident was the catalyst in setting off the sequence of actions that would realise an old dream of mine, the creation of the Foundation of the Hellenic World, an organisation which preserves and disseminates information on the history of Hellenism wherever and whenever this has manifested itself.

One of the Foundation's main programmes involves setting up a Data Bank, whose aim is to gather information on the history and architecture of Hellenic buildings and settlements and then record its findings electronically. For the time being, the programme focuses on Asia Minor.

The present book, which I am delighted to present, is the outcome of such work. Since it is the first time that an architectural study of an Asia Minor city has been published in Greek, I believe that Priene will fill a gap in our knowledge of the ancient world and that, in its broad treatment of the subject, its systematic presentation of architectural data and its use of modern electronic technology, it will be accessible to both general reader and researcher alike.

Priene is special in yet another way: it is the Foundation's first, truly in-house publication: the text, drawings, photographs, processing and art direction have all been generated by and produced from our own, internal resources.

We are particularly honoured by the fact that one of the world authorities on Priene, Professor Wolfram Hoepfner, has not only agreed to preface our book but also offered to write an introductory chapter; Professor Hoepfner was also kind enough to include previously unpublished material in his text. Our wish, in publishing the views of this eminent scholar on ancient architecture, is that this book will contribute to an ongoing dialogue and initiate fruitful debates, both through the Foundation's academic journal and through the organisation of international conferences on ancient Priene at our Cultural Centre in Pireos street.

Lazaros Efraimoglou

President of the
Foundation of the Hellenic World

CONTENTS

"Introduction" (Fritz Graf) *13*

"A modern approach to ancient Asia Minor" (I. Svolos) *17*

"Introductory Historical Note" (Dr. K. Ferla) *23*

"Old and New Priene – Pythius and Aristotle"
by Professor W. Hoepfner *29*

1. **INTRODUCTION** *49*
   A Brief History of Excavations
   Topography
   Water supply, Ventilation, Sunlight
   City Planning
   Streets
   Necropoles
   Defense System
   Acropolis "Teloneia"

2. **AGORA** *60*
   General
   Form
   Sacred Stoa
   South Stoa

3. **EKKLESIASTERION or BOULEUTERION** *74*
   The Building
   The Roofing

4. **PRYTANEION** *82*
   Location
   The Building

5. **SANCTUARY OF ATHENA POLIAS** *86*
   Location
   Temple
   Decoration
   Statue of the Goddess
   Colour
   Altar
   Floor
   Propylon
   Stoa
   The Area to the North – "Treasury"
   History of the Discovery of the Temple

6. **ASCLEPIEION or SANCTUARY OF ZEUS** 112
   Problems of Identification
   Location
   Description
   Temple
   Stoas
   "An inscribed anta" (Ioannis Arvanitis)

7. **SANCTUARY OF DEMETER AND KORE** 126
   Location
   Temple
   Bothros
   Houses
   Statues

8. **OTHER SHRINES** 132
   Sacred House
   Shrine of Egyptian Gods
   Shrine of Cybele
   Shrines at the Gates
   Shrine of Telon

9. **THEATRE** 140
   Location
   Historical Data
   Early Hellenistic Period
   Late Hellenistic Period
   Roman Period
   Colour

10. **GYMNASIA** 160
    General Introduction

11. **UPPER GYMNASIUM** 162
    Hellenistic Period
    Roman Period
    Christian Era

12. **LOWER GYMNASIUM** 166
    Propylon
    Exedra
    Palaestra
    Interior Courtyard
    Ephebeum
    Baths

13. STADIUM 176
      Description
      Running Track
      Seating
      Stoa

14. RESIDENTIAL AND COMMERCIAL DWELLINGS 180
      Typical House
      Access
      Spaces of the House, Oikos
      Andron
      Auxiliary Spaces
      Sanitation Facilities
      Upper Storey
      Storerooms
      Shops
      Courtyard
      Late Hellenistic Period
      House No. 33

15. CHRISTIAN BUILDINGS 196
      House No. 24 as Church
      Cathedral
      Single-hall Church
      Theatre Chapel
      Baptistery
      Ecclesiasterion Chapel
      Fortress

16. SCULPTURE – POTTERY (Eleni Zymi) 202

17. APPENDIX I 212
      The Orders of Priene

18. APPENDIX II 214
      Visual Glossary

19. GLOSSARY 217

20. BIBLIOGRAPHY 223

INTRODUCTION
by Prof. Fritz Graf

Priene, the small city on a terrace above the Maeander valley, did not have many claims to fame in antiquity, nor does it today. It was, after all, what one German archaeologist once called a *Kleinstadt*, Smallville, Ionia, possessing neither a far-reaching trade network such as Miletus or Phocaea had, nor an internationally famed sanctuary, such as the Artemision of Ephesus, the oracles of Clarus and Didyma, or the Asclepieum of Pergamum. Strabo, the geographer of the late first century BC, notes only: "From Priene, there comes Bias, one of the Seven Sages." This is all he has to say about the lasting fame of Priene; it is no small claim, since the renown of the Seven Sages stretched from Gaul in the West to Afghanistan (Aï-Khanoum) in the East, but it rests solely on the reputation of one man who did not even leave writings behind. Others, more interested in local history than Strabo, might have added that Alexander the Great sponsored Priene's main city temple, the temple of Athena, but only after the people of Ephesus had declined such a sponsorship with the diplomatic argument that "a god does not sponsor the temple of another god"; little Priene could not afford such pride. The neighbors of Priene also would have known that the city territory housed the Panionion, the federal sanctuary of the twelve Ionian cities—but presumably only because a city as small as Priene did not threaten to use this honor to further its own political claims, as larger cities in the federation were liable to do. It is the same reason that made Geneva and Vienna the favored cities for offices of the United Nations.

In modern times, Priene has not fared much better. Between 1895 and 1898, it was excavated by the German Archaeological Institute under the guidance first of Carl Humann, then of Theodor Wiegand. The excavations did not just explore some parts of the ancient city, they brought the entire city to light, its houses and streets, its temples and its city wall: suddenly, an entire Greek city became accessible to the modern gaze. Early scholars, especially in Germany, enthusiastically viewed Priene as a textbook city, comparable to the Italian cities Pompeii and Herculaneum, frozen in time by the eruption of Vesuvius. But unlike these famous cities, Priene has never entered contemporary consciousness or become part of our collective imagination about life in antiquity. Not that Priene lacks possibilities for such an undertaking. Here too, one can walk through city streets from city gate to city gate, and enter private houses and sanctuaries. As with the Campanian cities, there is the backdrop of a gorgeous landscape. Standing on the terrace of Athena's temple, the visitor looks over the wide Maeander valley that still preserves the shape of the vast bay it once was; and when the cotton is ripe on the fields and a breeze ripples its leaves and fruit, one still sees the waves ripple over its surface, and can image the harbor of Myus, far away on the southern side of the valley. Beyond the sweeping plain, there rise the hills and mountains of Caria, and far out to the west there is the Mediterranean, whose coastline now is miles further west than it used to be when Priene was founded. If the visitor then turns his gaze to the north, he looks at the towering cliffs that overlook the city and, at their foot, the small sanctuary of Demeter, whose excavations opened up new insights on the cult of this goddess, and that still fascinates historians of religion.

There is no easy explanation for the oblivion into which this beautiful excavation site has sunk, at least for a wider public of lovers of antiquity; scholars always were aware of the uniqueness of Priene and the possibilities it offered for insights into Greek city planning and city life in all its forms. Priene certainly did not meet the violent end of Pompeii that gripped the imagination of countless generations, from the time when the younger Pliny described his and his uncle's experiences on that fateful day in August 79 AD. Nor does it offer the religious fascination of early Christian sites, such as Ephesus or Pergamum: Paul never preached in Priene. That there is no easy harbor for cruise ships nearby, as in the case of Ephesus, is more a symptom than a cause.

Whatever the causes for this oblivion, the present book might help overcome it. It resurrects Priene in all its charm and glory; it lets us once again walk its streets and admire its buildings in the form they once had (or the form we can safely reconstruct, at least).

The scholar of antiquity thus acquires information and insights that not even the reading of the meticulous excavation reports could always provide. Admirers of ancient life are confronted with a splendid reanimation of how the city "once could have been," and gain an incentive to travel to Ionia themselves and let their own gaze roam through the narrow streets and sweep over the wide valley of the Maeander.

A MODERN APPROACH TO ANCIENT ASIA MINOR
by Ioannis Svolos

Over the last decade several Greek-language publications on Asia Minor have appeared in bookshop windows. This has meant that, for the first time in years, the Greek public has had access to a world that, for many centuries, had been one of the major cradles of Hellenism. For most Greeks born after the war this sudden influx of images not only claimed their attention but also provided new stimuli for their visual memory and changed the balance of their awareness in a variety of ways.

How and why this happened is simple and evident but by no means accidental. These books, focusing first on the inexhaustible and imposing Greek antiquities of Asia Minor and secondly, but no less importantly, on the recent "lost homeland of Asia Minor", have provided responses to the demand of post-war Greeks for a broader geographical, historical, and perhaps political, self-awareness at a critical moment. Certainly, the timing was not incidental: a post-war broadening of the horizons of modern Hellenism, progress in the science of history, the country's improved position on the international scene, the rejection on the part of the Greek people of various misguided assumptions about their history – all these factors prepared the Greeks for a more serious approach to the subject.

At the same time, the opening up of archaeology to a wider public – in itself part of the quickening pace of cultural achievement made possible by rising prosperity – turned the attention of the public towards antiquity. There can be no doubt, however, that the healing of wounds in the 70-odd years that had elapsed since the Asia Minor Catastrophe was another precondition for this shift in focus. But, notwithstanding, the first attempts at presenting the subject to a wider public appealed to emotional and aesthetic values, projected at best through a gamut of quasi-scientific, empirical observations of travel writers. What was (and still is) lacking, is a truly scientific approach that also embraces the layman within its scope – an approach such as that already available to German, British or French lovers of antiquity interested in learning more about ancient Asia Minor. This book is an attempt to fill this gap by focusing on the ancient city of Priene.

THE CONTRIBUTION OF PRIENE TO OUR PERCEPTION OF THE ANCIENT GREEK WORLD: Ionian Priene, the city-state in Asia Minor, is one of those rare cases in archaeology where a single excavated site provides almost complete information about life in an ancient Greek city. The city was founded in 334 BC after the relocation of an older city (whose site is unknown). In contrast to other cities of the ancient world, where historical evidence has been destroyed by successive disasters or obscured because of historical changes, short-lived Priene presents a relatively integrated picture – most of the ruins date back to the late Classical and Hellenistic period. Although the city declined and was deserted in the late Byzantine period, it was never destroyed completely, unlike Miletus, nor was it ever reconstructed from scratch, unlike Ephesus. Thus, the basic town-planning layout, the main public buildings and its walls – all these belong to a single period of vigour, the 2nd century BC, and provide the researcher with an unusually clear and complete picture. Throughout the eight centuries of its existence Priene changed very little, due to its small size and minor political significance, the high inclination of the ground and the fact that from the beginning it was completely enclosed by walls. Inevitably, some buildings were added, extended or altered in the first one hundred and the last two hundred years of its existence; but the basic structure remained the same, preserving the order of the original planning.

German archaeologists carried out excavations, discovered all the main public buildings, and revealed its road and town-planning system. They were also able to excavate and study an impressively large number of houses.

To the archaeologist-historian Priene is a model of the ancient Asia Minor city in which philosophical and political thinking, fully developed during the Classical period, was applied to the physical environment and led to the construction of a coherent and balanced entity.

To the architect, whether student or professional, the study of the monuments of Priene provides a view of a complete and homogeneous residential entity that includes typical specimens of a great variety of buildings. The Ekklesiasterion is one of the most famous examples of its kind; the Temple of Athena Polias is considered a milestone in the development and standardisation of Asia Minor architecture, and its treatment in early archeological publications has greatly enriched our vocabulary concerning the morphology of Neoclassical architecture.

Ancient Priene is still being studied, since only one third of the city has been excavated so far. For various reasons and with few exceptions (e.g., the study of the Ekklesiasterion), published studies on Priene are elementary and incomplete. This is due to the fact that the main excavations of the city took place many years ago, using methods that have little to do with modern archaeological research. It is therefore possible that modern excavations may reveal unexpected information that radically change our current views about the city. This book focuses mainly on the peak of the city's development based on the information collected to this day.

THE CONTRIBUTION OF THIS BOOK: Until quite recently, and for various reasons, financial, pedagogical and even political information about the ancient world was accessible only to those specialised in the field. Stored (one could even say imprisoned) in specialised libraries, it remained within reach of the very small group of experts whose academic qualifications enabled them to understand it. However, the situation has changed: more people now have access to higher education and a new conception of education has prevailed more recently, according to which the average person is entitled to knowledge and information. These changes have led to the publication of a significant number of books which present archaeological knowledge to a wide public in a way that is both instructive and scientifically accurate.

This book is based on our present knowledge of antiquity and makes use of modern media in order to present the basic elements of each building in an intelligible and clear way. The text and visual material will help students of archaeology and architecture to overcome the difficulty of studying the basic bibliography, which is in German. Moreover, without compromising its high standards, this book enables the non specialist to grasp the elements of a typical ancient Greek city.

Today Priene is a fascinating, large but unfortunately abandoned archaeological site. Without an "entrance", practically unfenced and unguarded, without any signs, the invaluable architectural material of these magnificent monuments deteriorates on the ground, at the mercy of God and whoever else...

METHODOLOGY: Instead of photographically reproducing the drawings of archaeological plans and restorations, these were copied. The drawing conventions were unified and systematised, and wherever possible, the restorations were completed. In an attempt to summarise their identity and to facilitate comparisons, the architectural plans of each building are followed by a presentation of metrical data and stylistic elements. To these drawings, made by architects-archaeologists of the past, colour has been added to give a more faithful rendering of the appearance of ancient buildings. The architectural plans were designed using Autocad 14 software and were processed with Corel 7. The graphics were processed with Photoshop 4. The 3-D model of the city was designed using the Arc View (3D-Analyst) software.

The representation of the ancient city through drawings is supplemented by photographs of the site in its present condition and by photographs from the time of the German excavations, thus providing a complete picture of Priene in all its phases of development and discovery.

DRAWING CONVENTIONS

- The drawings accompanying the text accurately reproduce the views of early researchers concerning the architectural plan of the monuments. In rare cases, elements from different reconstructions are combined, or additional drawings are included, which had not been shown in the original publications for reasons of economy (e.g., side views).

- In cases where no drawings are shown (e.g. the colonnade in the Sanctuary of Athena Polias) this means that for that particular monument no reconstructions have been published, or that the existing drawings of isolated members are not adequate for its full depiction.

- Due to lack of published drawings or information, the pattern of roofs is depicted in a general and schematic way, without corner or central acroteria. However, detailed graphics do appear in some cases (e.g. the Ekklesiasterion) where these express the view of a specific researcher, formed on the basis of estimates of existing information.

- In cases where a building is surrounded by minor structures, such as altars in agoras and shrines, these structures are only shown in the ground plans. The hypothetical appearance of such a location in antiquity, including the many existing statues and offerings, is depicted in various coloured perspective drawings taken from previous publications.

- The only decorative elements shown are the repeated motifs of mouldings, epistyles and simas, as well as the decoration of the capitals of Ionic antae. Sculptures or deep reliefs depicting scenes (as in the altar of the Temple of Athena Polias) are indicated in an abstract or symbolic way.

- The repeated decorative motifs on the capitals of antae and simas of the buildings were either taken from archaeological publications (e.g. Sacred Colonnade, Temple of Athena Polias) or are drawings based on photographs of the same publications (e.g. antae and horizontal simas of the Temple of Asclepius). In several cases the details of the corners of these motifs are hypothetical, since they have not survived intact.

- Since the present book is intended for a wide public, in some cases drawing conventions are bypassed. In drawings where ground plans, elevations and sections appear together, no reverse projections are shown. On the contrary, all the drawings are shown "flat".

- In the drawings that classify the architectural orders (following the architectural drawings of each monument), the referred dimensions were either taken from existing publications (and therefore refer to measurements of specific elements) or are measurements based on scaled published drawings.

- The colours of architectural elements shown in three-dimensional drawings are either based on the publications or are indicative of and in accordance with what generally applied to ancient buildings.

- The three-dimensional drawings of the Theatre, as well as the digital model of the entire city, have been created by FHW.

INTRODUCTORY HISTORICAL NOTE
by Kleopatra Ferla

To trace the history of ancient colonial cities is no easy task. Written references are fragmentary and oblique: they generally exist only when the colony's affairs touch upon the history of the metropolis, and when the colonies do not play a significant part of their own in historical developments, they are insignificant. To reconstruct such a city's history becomes even more difficult when archaeological data is not available and when other types of relevant information make no clear distinction between the real and the mythical. The city of Priene is a case in point.

Priene was an ancient city, built on the slope of Mt Mycale, near the Gulf of Latmia. It seems to have been a colony of Thebes, its founders being Aepytus, son of Neleus, and Philotas of Thebes.[1] A member of the Panionion,[2] the city reached its prime in the 6th century BC, when Bias of Priene, one of the Seven Wise Men of antiquity, appears to have been the civic leader.

In the 7th century, King Gyges of Lydia opened hostilities against the Greek cities of Asia Minor, but soon he had to face a newcoming enemy, the Cimmerians. The ensuing battles between Cimmerians, Lydians and Hellenes lasted until 630 BC, when the Cimmerians suffered repeated defeats by the Lydians and Assyrians. With the Cimmerians out of the way, the Lydians renewed their attacks against the Greek cities. Ardys, heir to Gyges, captured Priene and attacked Miletus. Alyattes, successor to Sadyattes and son of Ardys, unsuccessfully besieged Priene. The city's defence was organised by Bias.

In later years its citizens became involved in a war with the Samians, who suffered a major defeat and, after six years of peace, decided to form an alliance with Miletus against Priene. This time the Samians were successful, but Bias, ambassador of Priene to the peace conference, achieved favourable terms for his city.

1. Strabo 14, 1, 3 and Aelian Varia Historia 8, 5, 13-16: Pausanias 7, 3, 2: Diogenes Laertius Bias, Eustathius 823, 11. The city is referred to as Kadme in Strabo (14, 1, 12) and in Eustathius.

2. Panionion: league of several Ionian cities probably formed in 700 BC. It was named after the temple of Poseidon Helikonion in Mycale, where the representatives of 12 Ionian cities initially gathered to celebrate the festival of Panionia. It developed into a political league, with its primary aim being decision-making in case of war (e.g. the Ionian Revolt against the Persians).

In 560 BC Croesus became king of Lydia and forced all Aeolic and Ionian cities, except Miletus, to pay tribute. At this time Cyrus II became king of Persia, later defeating Croesus and succeeding him as suzerain of the Greek cities. Cyrus' commander, Mazares, campaigned against Pactyes of Lydia, who besieged Sardis with the help of the Hellenes of the coastal cities. On learning that Mazares was approaching, Pactyes abandoned the siege and left for the Aeolic city of Cyme, while Mazares, wishing to punish Pactyes' allies, captured Priene, enslaved[3] some of its inhabitants (545/544 BC) and then sacked other cities. At this point Bias, seeing no chance of freedom, during a conference of the Ionian League of Panionion suggested that all Ionic cities should colonise Sardinia. But his views were not accepted[4].

Already at this point Priene's history presents problems. We know nothing of the city after the enslavement of its inhabitants. In the Ionian assembly of the spring of 499 BC, Aristagoras, the tyrant of Miletus, announced his plans for a revolt against the Persians, which were accepted with great enthusiasm. The crucial moment of the revolt was the naval battle of Lade (494 BC), an island off the coast of Miletus, in which the Persians defeated the Ionians. Priene's contribution of twelve ships allows us to estimate the city's free population in around 500 BC at about 10,000. While we know that the Persians destroyed Miletus and chased its surviving inhabitants inland, there is no reference to the fate of Priene. The fact that the ancient sources make no mention of Priene may mean that the city did not play a leading role in developments after the Persian wars. Priene appears in the member lists of the Delian League[5] with a tax contribution of one talent.

In 441/440 BC Priene and its surrounding region was a *casus belli* for Samos and Miletus, though the causes are not known. After seeking help from Athens, Miletus won; but we do not know what happened to Priene.

Xenophon (*Hellenica*, 3, 2, 17) refers to Priene in his account of events in 397 and 392 BC, when the soldiers of Priene and the other Ionian cities dropped their weapons and

3. Herodotus 1, 161, Polybius 33, 6. Polybius makes a comparison between Myus and Priene: despite the catastrophe, the inhabitants of Priene remained in their city, unlike the inhabitants of Myus, who took refuge in Miletus.

4. Herodotus 1, 170.

5. The Delian Confederacy/League was founded in 478/7 BC. Representatives of Athenians and their Ionian allies met on Delos with the intention of taking revenge for their sufferings on the barbarians by sacking the lands of the Persian king. Later on the Athenians used the League as a means of establishing their dominance over Greece and Asia Minor.

refused to follow the Lacedaemonians under Derkylides against the Persian satrap Pharnabazos. We do not know why Xenophon singled out Priene from the other Ionian cities for special mention[6]. Another contemporary reference mentions Priene as being at the mouth of the River Maeander[7]. From this time onwards until 330 BC there are only a few problematic references to Priene[8].

When combined with the lack of archaeological data, this evidence does not give a trustworthy account of the history of the old city. Various theories have been put forward concerning the early history and the relocation of the city, although none has been generally accepted[9], since late 19th century excavations have brought to light only one third of the city from the late Classical and Hellenistic periods. Firm conclusions cannot therefore be reached about this period, and it is impossible to reach any conclusions at all on the old city.

Under discussion here is the new city of Priene, whose ruins this volume presents. There is no consensus among the academic community about whether or not it was refounded in the same location as its predecessor, or about the circumstances that led to the refounding. Even the date of foundation is in question[10], and it is an undeniable fact that the ancient sources available do not mention the relocation of Priene – on the contrary, Polybius stresses that the inhabitants of Priene, in contrast to the people of Myus, were proud that there had been no destruction which would have forced them to abandon their city. Nor is there reference to any relocation of the city due to the alluvial deposits of the River Maeander, as is the case with other cities. In the absence of other data, the interpretation of inscriptions and the debate on the edict of Alexander the Great continues[11]. However, it is certain that the Priene whose monuments are presented in this volume was built around 370 BC.

The dating of monuments and other archaeological findings still remains insecure. Since the excavations were limited in scope and conducted at a time when modern means of evaluating archaeological data were not available, it is difficult to draw safe conclusions.

6. Xenophon mentions Achilleion separately, probably the name of a port which has not yet been located.

7. Oxyrhynchus 12, 3. (396/5 BC).

8. Demand, N. H., The Relocation of Priene Reconsidered, Phoenix 40, 1986, pp. 35-44.

9. See among others, Regling, K. L., Die Münzen von Priene, Berlin: H. Schoetz & Co., 1927; Demand, N.H. op. cit.

10. These views are presented by Demand, N.H. op.cit. For the period after Alexander, see Lund, H. S., Lysimachus: A Study in Early Hellenistic Kingship, London/New York 1992, Krischen, F., Die griechische Stadt, Berlin 1938, Crowther, C. V., Priene 8 and the History of Priene in the Early Hellenistic Period, Chiron 26, 1996, pp. 195-239.

11. Cf. below, Hoepfner's article, pp. 28ff.

Dating the Temple of Athena, and therefore the city itself, is a typical example. Re-examining the inscriptions has led to new assessments and new dates have been suggested[12].

The planning of Priene is also a matter of controversy: everyone agrees that the Hippodamian system was adopted, but there are many contradictory views on the identity of the planner. According to some scholars this was Pythius, whom Vitruvius, the 1st century BC Roman historian, credited with writing a study on architecture as well as planning the Mausoleum of Halicarnassus. Since there are similarities between the Mausoleum and the Temple of Athena in Priene, many scholars, but by no means all, accept the view that Pythius was the temple's architect, but there is disagreement about whether the planner of the city was the same person[13].

Historical references to the period after Alexander are fragmentary. Priene was subject to the border changes of the Hellenistic states. It came successively under the rule of Demetrius Poliorcetes, Lysimachus and the Seleucid and Ptolemaic kingdoms. There were many frontier disputes in the region between Priene and Samos. In 277 BC the area around Priene was destroyed by the Celts. In 155 BC the city confronted Ariarathes, king of Cappadocia, and Attalus II, king of Pergamum, and suffered serious damage, including to the Temple of Athena. At the beginning of the 2nd century BC it came under the influence of Rome and after 129 BC it belonged to the newly established Roman Province of Asia.

The Mithridatic Wars of the first half of the 1st century BC dealt a severe blow to Priene's economy. The Maeander's alluvial deposits meant that Priene was no longer a coastal city. In the years to come the city shrank, the Temple of Athena and the Gymnasia were abandoned and their building materials were used for the construction of a basilica in the centre, as well as for residences on the site of the old Gymnasium. Very little is known of the time between the 6th and 10th centuries[14]: because of Arab raids in the region, the ancient city was abandoned around the end of the 7th century.

---

12. Among others see: Berchem, D. van, *Alexandre et la restauration de Priène*, MusHelv 70, 1972, pp. 198-205; Botermann, H., *Wer baute das Neue Priene? Zur Interpretation der Inschriften von Priene Nr. 1 und 156*, Hermes 122, 1994, pp. 162-187; Carter, J. C., *The Sculpture of the Sanctuary of Athena Polias at Priene*, London 1983; Hornblower, S., *Mausolus*, Oxford: Clarendon Press/ New York, 1982; Sherwin-White, S. M., *Ancient Archives: the Edict of Alexander to Priene: a Reappraisal*, JHS 105, 1985, pp. 69-89.

13. Apart from the above-mentioned, see Carter, J. C., *Pytheos*, in Akten des 13. Internationalen Kongresses für Klassische Archäologie, Berlin 1990, pp. 129-136.

14. An outline bibliography for the Byzantine period would include: Brandes, W., *Die Städte Kleinasiens im 7. und 8. Jahrhundert*, Amsterdam 1989; Cheynet, J.-C., *Pouvoir et contestations à Byzance (963-1210)*, (Byzantina Sorbonensia 9, Paris, 1990); Jones, A., *The Cities of the Eastern Roman Provinces*, Ahrweiler, H., "L' histoire et la géographie de la region de Smyrne entre les deux occupations torques (1081-1317) particulièrement aux XIIIe siècle" TM 1 (1965), 1-204; Foss, C., "Archaeology and the 'Twenty Cities' of Byzantine Asia" AJA 81, (1977), 469-86; Müller-Wiener, W., *Mittelalterliche Befestigungen im südlichen Ionien*, IM 11, (1961), 46-56; Orgels, P., *Sabas Asidenos*, Byzantion 10, 1935, pp. 67-80

But from the middle of the 10th century Priene flourished again. It is reported as one of the twenty most important cities of the Thracian theme[15]. Between the 11th and 13th centuries Priene became known as Sampson and it was the centre of important imperial episkepsis[16] in the Maeander valley. Its significance is proved by the fact that after 1204, when the crusaders occupied Constantinople, the Latins claimed Priene. It became the "capital" of the short-lived state of Sabbas Asidenos (1204-08) and was finally incorporated into the Nicaean empire. In the second half of the 13th century the Seljuk Turks threatened to capture the Sampson area; and despite the ambitious, and temporarily successful, efforts of Ioannis Palaeologos (1264) and Alexios Philanthropinos (1295) the city came under the control of the Turks. From these time onwards and until 1673 when English tradesmen from Smyrna discovered Priene, the lack of literally and archaeological testimonies do not allow us to speculate about his history. By the end of 18th and during the 19th century the Temple of Athena has been excavated by the "Society of Dillenti". In 1898 systematic excavations have been directed by K. Humann and later by Th. Wiegand.

There is at present an ongoing debate about the history of Priene and other Asia Minor cities and new research is being conducted. On the basis of the information presented in this brief historical note, it should be evident that, for the time being at least, our certainties are few in comparison with the host of questions to which the academic community is expected to provide answers.

15. Theme: a Byzantine province.
16. Episkepsis: a fiscal unit.

OLD AND NEW PRIENE – PYTHIUS AND ARISTOTLE
by Prof. Wolfram Hoepfner

Where was the early city of Priene located? The question has remained unanswered for the last hundred years. Recently it has been suggested that the archaic city of Priene lay under the ruins of the late Classical/Hellenistic city[1]. The ruins of the older city had to be removed, according to this view, so as to leave the free space required for the rebuilding of Priene in the mid-4th century BC, which explains why no findings or walls belonging to the earlier city were discovered during the excavations. On the other hand, no traces of the walls of the older city or of an archaic necropolis have been found. Moreover, there is no written reference to the earlier period on findings of the new settlement, nor are there any portable objects, such as vases or tools, which could have been preserved and used by the inhabitants in their new houses. Thus, it is safe to conclude that the earlier city was located at a different site; besides, written sources provide indications about the location of the earlier settlement.

In the record of his travels, written after the mid-4th century BC, Scylax mentions the following:

```
"The city of Priene has two harbours, one of which is closed".
```

Later he refers to the nearby River Maeander. Up to now, it was believed that the text referred to the new Priene which was a city-state with two harbours. It is, however, more likely that the word "harbours" did not refer to coastal cities but to natural bays. In such a case the city referred to could not have been the older city of Priene, as already pointed out by the scholar Hiller von Gaertringen[2], a suggestion mostly ignored by other scholars. Given that Scylax does not refer to the foundation of any city by Alexander, not even Alexandria, the text must have been written before 336 BC[3] and, on the basis of other evidence, after 370 BC. Thus, it is almost certain that the city referred to is Priene.

Therefore, the most probable assumption is that "Naulochus", Priene's only sea port, is the same city as the older Priene which, after the foundation of the new Priene, was renamed "Naulochus" or "Naulochon" after an eponymous hero. In fact, the place-name Naulochus does not appear in the older sources[4].

---

1. Schipporeit, S. Th., *Das alte und das neue Priene*, Ist. Mitt. 48, 1998, p. 193 ff. After Demand, N., *The Relocation of Priene Reconsidered*, in Phoenix 40, 1986, pp. 35-44.

2. Hiller von Gaertringen, F., *Inschriften von Priene*, 1906, 4 zu Inschrift No. 1.

3. RE, 2nd series, 3,2, 1927, Skylax, p. 64 ff. (von Arnim).

4. RE, 16,2 (1935) 1669, "Naulochon", No. 2 (Ruge. W).

On one of the oldest inscriptions of Priene, on the South Gate of the new city's walls, there is a reference to Demeter and Kore but also to the Hero Naulochus, who must have been honoured in the new city as well[5].

Therefore, the archaic city of Priene was not located, as has often been supposed, in the valley of the River Maeander[6] or under the new city, but was built on the coast. The fact that Scylax mentions the existence of two harbours leads to the hypothesis that the city was built on a peninsula with a topography similar to that of Miletus, with a harbour on either side. Today the coastline has receded considerably to the west as the deposits of Maeander transform the landscape continuously. Mount Mykale rises steeply above the river and therefore it is easy to determine accurately the position of the older coastline. However, the exact location of the peninsula mentioned above cannot be easily determined.

According to Strabo (12, 8, 17) Priene was at a distance of 40 stadia (approximately 5.5 kilometres) from the sea. Thus, Wiegand's hypothesis that Naulochus (which he did not associate with old Priene) was at least 40 stadia away from the new Priene is correct. A precondition for the foundation of the earlier city must have been the existence of a passage leading over the mountains to the famous Sanctuary of Panionion but also to other sites on the other side of the mountain ridge. The valley of Maeander was probably easily reached via the track leading to older Priene. In the area of Priene there are two tracks leading over the mountain. The western one is close to the area that belonged to Samos, and the second one is 5 kilometres to the east and leads to the gorge of Akbogaz. In this area Wiegand did make archaeological discoveries, which led him to the assumption that the settlement was Naulochus. Only a new excavation can show whether the older Priene is situated 5 more kilometres towards the west.

THE FOUNDATION OF NEW PRIENE: It is known that an edict regarding the foundation of the new city of Priene was issued by Alexander the Great. A very interesting inscription of 334 BC[7], which has only been partially recovered, mentions that the inhabitants of Naulochus, as long as they are citizens of Priene, should be independent and free. The plots of land and houses in the city and the countryside should be theirs, too, as in the case of the inhabitants of Priene itself. "The rest should return to the villages, where the land ownership is under the control of the king" (according to Wilamowitz)[8].

---

5. Hiller von Gaertringen, F., Inschriften XIII, 139 No. 196. A dedication to Naulochus is also known from Rhodes. Kontorini, V., Inscriptions inedites relatives a l' Histoire et aux cultes de Rhodes au IIe et au Ier av. J. C., Rhodiaca I, 1983, p. 65 ff. I would like to thank Ms Tassia Dreliozou for this remark.

6. Thus it is unfortunately quoted in Hoepfner, W. – Schwandner, E. L., Haus und Stadt im klassischen Griechenland, 2nd ed., 1994, p. 189.

7. Hiller von Gaertringen, F., op. cit., No. 1.

8. Translated and supplemented by Hiller von Gaertringen, F., op. cit., p. 4. Other supplements in Heisserer, A. J., Alexander the Great and the Greeks. The epigraphic evidence, 1980, p. 145 ff. and Sherwin-White, S. M, Ancient archives: The edict of Alexander to Priene, a Reappraisal 81. In this excerpt emphasis is (wrongly) put on royal land: "Since I decide that the villages (komae) of Myrseloi and Peidieoi and the land are mine and those inhabiting these villages have to pay taxes, the inhabitants of Priene are no longer bound by 'pension'..."

Various views have been expressed concerning this piece of evidence[9]. However, one can grasp its full meaning by studying the coins minted in Naulochus in 350 BC, which prove the independence of the city[10]. This was probably merely the result of the departure of the inhabitants of Priene for the new city. Foreigners were apparently a majority in Naulochus and managed, through some kind of revolution, to become independent from the city-state of Priene. Thus, they became citizens of the small city-state of Naulochus with full rights and were able to claim ownership of land and residences, while the old inhabitants of Priene lost their property to the new owners. This is the only explanation for the independence of Priene[11]. It also explains the earlier relationships that were restored by Alexander the Great.

The rights of foreigners in cities were clearly defined: even if they had been residents of a city for many years, foreigners, with few exceptions, could not acquire citizenship. They had to pay rent and never acquired the right of owning land or property. Most metics were merchants, many of them trading in products of their native land. Some of them were craftsmen or artists.

Apparently the wealthy foreigners living in old Priene were numerous enough to form an influential group making considerable claims. The citizens of Priene could not deprive foreigners of the right of ownership. Such an action would be at least against moral standards. Conflicts between different groups were very frequent in cities of the Hellenistic period. The citizens' rights were under firm control in cities of the classical era, since they were closely related to the identity of the city-state itself. In cities with a high percentage of foreigners it is possible that problems arose. Nevertheless, the specific cases that can be mentioned are few (e.g. the cases of Colophon and Notios)[12]. Thus, the case of old Priene becomes even more significant.

The arrival of Alexander the Great must have been like a God-sent gift to the first inhabitants of Priene. Busy as they were with the construction of the new city they could not claim their rights concerning ownership in the older city.

9. Berchem, D. van, Alexandre et la restauration de Priène, in Museum Helveticum 27, 1970, pp. 198-205, considered it a "curieuse condition", the fact that the inhabitants of Priene probably possessed a second house in Naulochus, "à laquelle ne consent toutefois aucun des commentateurs". The existence of a second house is easily explained if Naulochus is identified as old Priene.

10. Hiller von Gaertringen, F., op. cit., p. 4. Wiegand, Th. – Schrader, H., Priene. Ergebnisse der Ausgrabungen und Untersuchungen in den Jahren 1895-1898, 1904, p. 16.

11. Gehrke, H. J., Stasis. Untersuchungen zu den inneren Kriegen in den griechischen Staaten des 5. und 4. Jhs v. Chr., 1985, p. 133, supports the self-rule of the inhabitants of Priene and their independence from the Persians.

12. Osthues, E. W., in Hoepfner, W., Geschichte des Wohnens I, 1999, p. 281 ff. Following the expansion of the original settlement, Notios was renamed "Colophon-on-Sea".

The view that Alexander the Great himself was the founder of Priene has often been expressed. The inscription on the pronaos of the temple of Athena Polias seems to confirm this[13]:

" King Alexander dedicated this temple to Athena Polias" .

©DAI Istanbul

This is one of the oldest inscriptions in Priene and, like the edict found exactly below it, denotes the king's involvement in the city. According to this view, if Alexander financed the construction of the temple, then it undoubtedly started to be built during his rule. And since the sanctuary was probably one of the city's first buildings, the city itself must have been founded during the same period. Nevertheless, Hiller von Gaertringen interpreted the inscription in a different way: he concluded that Alexander "undertook the expenses of part of the temple, which had already been completed". Indeed, both the pronaos and the cella of the building must have already been constructed, since the inscription is engraved using symbols of the alphabet that evolved around 334 BC. Therefore the construction of the sanctuary must have begun at least 10 years earlier, which is in agreement with what was mentioned above about the changes in old Priene-Naulochus in the middle of the century.

The refounding of a city was quite common in those days. In northwestern Greece many cities evolved out of earlier settlements. Such cases also include the sizable cities of Messene and Megalopolis in the Peloponnese, as well as some important cities of the southeastern Aegean Sea. Rhodes, founded in 408 BC, with five harbours and a dense road network, soon became a dominant economic power. The development of the newly founded cities of Cnidus, Cos and Halicarnassus was similar. These large cities transformed the area into a new and important economic centre, which could also include Ionia.

However, new Priene does not belong to this group of new cities founded for economic reasons. The area enclosed by the walls of new Priene is not very large. Besides, the natural boundaries of the city did not allow it to expand. It is not likely that the new city was built on the ruins of the old one due to lack of space. Neither can it be assumed that the new city was founded in order to improve living conditions, since the houses in new Priene are very modest and access to the

13. No. 156 in Hiller von Gaertringen, F., op. cit.

city was particularly difficult, since carriages were excluded from its streets, which have many steps because of the sloping ground.

Therefore, nothing confirms the hypothesis that social upheavals in the old coastal city were the reason for the foundation of a new one in the hinterland. Naturally the citizens of Priene wished to preserve their properties in the coastal city.

Obviously the new city was not built overnight but took several decades and required great amounts of money and human labour. For this reason, various patrons or sponsors of the city have been suggested by archaeologists, including the city of Athens, Alexander the Great, and Artemisia, Queen of Caria and widow of Mausolus. These assumptions, however, are totally unfounded. The new cities of Rhodes, Cnidus and Cos were built and sponsored by their own inhabitants. Moreover, it is known that in Priene the completion of the temple of Athena Polias took another 200 years, despite Alexander's donations. Other parts of the city were never completed due to economic reasons[14].

It is possible, on the other hand, that Artemisia, who had employed the famous architect and sculptor Pythius for the construction of the Mausoleum, released him from that obligation so that he could work on the building of new Priene. She was certainly a benefactress of the city in some way, because the head of one of her statues has been found in the sanctuary of Demeter.

THE INTEGRATED WORK OF ART BY PYTHIUS: Pythius, one of the old architects ("de veteribus architectis") according to Vitruvius (8, 4), designed the temple of Athena exceptionally "nobiliter". In book 7, preface 11, Vitruvius names 13 architects who published books about their works (edited volumen). One of them is Pythius and his temple of Athena Polias in Priene. It is astonishing that in this city a temple was built which is mentioned in the same breath as the Parthenon even three hundred years later, for Vitruvius lived in the times of Augustus. It is even more astonishing that the whole city is a gigantic, integrated work of art (*Gesammtkunstwerk*). In a chapter related to the training of architects, Vitruvius (8,4 and 9,7) refers indirectly to the city of Priene by having Pythius say that an architect must know more about all fields of his art and

---

14. *In the middle of the road to the west of the Agora there are massive blocks of stones, which remain an obstacle to this day. Hoepfner, W. – Schwandner, E. L., op. cit., p. 196 ff.*

science than any other expert. Pythius was in fact a sculptor; according to Vitruvius, he not only wrote, together with Satyrus, a book about their work in the Mausoleum, but also created, as mentioned by Plinius, the quadriga crowning the pyramid of the Mausoleum. Pythius did not, of course, imply that an architect should know more than a doctor or a musician in their respective fields. His statement probably meant that what is most important for a well-rounded architect is not only the form of each individual object, but also its function and relations to other objects. Just as an inhabitant of a city is part of the *demos*, so a house is part of the city. The parallel sequences are clear: citizen, "phratria" (clan), "phyle" (tribe), demos, and respectively of house, block of houses, residential area, community and city. As legality is important for the co-existence of citizens, a similar order must prevail in all the spaces and buildings used by these citizens.

It is definitely no coincidence that the temple of Athena Polias is incorporated into the network of building plots. The exterior columns of its south side are exactly in the same positions as the corners of a regular building plot. The design of the temple, therefore, is not independent but integrated into the overall planning of the city. This is very important, since the obvious conformity of the temple to the laws of the city indicates that the architect was a Pythagorean. Like his famous ancestor, Hippodamus of Miletus, Pythius must have belonged to the Pythagorean school.

The characteristic symbol used by the Pythagoreans was the tetraktys. Ten points forming a triangle represent the harmony of the most important proportions in geometry and the corresponding proportions in music. It is no coincidence that the most important rectangles in the planning of Priene follow the pattern of the tetraktys. The proportions of the blocks in the zone of private residences are 3:4, of the public area of the Agora 2:3[15] and of the Temple of Athena 1:2. Thus, the intervals of the fourth, fifth and eighth give order to the form of the city and to the relations between citizens.

The Agora was a large open space in the city centre, intersected by the central street. In order to achieve a ratio of 2:3 between its sides, its north side would have to be extended by 10 feet (see drawing p. 56).

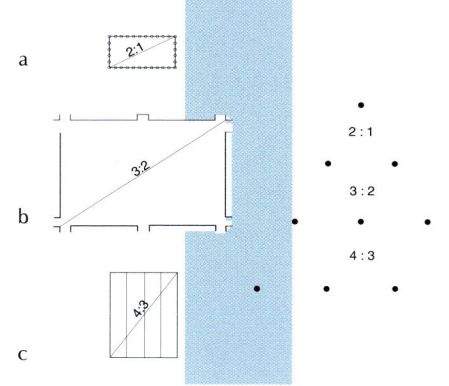

The most important rectangles of the town planning system conform to the pattern of the tetraktys, symbol of the Pythagorean school.
a. Temple of Athena
b. Agora
c. Residential plot

15. The development of the Agora, as described by Koenigs, W., in Ist. Mitt. 43, 1993, pp. 381-396. Based on "accurate research" is definitely wrong, as in this study neither the Bouleuterion nor the Prytaneion or the propylon of the Agora are related to the outdoor space of the Agora. Compare, on the other hand, my own "pure fantasies" (Koenigs, op. cit., p. 396) concerning the Agora of Priene in Hoepfner, W., 1999, op. cit., pp. 338-351. It must be noted that this more extended Agora has been already accurately represented by Steuben, H. von, Zur Agora von Priene, in Altertumskunde des Vorderen Orients 7, 1996, p. 275 ff.

The notion of a typical house was probably introduced by Hippodamus of Miletus in his planning of the new cities of Miletus and Piraeus. Its relation to the political system of Isonomy, which was later called Democracy, cannot be ruled out, as harmonious relationships between citizens were essential in Classical antiquity. Uniform housing conditions for everybody could contribute to the reinforcement of the social fabric. Apparently this applied to the new cities of conservative Macedonia as well, although typical houses in wealthy Macedonia were quite luxurious (see drawing p. 179).

The existence of a typical house in Priene must be considered certain, since it is evident in the ground plans made during excavations dating the city to a later phase. In 1983 Ernst-Ludwig Schwandner and I discovered traces of displacement, in the form of letters, on the walls of the houses in the street leading to the theatre[16].

The sequence of the letters leads to the conclusion that the plots of these houses were exactly of the same dimensions as a typical house, i.e., they were 30 feet wide (8.82m) and 80 feet deep (23.52m). Archaeologists who work on the site and insist that at the time of the city's foundation no houses of the same size existed, have not yet found evidence supporting their view[17] (see drawing p. 179).

The house unit introduced by Pythius was built on a narrow strip of land facing south, which ensured that the anteroom was always cool in summer and the sun could reach its interior in winter. The houses generally consisted of the ground floor, which included the oikos (a space used in daytime), the anteroom, a lateral room that served as a bathroom, and the andron (reception-room). The top floor included a bedroom, the women's quarters, and a gallery. Given that traditionally the hearth was in the oikos, one may conclude that the oikos was a very large space, which, according to a valid reconstruction of the residence in the settlement of Orraon[18], must have been two-storeyed. In House No. 32 the size of a marble capital that has survived on the wall of the andron indicates that it was part of a wooden structure supporting the ground floor or the floor above the vestibule.

View from House No. 32d of the street leading to the Theatre. The letters on the stones define the excavation layer and the position of stones. The building plot extended from the point above the steps on AA.

Prostasis of House No. 32. The marble capital now stands in the position of a wooden support separating the entrance from the hall.

16. Hoepfner, W. – Schwandner, E. L., Haus und Stadt im klassischen Griechenland, 1986, p. 169 ff.

17. Rumscheid, F., Priene. Führer durch das "Pompeji Kleinasiens", 1998, p. 31 ff. (Koenigs W.).

18. Hoepfner, W., 1999, op. cit. p. 384 ff.

The houses of Priene take full advantage of the available space but one of their striking features is their small size and austerity: their plots are only 208m². Around the middle of the 4th century the houses were built with larger rooms enclosed by peristyles. This is why it is hard to explain the oblong shape of the plots, which does not allow the incorporation of peristyles in the courtyard after construction. The small androns, with room for only three couches, are also unusual. Androns that accommodate up to six persons (two per couch), have been found only in older cities such as Athens[19]. Later on, while designing a model house for Piraeus[20] Hippodamus suggested a house with a three-couch andron. However, this plan was later turned down. Perhaps Pythius, with the approval of the inhabitants of Priene, decided to adopt this plain model.

The residents of Priene must have decided to adopt the modest houses of the early Classical and Classical eras and reject the luxurious houses of their own time.

In 1906, Hiller von Gaertringen was the first to express and substantiate the view that Pythius not only designed the temple of Athena but also planned the whole city of Priene[21]. He called this city plan "an integrated work of art" (*Gesammtkunstwerk*) of which the temple was an "organic part". Later, G. Kleiner, although unaware of the proportional relations connecting the temple, the agora and the houses[22], also expressed the view that Pythius was responsible for the whole city planning of Priene.

PYTHIUS' BOOK AND ITS READERS, ARISTOTLE AND VITRUVIUS: It would be extremely interesting to know exactly how Pythius had structured his book on the temple and what was most important for him. Unlike Vitruvius, Pythius certainly did not intend his book to be didactic; it is more likely that it was a description. As a consequence, it must have been quite detailed, providing sufficient information for experts. One should bear in mind that in those days a book could not contain complex and elaborate plans, since they could not be reproduced by copyists. It probably included simple plans with proportions and metrical data. The text, therefore, must have been so detailed that the reader would be able to visualize its descriptions with accuracy.

One can easily conclude that Pythius was interested not only in the function of his work but also

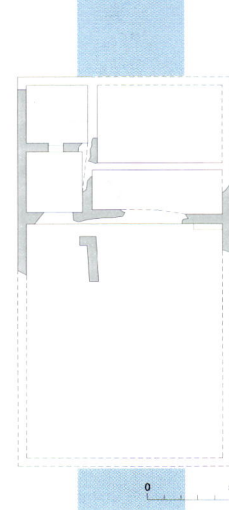

Piraeus: The oldest house, dated around 470 BC, in the vicinity of the Agora, served probably as a model for Hippodamus.

19. Op. cit., p. 234 ff.

20. Op. cit., p. 217 ff.

21. Hiller von Gaertringen, F., op. cit., p. 11.

22. Initially in Hoepfner, W. – Schwandner, E. L., Haus und Stadt im klassischen Griechenland, 1986, p. 144 ff., with a representation of the Agora and the Temple of Zeus that had not yet been correctly pronounced.

in its proportions and artistic form by focusing on certain important details of the temple of Athena Polias. They appear in an almost identical form in the Mausoleum of Halicarnassus and are apparently the artist's personal stamp. Pythius created a basic formula for the Ionic capital, its proportions remaining dominant until late antiquity: a ratio of volute height to depth and to maximum width of 1:2:3.

Order, grid, repetition of similar elements and alternating repetition of other elements are the basic features of Pythius' works. In the temple of Athena Polias the side of the plinths on the bases of the columns as well as the distance between them are equal to the "embates' (dimensional module), and the relation of the columns to their inter-axial distances is 4:7.

In the Mausoleum and the Temple of Zeus in Labranda of Caria, which was probably also a work of Pythius, there are variations of the same proportions.

These figures show that Pythius took interest in minute details, which he always related to larger units. The characterisation of the city and its buildings as an integrated work of art (*Gesammtkunstwerk*) is therefore justified.

The similarities between the Ionic capitals of Vitruvius and those of Pythius are so obvious, that one can conclude that Vitruvius had Pythius' book in mind. The same seems to apply to many other details. Thus, the lower diameter of the column is a kind of basic unit for the design of the columns and the entablature. It is probably no coincidence that Vitruvius claims that the Greek agora should be designed with side proportions 2:3, which happen to correspond to the metrical data of Priene.

It is even more striking that the data of Priene coincide with those cited in book 7 of Aristotle's *Politics*, where the city-state is discussed. These observations are presented here for the first time. Aristotle (7,6) wonders whether cities should be founded near the sea: "It is said that the arrival of foreigners raised under different laws, as well as the increase of population are not beneficial to order in the city". Both these factors seem to have led the inhabitants of older Priene to build

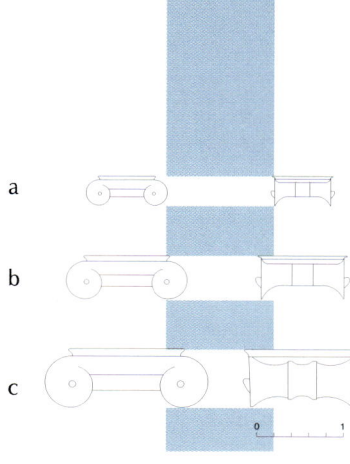

Metrical data of Ionic capitals from the
a. Temple of Zeus in Labranda
b. Mausoleum in Halicarnassus
c. Temple of Athena in Priene

their new city in the hinterland. It is therefore likely that Pythius referred to these problems in the introduction of his book. In chapter 7, 8 Aristotle does not approve of the foundation of large cities such as Rhodes, Kos, Halicarnassus and Cnidus. On the contrary, he emphasises the importance of self-sufficiency, which can only be achieved in states that are not very large. The size of a man is also unimportant, explains Aristotle. In chapter 7, 11 he refers to the necessity of walls since "catapults of great precision and battering rams have been invented". It is known that these weapons were widely used after the middle of the 4th century. Thus, Aristotle must have referred to an earlier source, possibly the book of Pythius on Priene. Although Priene was protected by the steep hills surrounding it, it was enclosed by walls, which even included its acropolis that stood much higher. The triangular fortress to the north was a pioneering construction for that time, with three large towers that had room for heavy catapults. In times of peace, the acropolis accommodated a garrison commander and soldiers guarding the city[23].

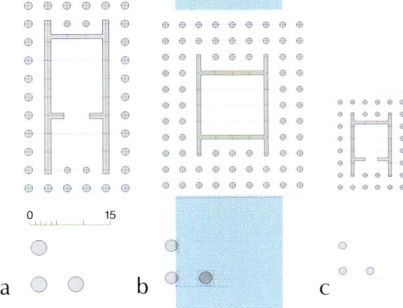

a. The Temple of Athena in Priene
b. The Mausoleum in Halicarnassus
c. The Temple of Zeus in Labranda in grid showing the basic relations of columns

Smaller towers stood to the east and west. The south walls were built in a saw-tooth pattern. Towers were not essential here; the wall was not continuous, but consisted of sections with gaps between them, a fact indicating that the architect, probably Pythius, had foreseen the danger from heavy shots of stone-throwers from the valley. If the walls were hit at one point, then each of these independent sections of 30 to 40 metres would fall down without causing the collapse of the whole wall.

According to Aristotle, chapter 7,12, the site of the most important sanctuary of a city "must be as conspicuous as is required by its significance" and must stand on firm foundations. The temple of Athena in Priene stands out as the symbol of the city on its most conspicuous site. It is supported by an imposing retaining wall, which is "stronger than the neighbouring sections of the city". In the next phrase, Aristotle mentions that below the temple an agora must be constructed which should be of the type called "free" in Thessaly. It should be free from commercial stores and uncultivated people, such as peasants, should be excluded from the area unless invited by the "archons". Priene suits this description perfectly. The peculiar regulation that the Agora is a place only for citizens may have reflected the fear of riots and the increase of the immigrant

23. RE Suppl. 9, 1962, p. 1193.

population in Priene.

Aristotle goes on to say that a well-planned city should include nearby Gymnasia for men. This also applies to Priene, where the Gymnasium is next to the Agora, on its northeastern side, which has not been excavated yet. As far as houses are concerned, Aristotle's statement in chapter 7, 11 is well-known: "the distribution of houses is better and generally more practical when it is rectilinear and follows the principles of the new Hippodamian system". This does not only mean that the building plots should be equal in size (which had been the case in the new colonial cities since the 7th century), but also that the houses should be built in a standard way, a fact proven beyond all doubt by excavations in Piraeus, Olynthus, and naturally Priene. This passage may also have been echoing Pythius' book.

Aristotle undoubtedly used hundreds of sources. He must have possessed one of the richest libraries of his day. Copies of new publications circulated fast and reached Athens without delay. Naturally, the work of Pythius concerning a major Ionic temple and probably a whole city and its major buildings would have been of interest to architects, philosophers and those involved in science. Thus it is safe to assume that the work of Pythius reached the library of Aristotle soon after its publication. Be that as it may, it is astonishing that Aristotle's ideal city bears such a close resemblance to the findings of Priene.

DEVELOPMENTS IN HELLENISTIC TIMES: Living conditions for the rural population of antiquity were not unchanging. It seems that many of the inhabitants of Priene soon felt that their houses were too small. This became evident first with the reception-rooms (androses). Already in the Archaic era private symposiums were a very significant part of social life, to such an extent that androses were added even to single-room houses, restricting the rest of the family activities to a small room with a hearth. This can be clearly seen in the excavations on the islands of Tenos and Andros[24].

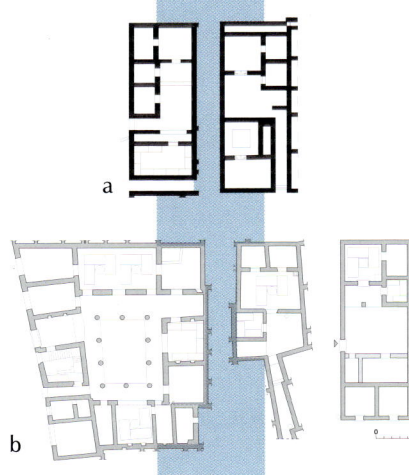

a. Since the androses, according to their initial design, were small, some owners added larger ones on the southern section of the plot. Examples are Houses No. 8 and No. 25.

b. Delos and Priene. House No. 6-1 and House No. 3F in Delos, as well as a restored house on the central street of Priene. In the 2nd century BC, the larger rooms of houses were used as reception rooms, where triclinia could be placed. Doors and windows allowed guests to have full view of the peristyle or the courtyard.

Left to right: House No. 6-1 and House No. 3F in Delos, as well as a restored house on the central street of Priene

24. Wiegand, Th. – Schrader, H., op. cit., p. 39.

In Priene, some citizens extended their houses by adding a larger symposium hall on the south section of the courtyard, next to the street. A large andron of this type with seven couches accommodating fourteen people and beautifully decorated with mosaics was discovered in House No. 8[25]. In House No. 25, moreover, the andron extended along the entire width of the plot and could accommodate ten couches; it was later restricted by the construction of a wall. There was a lavatory next to the narrow anteroom (cf. p. 39).

Towards the end of the 3rd century a new trend demanded the replacement of built-in couches with portable furniture that could be placed in the open-air or on platforms. Thus, the small andrones of the early years, which had a narrow door opening onto the vestibule and not the courtyard, were inadequate. In certain cases some wealthy citizens purchased adjoining plots and extended their houses by constructing open-air platforms. House No. 33 (cf. p. 188) was extended towards the east during the Hellenistic era by the construction of a three-sided peristyle. On the south section of the courtyard, stands a platform with a triclinium. These triclinia could accommodate three people on a couch 1.25m wide. Three couches were placed around each table. The fourth side remained free so as not to obstruct the view. The view through doors, windows or the openings of the platforms, was very important. The servants could now approach the guests and hosts only from the outside, and contrary to what happened in earlier years, the couches were placed in the centre of the room while the space between the couches and the walls remained unoccupied. For each couch a space of 4 metres was necessary.

In the late Hellenistic era the use of triclinia became more widespread and the usual andrones were replaced in most cases. Examples showing the change in the design of late Hellenistic houses are the houses of Delos, which were built after 166 BC [26]. In these houses one can see that the earlier oikos, the space including the hearth where the family assembled, has been converted into a large reception room with a door and windows. One or two triclinia, according to the residents' needs, could be placed in this room.

Andrones of the older type, with built-in couches, were probably used mainly in intimate gatherings. They are rarely absent from the houses of Delos. The same development is to be seen

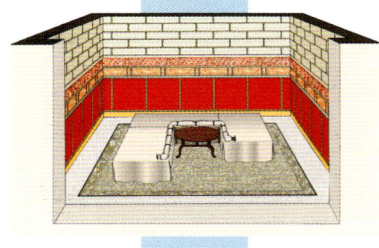

Graphic representation of an "andron" in a house in Delos during the Hellenistic period

25. Hoepfner, W., 1999, op. cit, p. 163 ff. and 190 ff.

26. Rumscheid, F., op. cit, p. 101, claims that this andron was for renting.

in Priene. After the 2nd century the family and guests gathered in the oikos, which in earlier times was reserved only for the family's private life. In some houses, as in Houses Nos. 13 and 19, built-in bases, about 1m wide and 53cm high, have been preserved in the centre of the oikos. These bases supported the table of the triclinium[27]. The plates that covered the table are missing. These rooms, 4.50m wide, were large enough to accommodate three couches. Naturally, couches were only placed there whenever they were needed for a symposium. During daytime the couches were stored in a lateral room of the oecus maior (Vitruvius).

It seems that this new arrangement was established in many houses. The stable, built-in tables were replaced by portable, round ones, of which, of course, there are no traces. However, there is some evidence of this change: in the old oikoi of private houses there was normally a low hearth in the centre, the flame of which symbolised family unity. No such hearths have been found in any house in Priene. In subsequent years the hearth was moved to one of the corners of the oikos (House No. 3) or to a corner of the vestibule. In House No. 4 the hearth was transferred to the upper floor so that free space for the triclinium was left in the ground floor. The staircase led straight from the courtyard to the upper floor[28].

Doing away with the separation of the space reserved for the family (oikos) from the space for the symposia (andron) is a social phenomenon of that period, even in the large Hellenistic cities of the East[29].

THE SACRED HOUSE: Among the ruins of Priene a building complex survives that offers invaluable information about social life in ancient Greek cities. It concerns private religious societies, the "thiasoi", which increased in number and power after the 4th century. Since the demos only concerned itself with public celebrations and did not provide space for private ones, the founders or sponsors of such societies purchased houses and converted them to suit their purpose.

The Sacred House in Priene is on the central street leading west, near the city's West Gate. Due to frequent alterations it is impossible to make out the original building plots in the part of the House close to the wall and towards its steep south side.

a

b

c

a. Oikos in House No. 13. Base of a table at the centre of the room, where a triclinium was placed.

b. Oikos in House No. 13. The base of the table from a height of 53cm.

c. Oikos in House No. 19. Base of a table in the centre of the room.

27. Hoepfner, W., 1999, op. cit., p. 507 ff.

28. No altars could be located in the middle of such spaces. Besides, there are no traces of fire whatsoever.

29. Hoepfner, W., 1999, op. cit.

The Sacred House stands on one of the lateral secondary streets and extends on both sides to the adjacent plots. It can be reached by a small street that does not belong to the original street network.

The findings of the excavations are described in the study published in 1904[30]. The ground plan provided in this publication takes into account all observations made after the end of the excavations in 1899. It is evident that the building has undergone several modifications. What remains is a complex made up of three parts: the middle section includes the courtyard with the spaces on its east; the north side consists of a large space that was later divided to include a worship bench and an altar, and the south side consists of two halls of approximately equal size.

The character of this complex is described in an inscription on the anta of the entrance, of which unfortunately only a fragment survives and is now in Berlin. On the lower part of the inscription one reads that only those who were pure and dressed in white were allowed to enter the sanctuary. It is obviously a private religious society. Further up, beyond the missing lines, one reads that the priests had drawn lots and appointed Anaxidemus, son of Appolonius, to some high office. However, it is unlikely that he was appointed as priest or high priest, since these positions were associated with financial obligations and therefore could not be assigned by lot.

Both the precise character of the sanctuary and the deity to which it was dedicated remain unclear. M. N. Tod in his concise history of the development of thiasoi suggests that during the 4th and 3rd centuries citizens organised societies whose members gathered to pray in private, make offerings and take part in ritual dinners[31], usually in honour of a hero such as the hero Amynus, who was honoured on the west side of the foot of the Acropolis of Athens. The guests of private symposia were usually relatives and neighbours. In this way the internal bonds of a phratria (clan) were strengthened. A statuette of Alexander the Great has been found in the great hall of the Sanctuary of Priene. For this reason it is assumed that the hall was an "Alexandreion".

---

30. Wiegand, Th. – Schrader, H., op. cit. p. 172 ff.

31. Tod, M. N., Klubs und Vereine in der griechischen Welt, in Streiflichter auf die griechische Geschichte, 1964, p. 45 ff. ibid.

Similar places of worship must have existed in many cities. As indicated earlier, the inhabitants of Priene had special reasons for expressing their gratitude to Alexander, to an extent that could justify even the construction of a public place of worship with a temple dedicated to him. But even though it was common, even in some of the greatest sanctuaries, to worship demigods along with important deities in the same temple, sanctuaries were never dedicated exclusively to them. Thus it is possible that this private sanctuary, built on restored older houses, was indeed an "Alexandreion". The dimensions of the complex are 20 x 25m (a surface of 500m^2), and the area reserved for worship of the demigod is 19m long and 9m wide, i.e. larger than the cella of the temple of Athena Polias. The letter symbols of the inscription on the door, including a "Sigma" with diverging ends and an "Alpha" with a straight middle line, belong to the 3rd century. The form of the walls provides clear indications about the form of the sanctuary in its original phase.

In those days the visitor would enter the courtyard through a covered propylon. Symmetrical colonnades enclosed the three sides of the courtyard. Two of the columns of this peristyle as well as part of the stylobate on the northern section still survive in their original positions. On the basis of this arrangement and an inter-axial distance of 10 feet or 3m, one can conclude that there were four more columns towards the east and five columns towards the north and south. In the middle of the courtyard, the archaeologists have noted the "foundation of a statue pedestal". But since statues, especially marble statues, were preferably placed in covered halls, it is possible that this was an altar base.

The two halls in the southern section were probably used for symposia, since such sanctuaries always included halls for this purpose. Of these two halls, the one on the east side had an entrance slightly moved towards the west, so as to allow a better arrangement of the couches. There is no doubt that this was a symposium hall that could accommodate the usual 11 couches[32]. The ritual meals were very important for the "thiasoi", which consisted of people belonging to the same professional group or social class, such as the metics (foreigners organised according to their origin), women and slaves. Providing wine for the symposia was one of the basic responsibilities of the society.

The statuette of Alexander the Great found in the Sacred House
©DAI Istanbul

32. *Examples are cited in Börker, Chr., Festbankett und griechische Architektur, 1983. Also, e.g. in a three-room symposium house behind the Temple of Dionysus in Pergamum. Hoepfner, W., in Heilmeyer, W. D. (ed.), Der Pergamonaltar. Die neue Präsentation nach der Restaurierung des Telephosfrieses, Catalogue of the exhibition in Berlin, 1997, p. 31.*

The large hall had three axial supports with an epistyle, which supported the short, diagonal beams of the roof. Towards the east, a built and plastered podium, only 1.20m high, has been discovered, which can be reached through three small staircases of four steps each. In this area and around the podium, statuettes of baked clay and marble have been found, probably offerings of the members of a thiasos. A marble table for offerings was placed approximately in the middle of the west side of the podium.

It is worth noting the size of the area reserved for worship. In contrast to other temples, this building not only accommodated the cult statue, but was also a gathering place for the faithful, who followed a specific ritual. The two halls with the couches could host 24 people, and an equal number of people could attend the rituals standing in the large hall. It is assumed that the statue was originally placed on a pedestal on the narrow side of the hall. This podium probably served for depositing offerings. Through the small staircases one could reach the parts of the pedestal that were close to the wall, without interfering with the offerings placed on the front.

Large blood sacrifices were forbidden in these places of worship. The thiasoi worshipped heroes and daimones by burning incense and offering fruit and the like. Penalties for the members of the "society" included the provision of incense. Offerings were placed on the table in front of the podium. It remains unknown whether there was an altar in the courtyard of the peristyle in its early stage, when the sanctuary was dedicated to a single deity (see below).

The thiasoi used to gather for prayers and sacrifices in the temple of Drerus in Crete and the recently discovered temple in the Cathedral of Thessaly[33], which were both public. In the 7th century, and in some regions even in the 6th century, temples served as gathering places of the community[34]. As the population increased, their size became inadequate and rituals had to be held outdoors, in front of the temples. Thus the open space around the temple became more important; later, thiasoi organised ritual meals there. During the 3rd century the function of the large hall of the Sanctuary of Priene was similar to that of the temples of older times: it was important that only a limited number of members could enter, as in archaic communities. Some societies made a point of maintaining a stable number of members by including a relevant

33. Excavator: Intzesiloglou B., Architectural Study: Korres M.

34. Martini, W., Vom Herdhaus zum Peripteros, JdI 101, 1986, p. 23 ff.

statement in their Articles (as Academies do today). Only after the death of a member could a new one be elected in his place.

During the 2nd century the Sanctuary of Priene underwent significant changes. It was decided that from then on two heroes would be worshipped there. The place of worship of the older hero had to be restricted to a smaller area created by the construction of a wall. A new hall was constructed in the northeast corner of the courtyard for the worship of the new deity. For this reason a large part of the peristyle had to be removed. Only the colonnade on the northern side was preserved, because it served as an anteroom for the neighbouring places of worship and as a hall where cult statues were placed. Some bases of these statues survive to this day near the wall. The new cult statue was set on a round base and was probably not very large. A table for offerings stood in front of it. The members of the thiasoi, who waited in the courtyard, were only able to see the preparation of the offerings. The priest either alone or accompanied by an assistant brought the offering to a narrow room. The isolated hall on the west side of the older place of worship probably also served for the gathering of the faithful when the weather did not permit their assembly in the courtyard. In late Hellenistic times, worship of more than one deity also took place in other buildings belonging to societies. The statues of these gods were placed in small lateral halls. A good example is the Sanctuary of the Poseidoniastes of Berytos in Delos[35] where, around 110 BC, the goddess Roma was worshipped along with Poseidon of Berytos and two other deities, a fact that indicates a dependence on political conditions. The best example of a large number of private societies for the worship of gods and heroes during late antiquity is provided by Dura-Europus on the Euphrates River[36].

In order to explain the purpose of the two halls constructed on the east side of the courtyard in the Sacred House of Priene, one should take a look at the Heroon (hero-cult shrine) in Calydon.

According to archaeological findings, this Heroon dates back to the 2nd century and was a tomb outside the city but also a place of worship of an eminent citizen, who was recognized as a hero and who had probably founded the Heroon himself. It is conjectured that this person ensured that the cult rituals would be held indefinitely in the future, financed by a trust. E. Dygve,

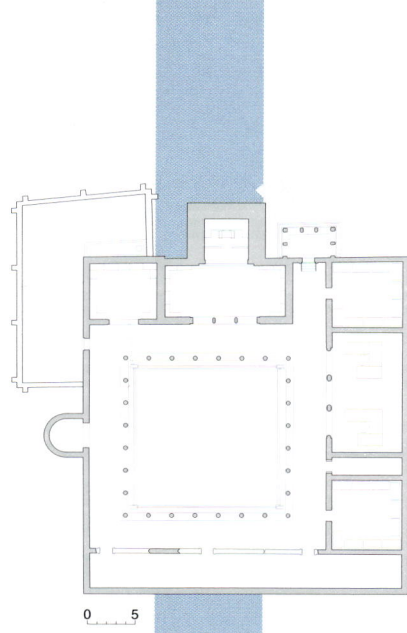

The Heroon in Calydon: plan by Dygve with new additions referring to the use of space.

35. Picard, Ch., EAD VI, L' Établissement des Poseidoniastes de Berytos, 1921.

36. Rostovtzeff, M. I., Dura Europos and its Art, 1938. Ibid, Die hellenistische Welt. Gesellschaft und Wirtschaft, 1955, p. 842 ff.

F. Poulson and K. Rhomaios carried out excavations and published their data concerning this monument, which is certainly not unique[37].

The similarities between this building and the Heroon of Priene indicate that the two constructions are related. Through a porch with a colonnaded propylon, the thiasos entered a large peristyle. The north side, built with thick walls, includes the worship pedestal, which is next to the place of worship and assembly. The vaulted funerary chamber of the hero-sponsor is in the basement. A pedestal for offerings is above it, and a sacrificial altar in front of it. The assembly hall includes benches and three openings that offer full view of the courtyard.

A square hall stands on the northwestern corner. This room does not have couches on the walls but benches instead, 70cm wide, as indicated by the survival of leg imprints on the mortar of the floor. The floor slopes towards the door, where there is a drainage tube leading to a canal at the end of the peristyle. Outside, towards the north, there is a cistern, and next to it a well. Everything points to the conclusion that here the members of the thiasos drank water and offered water libations.

In the corners of the west side of the Heroon stand two square halls, which are easily recognised as symposium halls with 10 couches each. However, the large platform between these halls is more recent and different[38]. It is 13m wide and its extension towards the peristyle is supported by two pillars and is 9m wide. Instead of couches around the walls, there were triclinia, three at the very most, which were groups of three couches arranged around each table. This way of having a meal while reclining was established during the last decades of the 3rd century, when it was considered essential that during a symposium the participants should have a full view of the courtyard through the peristyle. This applied to private houses, as indicated earlier, but also to every other occasion where common meals were necessary. The moveable couches could also be transferred to the peristyle, depending on the occasion. The covered spaces were used for meals only in winter.

---

37. Dygve, E. – Poulson, F. – Rhomaios, K., Das Heroon von Kalydon, 1934.

38. Hoepfner, W., 1999, op. cit., p. 446 ff., 515 ff.

The Sacred Houses of Calydon and Priene are quite luxurious and spacious. The dining-halls of Calydon could accommodate 20 couches, i.e., up to 40 people. The platform containing three triclinia could host up to 27 people. Therefore, a thiasos could not have included more than 30 members. This also applied to Priene, where the 2 x 11 couches could accommodate up to 44 people. Societies with up to 30 members were not unusual[39]. The Heroon of Calydon is more recent than that of Priene, which was altered in the 2nd century. Two makeshift platforms were arranged next to the hall of worship as triclinia facing the courtyard. Due to lack of space, these triclinia could be served only from the side of the courtyard. At a still later stage the northern one was turned into an enclosed space.

After a fire, which is undoubtedly related to a war around 130 BC[40], Priene declined to such an extent that ruined houses in the central street remained unused and uninhabited. The inhabitants were put to death or sold as slaves. Archaeologists were the first to discover hidden treasures of coins, headed by Theodor Wiegand. There are no findings of the Sanctuary dating from the Roman era. Apparently the Sanctuary did not survive the destruction of the late Hellenistic period.

---

39. Tod, M. N., op. cit., p. 55.

40. Hoepfner, W. – Schwandner, E. L., 1994, p. 189.

PRIENE

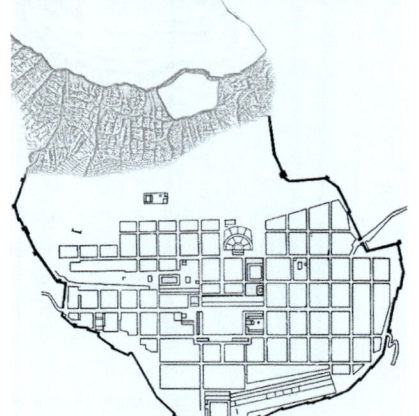

INTRODUCTION: The subject of the present publication is the architecture of Priene, a typical middle-size Hellenistic city of Ionia in western Asia Minor. The book focuses on the late Classical/early Hellenistic period (2nd half of the 4th century BC) until the end of the Hellenistic period (2nd half of the 2nd century BC – 129 BC).

A BRIEF HISTORY OF THE EXCAVATIONS: The excavations in the area of Priene have begun in 1894 by Karl Humann and Reinhard Kekule von Stradonitz, directors of the Department of Antiquities of the Berlin Museums. The aim was to locate not only the famous Temple of Athena Polias but also the entire city. After the death of Humann, the project (on behalf of the Department of Antiquities of the Berlin Museums) was taken up in 1896 by the archaeologist Theodor Wiegand who employed more than 100 workers. By 1899 approximately 1/3 of the overall surface of the city had been brought to light. The results of the excavations were surprising and the impressive findings provided invaluable information about the ancient world. Today research continues under the guidance of Wolf Koenigs.

TOPOGRAPHY: Although Priene remains the most extensively excavated Hellenistic city of Asia Minor and despite the abundant findings, our knowledge of the city's phases of development is incomplete. The built-up area of the city, which is the subject of the present publication, dates back to late Classical times and is situated at the foot of Mount Latmus, opposite the island of Samos. Its area is defined by natural boundaries: the foot of Mount Mycale and the River Maeander. The steep mountainside protected the city and supported its fortification. The city's acropolis, Teloneia, on the top of a steep hill to the north of the city, was used exclusively for military purposes as a fortification.

A navigable tributary of the River Maeander, flowing on the south side of the city walls, was one of the city's main resources and supported the economy of Priene's rural population. Today, due to Maeander's deposits, the shore of the Aegean Sea is quite far from the ruins of Priene. But in ancient times, Naulochus, the harbour of Priene, was only 6km away. The city of Priene had close relations with the city of Thebes towards the west and Mount Panionion towards the north.

WATER SUPPLY, VENTILATION AND SUNLIGHT: The site on which the city was founded was chosen according to criteria that applied generally to Hellenistic cities: to facilitate ventilation and to make the best possible use of sunlight, the building complex should face south and be built on different levels[1].

In the particular case of Priene, it is possible that an additional reason for choosing that site was its potential for good water supply. Written sources refer to the existence of a spring behind the acropolis which supplied the city with sufficient water. Thanks to the pronounced slope of the hillside, water was collected in a reservoir on the northeast side of Priene and chanelled through pipes to the whole city. Water was abundant in Priene; it gushed from numerous fountains at street corners and central points, creating an image of prosperity that was absent even from wealthier cities, such as Athens[2]. Wiegand and Schrader refer to the existence of lavatories in a building that was later turned into a Christian church[3].

An additional advantage of the site of Priene was the soil: there are many areas containing high quality calcareous rock suitable for carving stone architectural elements.

CITY PLANNING: According to estimates by Hoepfner and Schwandner[4], the original population of Priene, mainly rural, did not exceed 5,000 people in total, including immigrants, inhabitants and slaves. Approximately 1,500 of these people had the right to vote, since women, children and slaves were excluded. The city developed within the walls. The total territory of the city-state of Priene covered a surface of 400 km². The main city-planning complex covered the south side of the area and occupied a surface of 370,000 m², of which only 40% was built. The remaining free space could be occupied by the inhabitants of the surrounding area and their animals in case of danger. However, the existence of large uncovered areas within the walls is probably an indication of a long-term plan for future building.

The mouth of the River Maeander
1) 500 BC   2) 100 BC   3) Today

1. Hoepfner, W. – Schwandner, E. L., Haus und Stadt im klassischen Griechenland. Deutsches Archäologisches Institut, Architekturreferat. In Zusammenarbeit mit dem Seminar für Klassische Archäologie der Freien Universität Berlin. München: Deutsche Kunstverlag, 1994, pp. 193, 195.

2. Tomlinson, R., From Mycenae to Constantinople – The Evolution of the Ancient City. London and New York: Routledge, 1992, p. 87.

3. Wiegand, Th. – Schrader, H., Priene. Ergebnisse der Ausgrabungen und Untersuchungen von den Jahren 1895-1898. Unter Mitwirkung von G. Kummer, W. Wilberg, H. Winnefeld, R. Zahn. Berlin: Königliche Museen zu Berlin, 1904, p. 480.

4. Op. cit., p. 190.

General view of Priene looking towards the plain of Maeander at the time of the German excavations of 1896
©DAI Istanbul

General view of Priene, today

Unlike pre-historic or medieval settlements, Priene is not laid out in an arbitrary or random way, but follows a perfectly organised plan according to the Hippodamian system[5]. According to Hoepfner and Schwandner[6], it is most likely that its town-planning was the work of Pythius, who according to all the sources, was also the architect of the famous Temple of Athena Polias[7]. A strict geometrical layout has been followed despite obstacles caused by the geomorphology of the site. Priene is one of the most sloping cities in antiquity, with an average inclination of 20%. Since level areas were necessary for the construction of sanctuaries (such as that of Athena Polias), for public buildings (such as the Lower Gymnasium) and complexes (such as the Agora), large artificial terraces were constructed and supported by strong retaining walls.

It should be noted that, with the exception of the magnificent Temple of Athena Polias, Priene is not distinguished for its temples, but, rather, for its public buildings (gymnasia, stoas, the theatre), which are numerous and elaborately constructed.

The houses of Priene were 30 attic feet wide and 80 attic feet deep[8]. They were organized in blocks of 8 houses of equal surface area (in two rows of four houses), slight adjustments being made depending on their position in the block (i.e., in the middle or corner of the block)[9].

STREETS: The city's road system is clearly oriented towards the south. On either side of the basic east-to-west road axis there are five additional streets: three to the north and two to the south. As they intersect 15 narrower perpendicular streets, so building plots are formed.

In Priene the width of each street was related to its function and followed an elaborate scaling system. Thus, commercial streets were wider than streets of residential areas[10]. The main street leading to the West Gate from the north side of the Agora was the widest (24 attic feet). Three streets, 20 feet wide each, crossed the main street at right angles and defined the rectangle of the Agora.

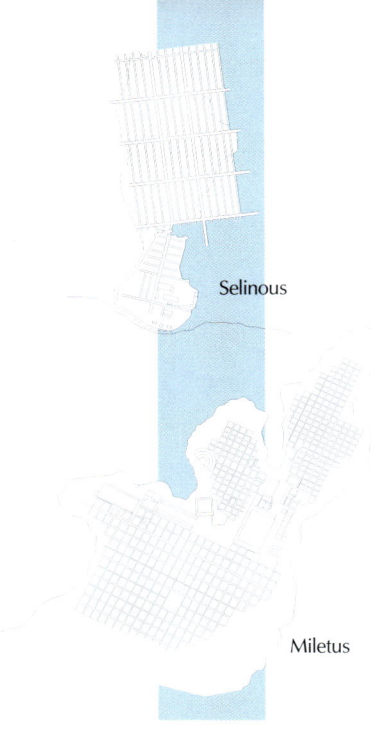

The Hippodamian system

5. The Hippodamian system is defined as a system of urban planning organised on the basis of a rectangular grid. This system, according to which cities such as Miletus, Olynthus and Priene were built, is attributed by historians to Hippodamus of Miletus, who first systematised and recorded its principles. However, it must be noted that in the western Doric and Archaic colonies (8th century) of the Hellenic world, in South Italy (Syracuse, Selinous, Acragas) a similar organisation had been encountered much earlier. Gruben, G., Die Tempel der Griechen, München: Hirmer, 1986, p. 376.

6. Op. cit., p. 196.

7. Reference to the problems regarding the identity of Pythius is made in the Introductory Historical Note of this publication.

8. 8.82 x 23.5m. According to detailed measurements the attic foot in Priene equals 29.46cm., Hoepfner, W. – Schwandner, E. L., op. cit., pp. 195, 198.

9. Due to the steep gradient of the ground only two houses could fit in depth of each plot, whereas the width, in a common dimension of 120 feet, could easily accommodate four houses. Thus, in each plot of 120 x 160 feet (that is a 3:4 ratio) 8 houses could comfortably fit. Op. cit., p. 198.

10. Mueller-Wiener, W., I Architektoniki stin Archaia Ellada. Thessaloniki: University Studio Press, 1995, p. 203.

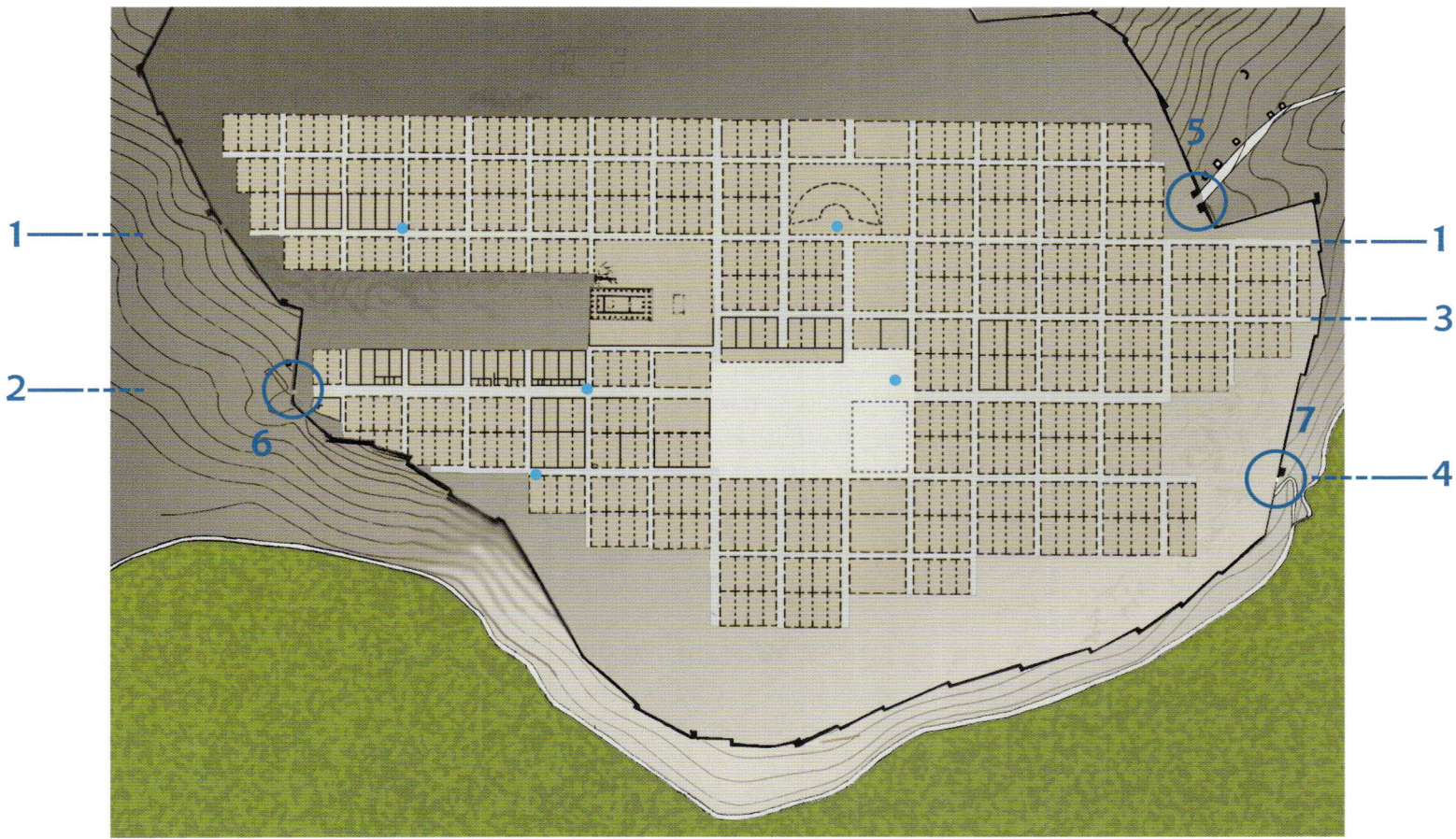

Plan of Priene
1. Theatre Street
2. West Gate Street
3. Street leading to the Sanctuary of Athena Polias
4. Spring Gate Street
5. East Gate
6. West Gate
7. Spring Gate
• Fountains

In Hellenistic times the middle of the street was blocked by the construction of buildings. Narrower streets, 16 attic feet wide, crossed the central streets at right angles and defined the area of building plots. In the perimeter of the city the streets were still narrower (only 12 feet wide). Due to the slope of the ground, carriages were restricted only to the streets running from east to west. For this reason these streets were paved with slabs. The streets that crossed them had steps and were narrower, since there was no provision for the circulation of carriages.

NECROPOLES: Priene's necropoles are situated to the east and west, outside the city gates. The most important necropolis is on the east side, extending for more than 1 km along the route to modern Sokia. There are few findings from Hellenistic times in this area. Some of the tombs were partly cut in the rock and then completed with masonry and sealed with large stones. A number of low-built funerary chambers from Roman times have survived. They are arranged along the uphill road leading to the East Gate of the city. Such structures have been discovered outside the West Gate and are similar to the "tholaria", which are quite common in the islands of the Aegean Sea, especially those near the shores of Asia Minor. In most cases they are vaulted funerary chambers with a main opening and three funerary couches on the other sides. Similar structures have been found in Amorgos (Katapola), Symi, but also in Lassos, on the coast of Asia Minor.

The most important Roman necropolis of the area has been located approximately 1 km east of Priene. It consists of an underground, oblong, paved corridor, accessible by 12 steps. At the end of the corridor there is a funerary chamber. There are alcoves on the walls of the corridor and the chamber.

THE DEFENSIVE SYSTEM: Priene was surrounded by walls 2,500 m long including the 600m of the perimeter of "Teloneia", the acropolis. Between the acropolis and the city the walls were interrupted at the points where the steep ground provided sufficient defensive protection. The walls were saw-like in plan, i.e., they consisted of small and large parts put together in acute angles. This was particularly useful in defense and especially for archers[11].

11. Schede, M., Die Ruinen von Priene. Archäologisches Institut des Deutschen Reiches. Abteilung Istanbul, 1964, p. 21

View of Priene during the late Hellenistic period (after Zippelius)

There were very few two-storey towers that were independent structures, i.e. whose masonry was not part of the walls. In this way, the destruction of a tower would not cause a gap in the defense system of the city. The walls, always founded on rock, had a core of rubble masonry backed up on both sides by masonry following the pseudo-isodomic system, with rough external surfaces. For greater stability there were intersecting stones connecting the two faces of the wall. The construction material was gray-blue marble[12]. The walls were probably 1-2m higher than the 8m-high walls that have survived. Their average width was approximately 2m. Their upper surface was covered by slabs that formed the floor of the wall top, which could be reached through staircases or through the towers. People standing on the wall were protected from the enemies' shots by a continuous wall with openings for the archers. The city wall probably had only three gates (the East Gate, the West Gate, and the so-called "Fountain Gate"), whereas the acropolis had only one. The West and the East Gates were arched. The East Gate, which was the main one, was also protected on both sides by towers and, probably for strategic reasons, was not related to the Hippodamian system of the city. Finally, to the south, there were small openings at the lowest part of the walls for the draining of rainwater.

The Christian era witnessed a time of intense building activity in connection with the walls. These were reinforced for the improvement of the city's defensive system: for instance, the older northern wall was extended by adding round bastions.

ACROPOLIS "TELONEIA": To the north of the city stands the acropolis "Teloneia", named after the hero Telon. It is on the top of a rocky hill; indeed its sides are so steep that to a large extent no fortification is required. The walls of the acropolis included more two-storey towers, the ground floor of which accommodated the garrison. The garrison commander was elected every four months by the citizens of Priene and during his term of office he was not allowed to leave "Teloneia". The walkway on the walls of the acropolis has survived.

East Gate (outside the walls)

12. McNicoll, A. W., Hellenistic Fortifications from the Aegean to the Euphrates. Oxford Monographs on Classical Archaeology. With revisions and additional chapter by N. P. Milner. Edited by M. Roberson, J. Boardman (et al.). Oxford: Clarendon Press, 1997, pp. 49-50.

Tower on the walls of Priene
©DAI Istanbul

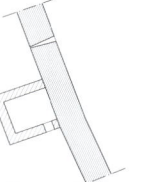
T4
Tower with window and wall opening for the discharge of rainwater

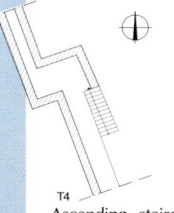
T4
Ascending staircase on the walkway

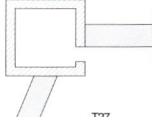
T27
Plan of the ground floor

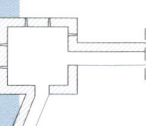
T27
Plan of walkway level

0 5

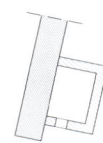
T10
Spring Gate and adjoining tower

Ground plans of fortification towers

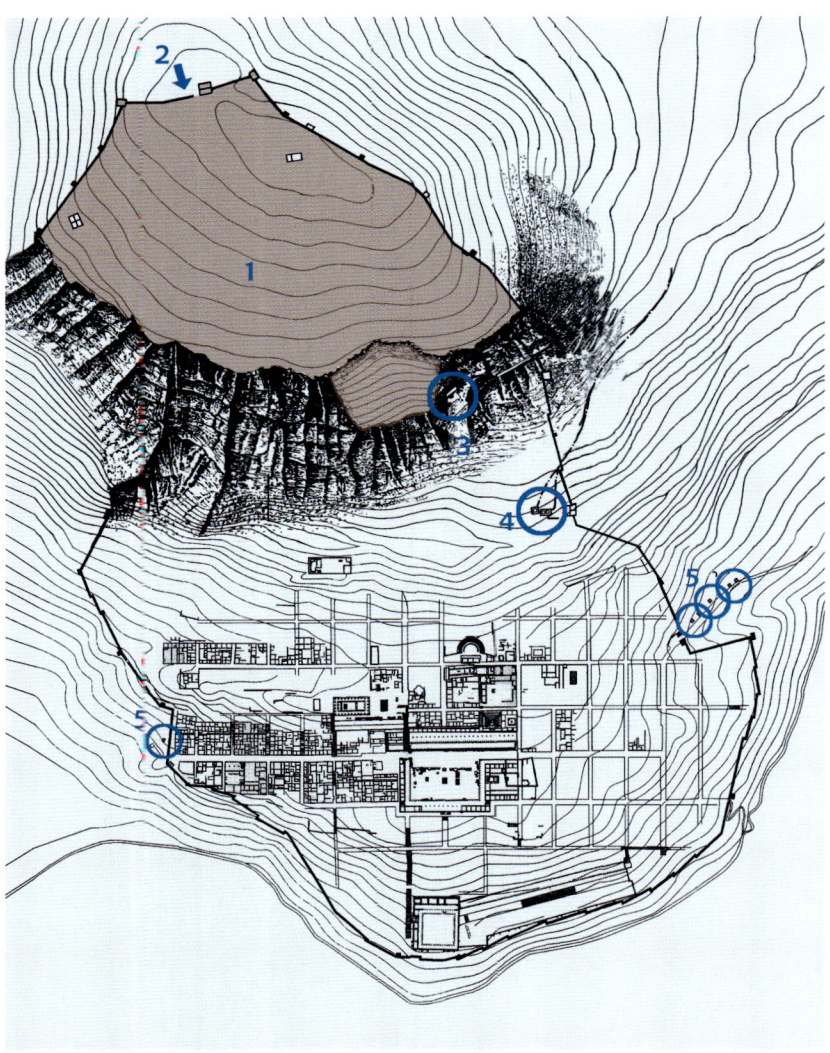

1. Acropolis "Teloneia"
2. Gate to the Acropolis
3. Shrine of Telon
4. Cistern and waterpipe
5. Tombs outside the city gates

General view of Priene to the east during the period of the German excavations (1896)
©DAI Istanbul

AGORA

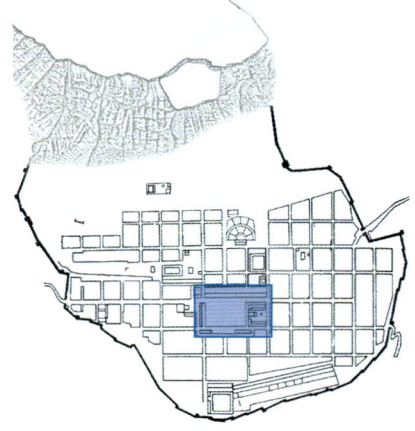

GENERAL: The Agora of Priene is situated to the south of the central east-west road axis. As in most Greek city-states, the Agora served mainly as the religious and political, rather than commercial, centre of the city. This fact is confirmed by the existence of a second, purely commercial, market situated right next to the Agora, westward.

FORM: The Agora's central position in the city seems to have been part of the initial city planning. In ancient cities the dimensions of the Agora usually reflected its social and political significance. In the case of Priene, the location selected for the Agora was a large open-air space where the ground was originally relatively even. Nevertheless, despite the natural evenness of the ground, it was necessary to construct terraces with retaining walls in order to fully achieve the desired result.

What we see of the Agora today dates back to the late Hellenistic period. One can still make out the "toichobates" which supported the stoas all around the central open-air space; parts of the chambers of the west side are also preserved. The original form can be traced back to the 4th century BC, when building plots were determined and the purpose of each section was identified. However, due to the bad condition of the ruins and insufficient archaeological research, it is still difficult to reach definite conclusions about its size and form. Thus, contradictory views have been expressed concerning the possible features of the Agora. Archaeological research, begun recently and is still being carried out, may soon provide us with definite answers on the matter.

Two different views have been put forward on the basis of the interpretation and evaluation of measurement data.

According to Hoepfner[1] the Agora was an open-air rectangular area in the centre of the city, with a ratio 3:2. It occupied 3 building plots in length and 1.5 plots in width. The Sanctuary of Asclepius (or Zeus), possibly consisting only of an altar at the time, was included in this area, as in other Hellenistic cities (e.g., Magnesia by the Meander River). The Agora originally included the area that was later occupied by the buildings of the stoas and the Sanctuary of Asclepius. The porch, at the northeast end of the area, was a symbolic entrance point to the Agora.

According to Koenigs[2], the Agora was almost square, with an altar (probably dedicated to Hermes) in the centre, and extending on either side of the road leading to the Western Gate. It occupied two plots south of the street and two half-plots to the north. Its dimensions, including the surrounding roads, were 82.75m (north to south) and 88.25m (east to west).

1. Hoepfner, W. (ed.). Geschichte des Wohnens, Bd. 1, 5.000 v. Chr - 500 n. Chr: Vorgeschichte, Frühgeschichte, Antike. Deutsche Verlags – Anstalt, Stuttgart, 1999, p. 343.

2. Koenigs, W., Planung und Ausbau der Agora von Priene, Ist. Mitt. 43, 1993, pp. 381-396.

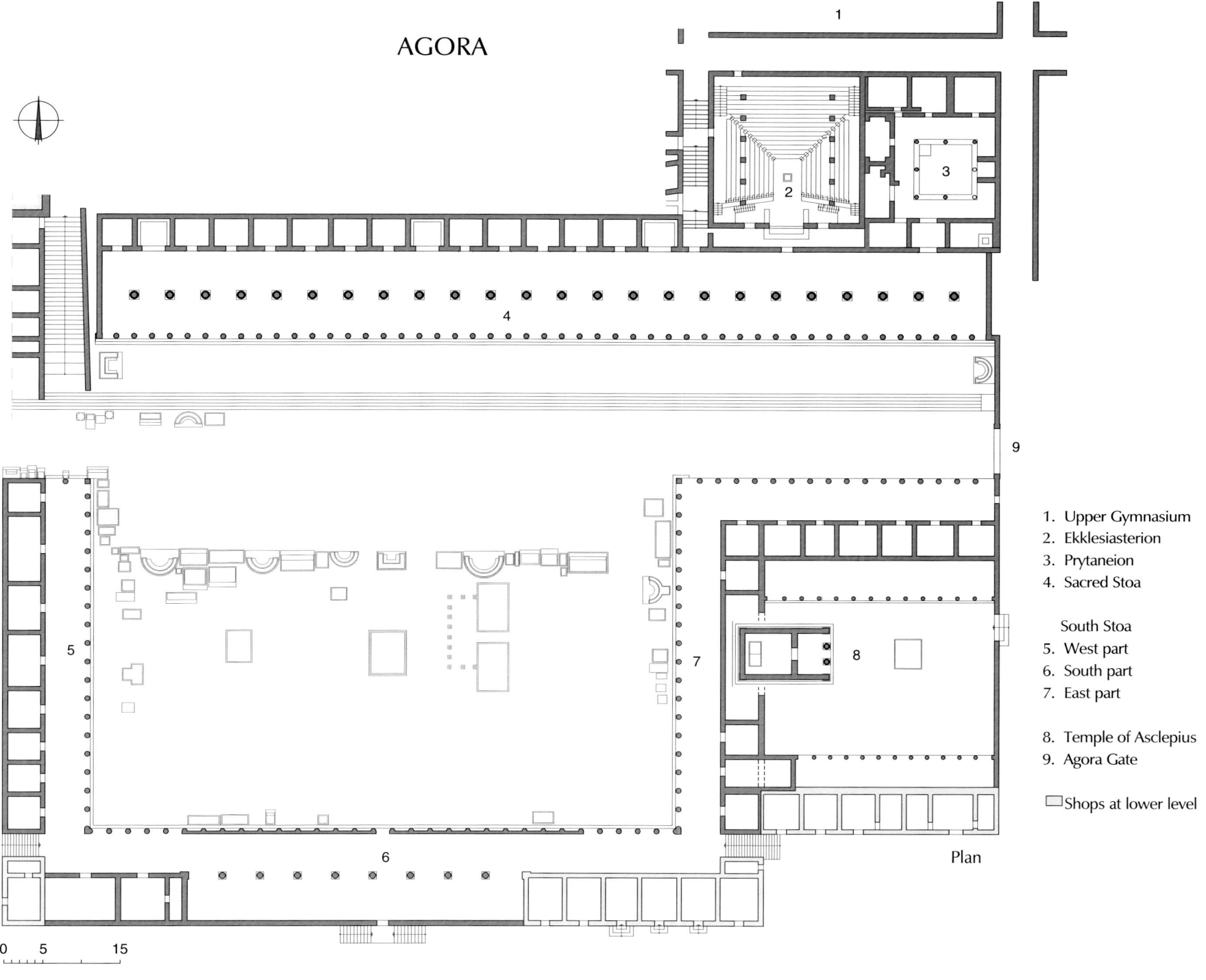

Plan

1. Upper Gymnasium
2. Ekklesiasterion
3. Prytaneion
4. Sacred Stoa

South Stoa
5. West part
6. South part
7. East part

8. Temple of Asclepius
9. Agora Gate

☐ Shops at lower level

number of votive offerings and statues were gradually placed around the stoas and along the road. Thus, as time went by, space became more and more restricted. Most of these offerings took the form of an exedra (pedestal for the display of votive offerings): that is, they consisted of a uniform stone surface of straight, semi-circular or polygonal shape. These stone surfaces were part of a pedestal on which marble or bronze statues were placed. These statues portrayed persons of importance to the history of the city, who had been thus honoured following resolutions passed by the "Boule" and the "Ekklesia of Demos".

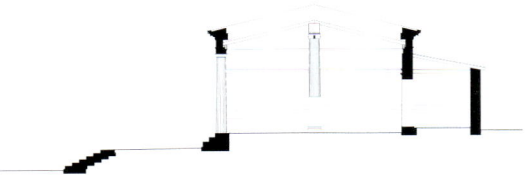

Cross section 1st version

More specifically, on an imaginary line halfway between the road north of the Agora (leading to the Western Gate) and the altar of Hermes, offerings connected with the city's history were arrayed. These monuments faced toward the front of the road and not toward the open space.

SACRED STOA: The Sacred Stoa was constructed in the second half of the 2nd century BC, in the same location as an older and smaller Stoa. According to an inscription on an offering, fragments of which have been recovered, its founder and sponsor was a Cappadocian king[5]. It is therefore estimated that the Stoa was constructed around 150 BC, and was renamed as the Sacred Stoa after the Wars of Mithridates, i.e., after 63 BC.

Cross section 2nd version

The Sacred Stoa, with an overall length of 116.46m, extends to the north of the Agora area, in front of the Ekklesiasterion and the Prytaneion. Both these buildings are connected with the Agora through the Stoa. The Sacred Stoa stood 2.40m above the main level of the Agora, which points out its importance. In order to reach it, one had to climb six steps, which extended all along the Stoa. A spacious corridor, 6.47m wide and 1.50m above the Agora level, extended between the steps and the main Stoa.

On the outside, the façade of the Stoa consisted of 49 Doric columns, whereas on the inside a row of 24 Ionic columns divided it into two aisles. The inside columns were taller, thinner, and arranged in such a way that there was one column behind every second external column. As was common practice in the late Hellenistic period, the lower one-third of the columns was not fluted. The Stoa was covered by a wooden pitched roof and the floor was probably of tamped earth[6].

5. *Op. cit., p. 90.* See also the Introductory Historical Note of this publication.

6. *Krischen studies two cases of different heights of internal columns and considers it more likely that, for aesthetic and structural reasons, taller internal columns were used. This revises the older view of Wiegand, according to which the internal columns were of equal height with the external ones. Holes located at a height of approximately 1.50m from the base of the Ionic columns, still with traces of leading, have not been explained. They probably constituted supports displaying painted tableaux of portraits of dignitaries.*

Sacred Stoa

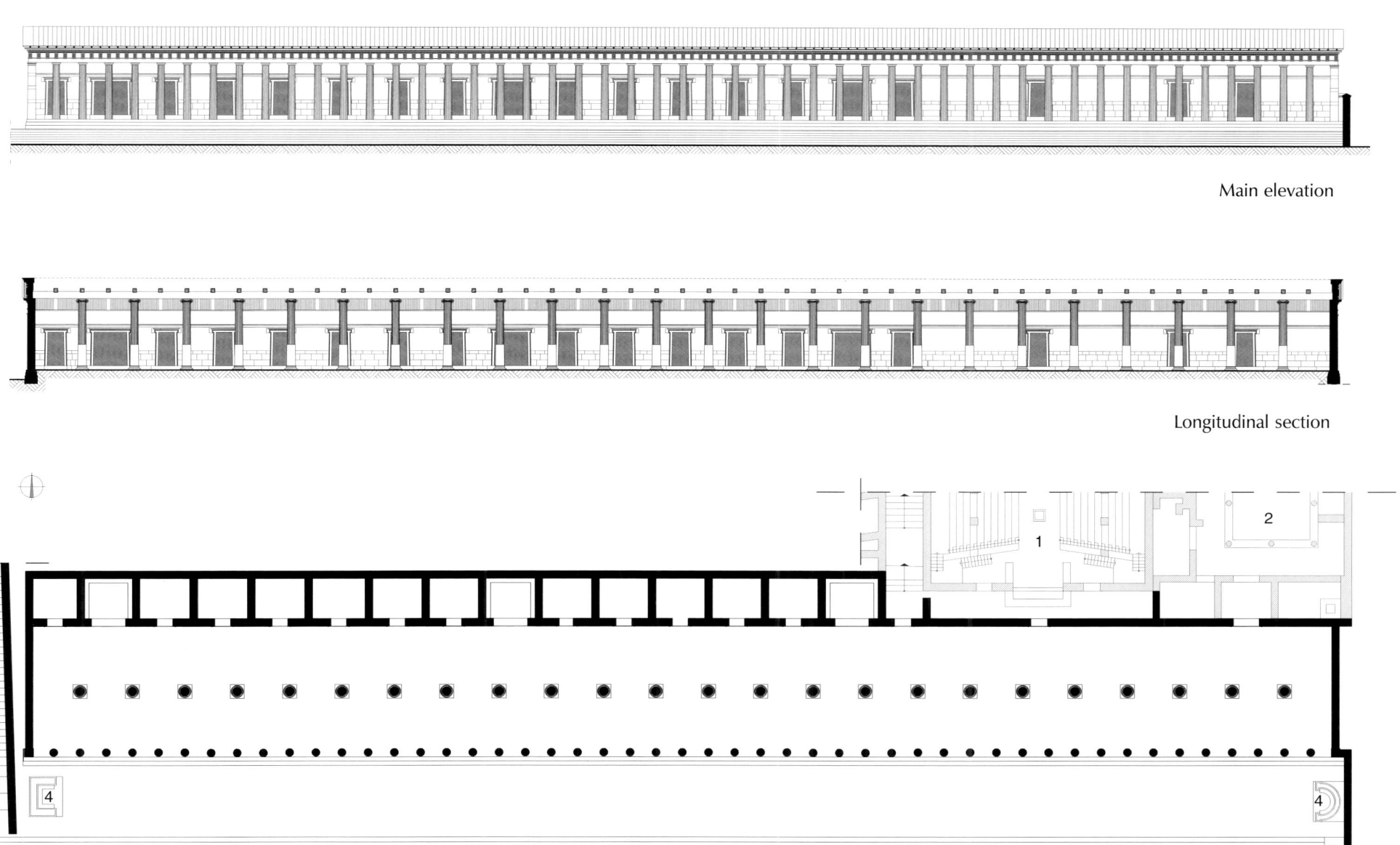

Main elevation

Longitudinal section

Plan
1. Ekklesiasterion 2. Prytaneion 3. Fountain 4. Exedra

AGORA GATE

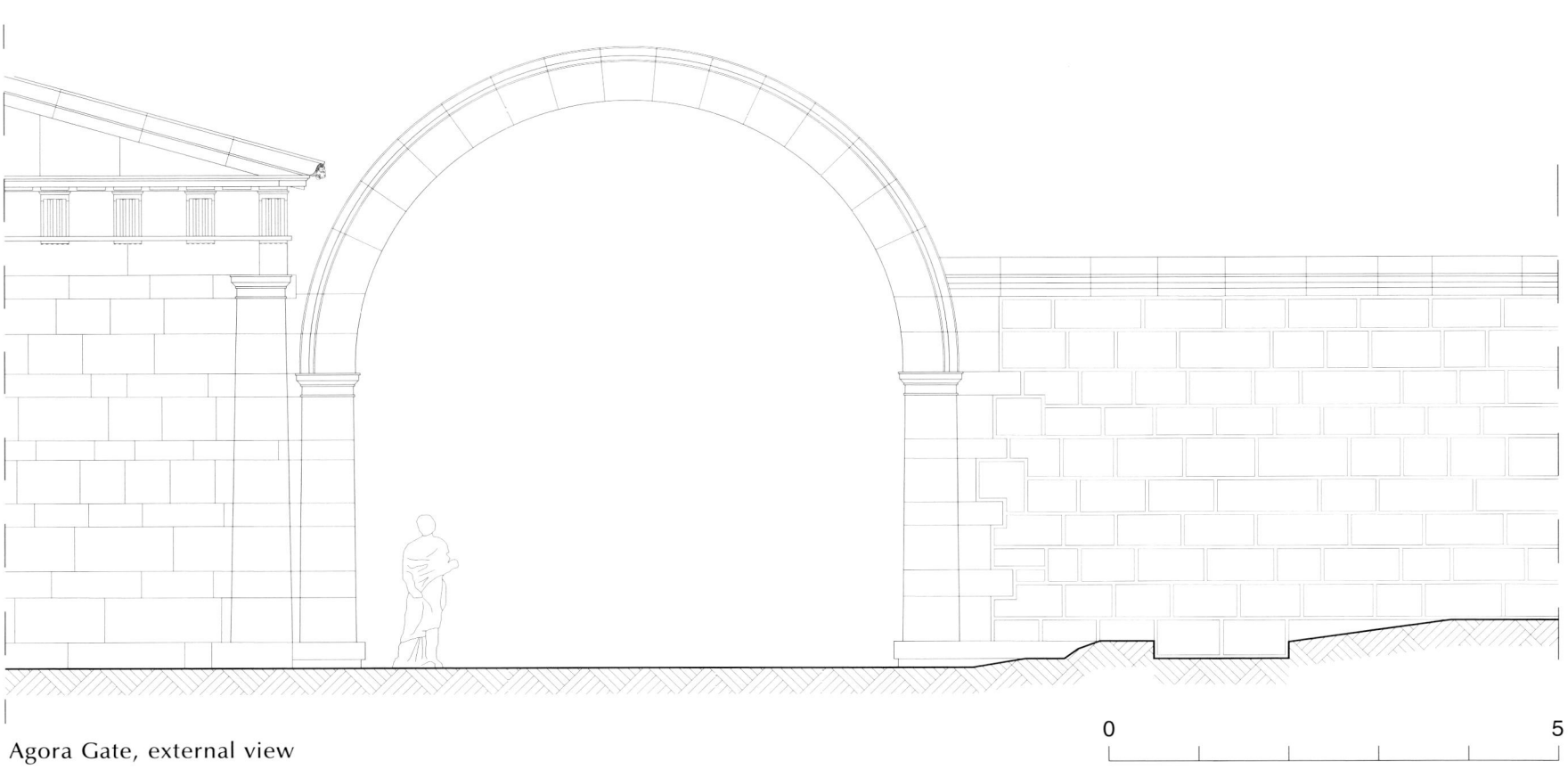

Agora Gate, external view

SACRED STOA

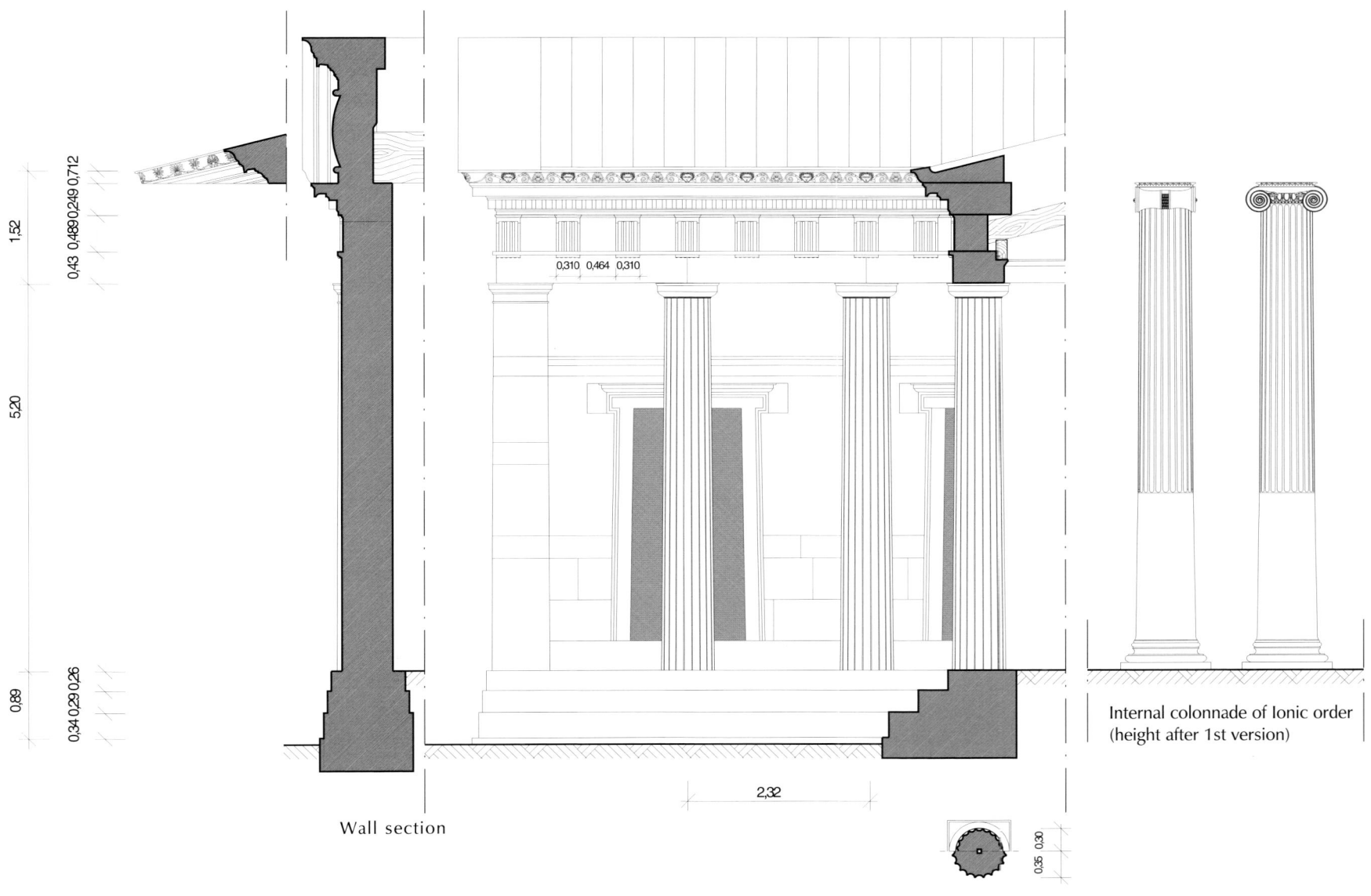

Wall section

Internal colonnade of Ionic order
(height after 1st version)

Architectural order

At the far end of the Stoa were 15 rooms, most of which had a door. Only three of them (the second, ninth and last room, counting from the west) had direct access to the Stoa. In one of these rooms there was a bench running round the walls, with marble bases that have been recovered. This room was probably dedicated to Rome.

The narrow walls at the east and west ends of the Stoa bore pediments decorated with a shield in relief. The inside of these walls was covered mainly with inscriptions in honour of important men. In the period between 130 and 50 BC the Sacred Stoa was the public archive of the city, a role earlier assigned to the Temple of Athena Polias.

Immediately to the north of the Stoa and along the back wall of its chambers, there was a corridor, 1m wide, for the draining of rainwater from the neighbouring residences. It also protected the rooms of the Stoa from excessive moisture.

SOUTH STOA: The South Stoa includes a group of three successive stoas arranged in a "Π" shape, built around the central area of the Agora on the east, south and west. The eastern aisle formed a curvature and extended along the north side of the Temple of Asclepius. It is not possible to draw conclusions about the exact date of its construction[7]. Assumptions can be made on the basis of the morphology of the ruins that have been recovered[8].

Each of the smaller stoas constituting the South Stoa complex had an external row of Doric columns. Behind this row, there was a corridor with chambers of dimensions similar to those of the chambers in the Sacred Stoa. These chambers were not connected with each other[9]. The east and west wings of the South Stoa have 18 columns each, and the central south section has 30, all of which are Doric. The east wing extended with a row of 16 additional columns along the north side of the Sanctuary of Asclepius[10]. In the northern corners of the east and west aisles, antae were formed, whose bases are still preserved in situ. However, at the meeting points of the east and west wings with the south section of the South Stoa there was no anta. Instead, there were pairs of half-columns joined to a common pilaster.

South part of the South Stoa
(drawing after Krischen)

7. Tomlinson, R., op. cit., p. 90.

8. Based on findings, W. Koenigs (cf. footnote 1) places the construction to the end of the third century BC.

9. The depth of the corridor – measuring from the external face of the stylobate to the external wall of the rooms – is approximately the same in all three sections. The internal measurement of the rooms is, on the east and west side, 1m shorter than the corridor, whereas on the south it is equal to it.

10. The proportions of size between the columns and the entablature appears "weightier" than in other cases of the Hellenistic period.

SOUTH STOA

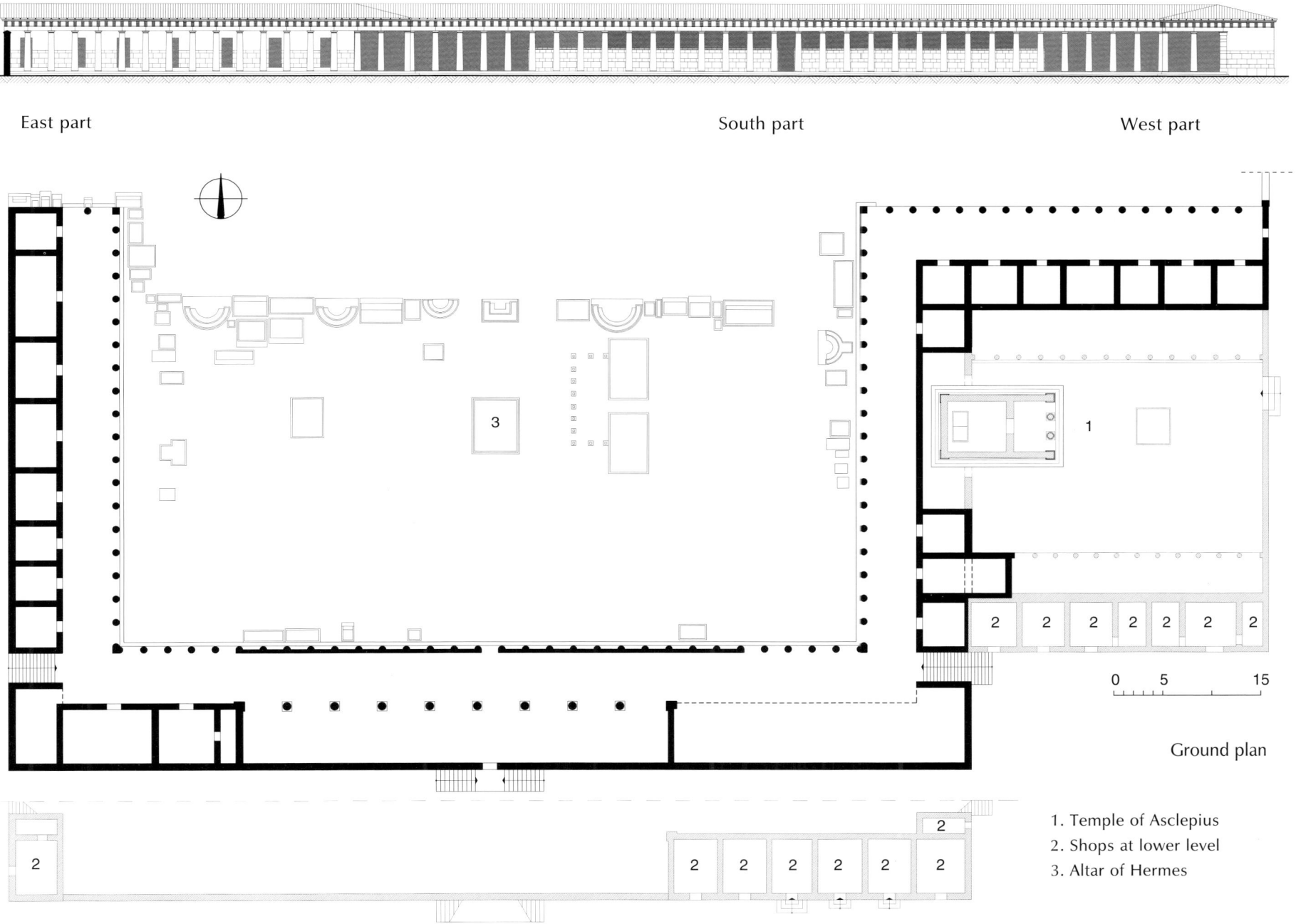

East part South part West part

Ground plan

1. Temple of Asclepius
2. Shops at lower level
3. Altar of Hermes

The columns of the east and west wings were probably not fluted; in those of the south aisle the carving of the flutes was never completed[11].

The capitals of the south external Stoa as well as those of the proscenium of the theatre are among the best and most complete findings of Priene: they are remarkable examples of the Doric order.

It is assumed that the roof of the Stoas was pitched, although in Schleif's reconstruction the roof appears to be monopitched and very slightly slanted, and was probably supported by the cornices of the chambers of the adjoining Temple of Asclepius. According to Krischen, the roof of the south section of the Stoa was probably pitched and slightly slanted[12].

The south section of the complex is of special interest. Between the central columns of the external row there was a wall up to 2.46m in height. Only the five last openings on the east and west ends, as well as the central opening, remained free. The wall was half as thick as the columns and was built in such a way that the columns gave the impression of being half-columns. The wall most likely was intended to protect the Stoa from the north winds. Its purpose, however, was probably not fully served since the wall is not as high as the columns – probably in order not to obstruct the light.

The overall design is of interest, since it was an attempt at protecting a large area from bad weather conditions, while at the same time providing plenty of natural light, which was necessary for the Stoa[13].

Behind this external row of columns there was a second one, also of the Doric order, which divided the central section of the Stoa into two aisles. This section contained a 43m corridor without any chambers. At the two ends (east and west) and at the central point of the southern wall of the Stoa, there were staircases leading to a lower level, to the road that led to the spring. The ground was slanted enough to allow the construction of some additional chambers under the rooms of the north section of the Stoa; these lower-level rooms were accessible from the street. The latter chambers are the only ones surviving to this day, and were probably independent shops, since there is no evidence of internal communication between the two levels.

Access staircase in the South Stoa from the southeast
(drawing after Krischen)

11. There are visible indications of the carved flutings on the lowest drums and also on the hypotrachelium of the capitals. It should be noted that instead of the characteristic 20 flutings of the Doric order, the 24 flutings of the Ionic order are found here. This is typical of the Hellenistic practice of incorporating elements from the Ionic into the Doric order. Wiegand, Th. – Schrader, H., op. cit., p. 190.

12. Kleiner, G., Priene, RE Suppl. IX, 1962, p. 1207.

13. This problem was never resolved in antiquity, since the wide use of glass as a transparent protective material was not known. Wiegand, Th. – Schrader, H., op. cit., p. 192.

SOUTH STOA

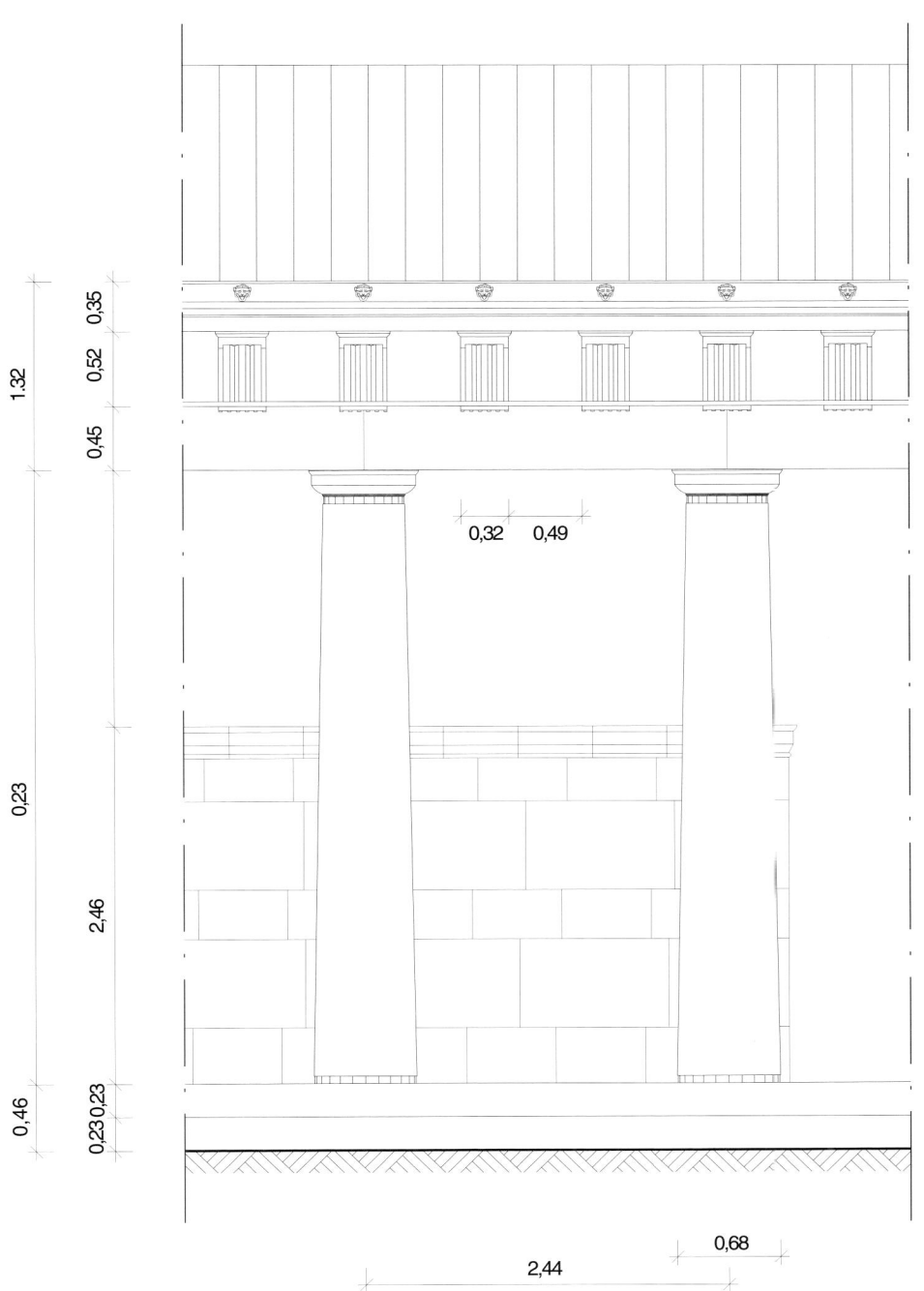

Architectural order

View of the west end of the Sacred Stoa
(drawing after Krischen)

View from the same angle

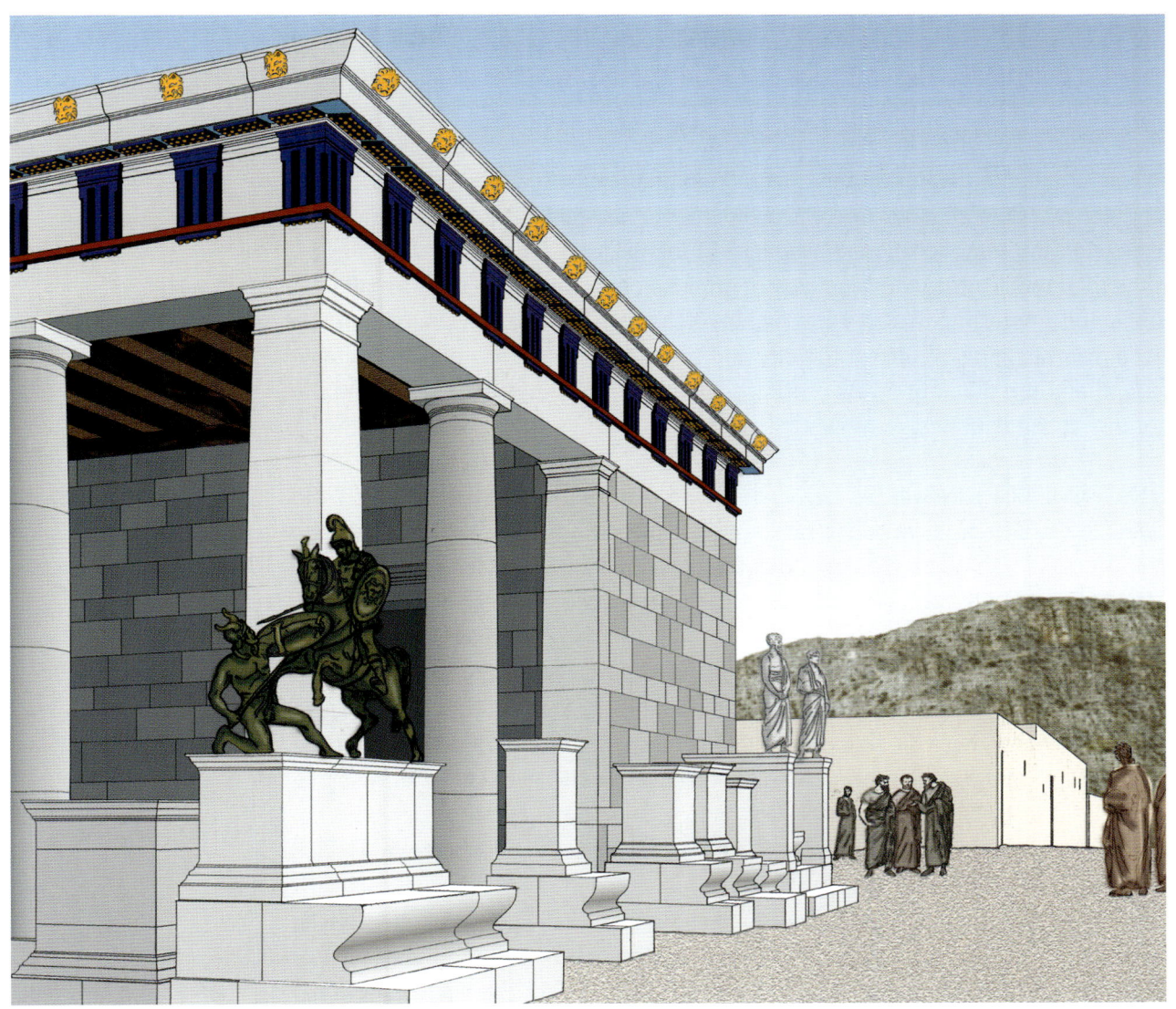

View of the west end of the Sacred Stoa (drawing after Krischen)

EKKLESIASTERION OR BOULEUTERION

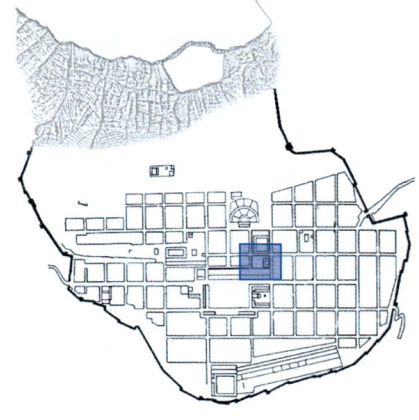

The Ekklesiasterion or Bouleuterion is the best preserved building of Priene. By studying its ruins one can draw some conclusions about its original form. The building was recovered during excavations from under a layer of mud and charred tiles[1], which suggests that it had probably been destroyed by fire. This layer protected the objects lying underneath.

The building was situated to the north of the Agora, behind the east section of the late-phase Sacred Stoa. It is probable that an open-air Bouleuterion, seating 300-500 people, had previously existed in the same location. To the east of the Ekklesiasterion is the Prytaneion, to the north the road that leads to the Sanctuary of Athena Polias, and to the west a road with ascending steps. It is interesting that an effort had been made to include this square building in the Hippodamian planning system of the city and to take advantage of the considerable slope of the land and the different levels of the surrounding roads in order to facilitate the movement of the citizens during assemblies.

DESCRIPTION OF THE BUILDING: It has been established that the Ekklesiasterion was built in two phases. First the roofing problem had to be solved and then efforts were made to make the seating more accessible through the construction of an additional staircase. However, archaeologists and architects disagree about the form of the building in each of these phases.

The almost square Ekklesiasterion building was the place of assembly of the Boule, which, along with the "Ekklesia of Demos", was the supreme political institution of the city. The marble seating (for 640 people) was arranged in a "Π" shape along three of the interior sides of the building. The architect took advantage of the sloping ground and the difference in the levels of the surrounding streets so as to facilitate the movement of citizens during assemblies. He also preserved the traditional rectangular ground plan which appeared in older buildings of similar purpose.

The south wall of the Ekklesiasterion had two doors. Between them was a large arch, under which Π-shaped marble seating was constructed, possibly with a back, that protruded from the building. According to Wiegand, this (at least in the second building phase) extended to the interior of the

1. Many fragments of roof tiles have been found. Their construction and colour decoration are meticulous.

View of the tiered seating

View to the southeast

building and was about 1m away from the wall of the side passageways. It was probably intended for the officials of the Boule. It is assumed that the part protruding from the building was protected from the sun and rain by cloth curtains. Special "partitions" had been placed between the seating and the walls of the side passageways in order to control, when necessary, the movement of the public to and from the altar at the centre of the building. Higher up above the arch, were windows, probably the only ones in the building, which provided the hall with natural light.

The core of the Ekklesiasterion was a rectangular space of 5m x 3.65m at the lower level, whose surface was probably covered with tamped earth. In its centre was a small marble altar decorated with bucrania (ox heads) and guilloches. Few traces of this elaborate decoration have survived the fire.

The tiered seating begins here[2]. There are ten rows of seats to the east and west, and sixteen to the north. There is also a perimetrical corridor behind the seating. Access to the seating was through four staircases starting from the four corners of the seating structure. The seating and staircases are defined by two slanting walls on their south side, similar to the "parodoi" of a theatre. The south staircases were supported on carefully constructed side walls, without penetrating them, which indicates that the staircases were constructed at a later stage.

It is obvious that the building had been planned carefully so as to facilitate access to and from the building. The architect's aim was twofold: on the one hand, to give the citizens eazy access in and out of the hall, and on the other, to keep them away from the altar so that their movements did not interfere with the orations of the public speakers. For this reason there were three entrances at each of the three sides of the building[3]. Thus citizens entered through the north and west entrances, passed through the perimetrical corridor and then walked down the staircases and reached their seats, or used the corridor between the Ekklesiasterion and the Sacred Stoa, entered through the doors of the south entrance at the lower level of the hall, and climbed the stairs to the seating. This last arrangement is similar to the movement of the audience in theatres, where spectators move through the parodoi at the orchestra level towards the seating. The majority of

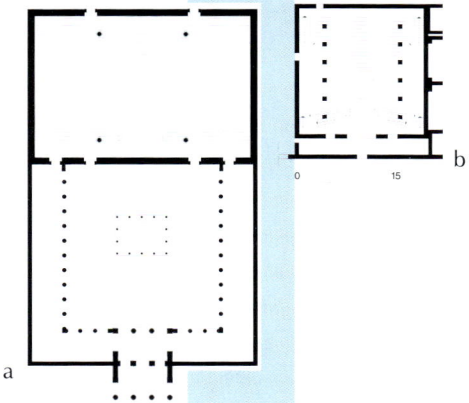

(a) Bouleuterion of Miletus
(b) Ekklesiasterion of Priene

2. The section of seating, 37-39cm high and with a seat width 27cm, is characteristic of ancient seats encountered in other cities, such as Miletus. There are no honorary seats. Probably the last row of seats had a back, as suggested by remains on the east side. The total number of seats, assuming that each spectator occupies a width of 0.50m, is estimated at 640.

3. In particular: a) a door on the street towards the Temple of Athena and the western end of the building b) one door on the west side and on the ascending side street and c) two doors on the south side, on either side of the semi-circular arch.

EKKLESIASTERION, PHASE A'

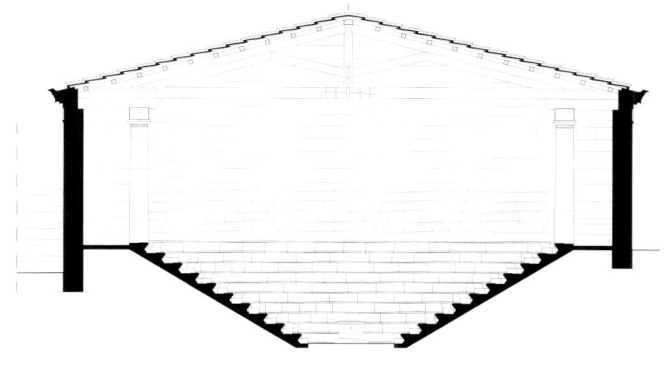

Section A - A'

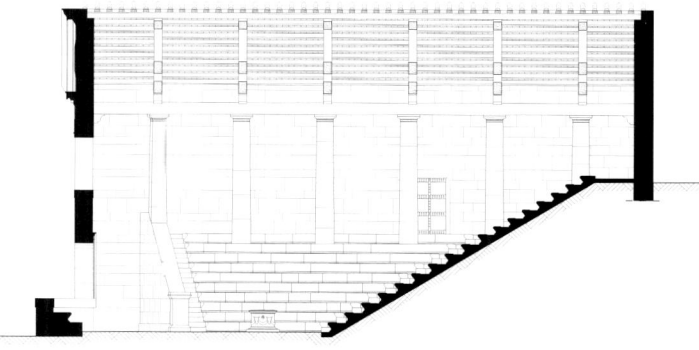

Section B - B'

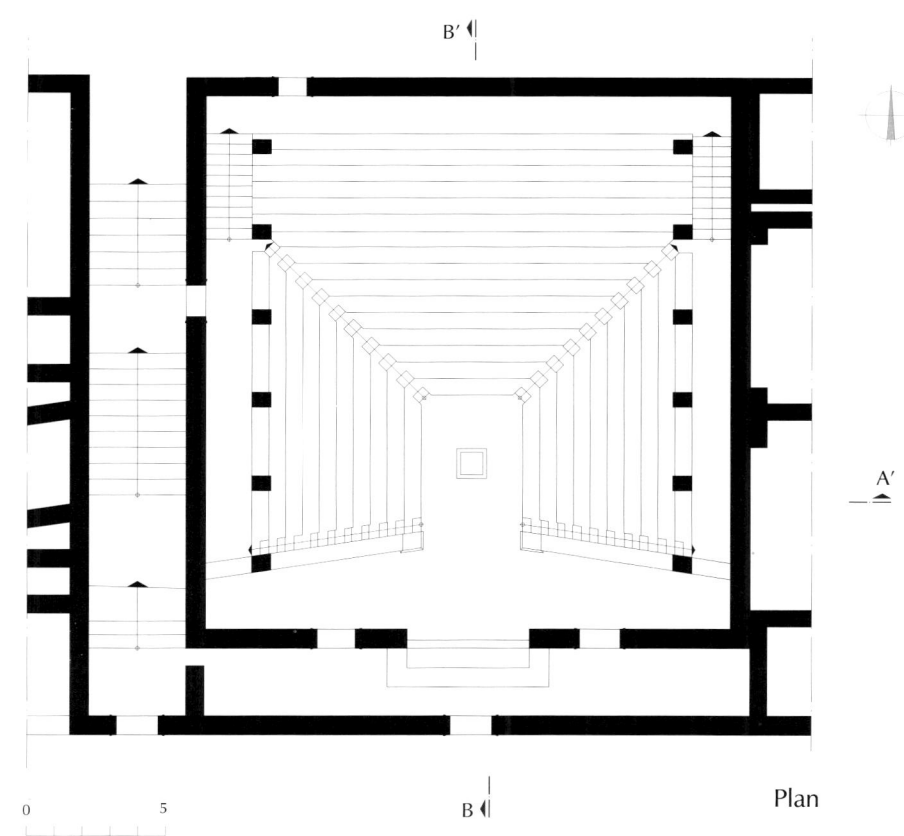

Plan

citizens probably used the doors of the Sacred Stoa leading to the adjoining uphill road. It is remarkable that the circulation of citizens was controlled through the construction of a transverse wall at the building's external corridor. The width of the corridor at that point was only 0.65m, allowing only one person to pass at a time.

THE ROOFING OF THE BUILDING: As indicated earlier, one can trace two building phases in the Ekklesiasterion. These relate to different solutions to the problem of supporting the wooden pitched roof. The surviving parts belong to the second phase.

In the initial phase the support pilasters of the roof stood on the perimetrical corridor. There were six pilasters on the east and the west sides. Their height is estimated to be at least 5m, while the height of the north corridor at 3m. The opening between the pilasters is 14.5m – whether this space could be covered by wooden beams is a point of contention[4].

In an attempt to solve the problem at a later stage, the pilasters were shifted by 2m towards the interior of the building and were reinforced, with the result that the gap in the roof was down to 10.65m. According to Wiegand, it is a moot point whether in the first building phase the north side had similar pilasters, since the upper tiers and the north corridor are totally destroyed. Assuming that he has located traces of two of them, Wiegand claims that in the second phase pilasters must have been constructed on the north side. According to Krischen the construction of pilasters on the north side was not necessary.

A third view, held by Bouras[5], claims that the building was roofed only perimetrically, that is over the corridor behind the tiers. The gap of 14m is considered too large to be bridged by wooden beams, and it is conjectured that a light construction of cloth probably sheltered the members of the assembly.

---

4. It should be noted that the net width of the cella of the Temple of Athena Polias is 9.38m, whereas the distance between internal columns of large Doric temples, such as the Parthenon, is 9.82m.

5. Bouras Ch., Mathimata istorias tis Architectonikis (A Course in the History of Architecture), vol. 1, 1st ed. 1968, 2nd ed. 1980, 3rd ed. Athens: Symmetria editions, 1991, p. 311.

EKKLESIASTERION, PHASE B'

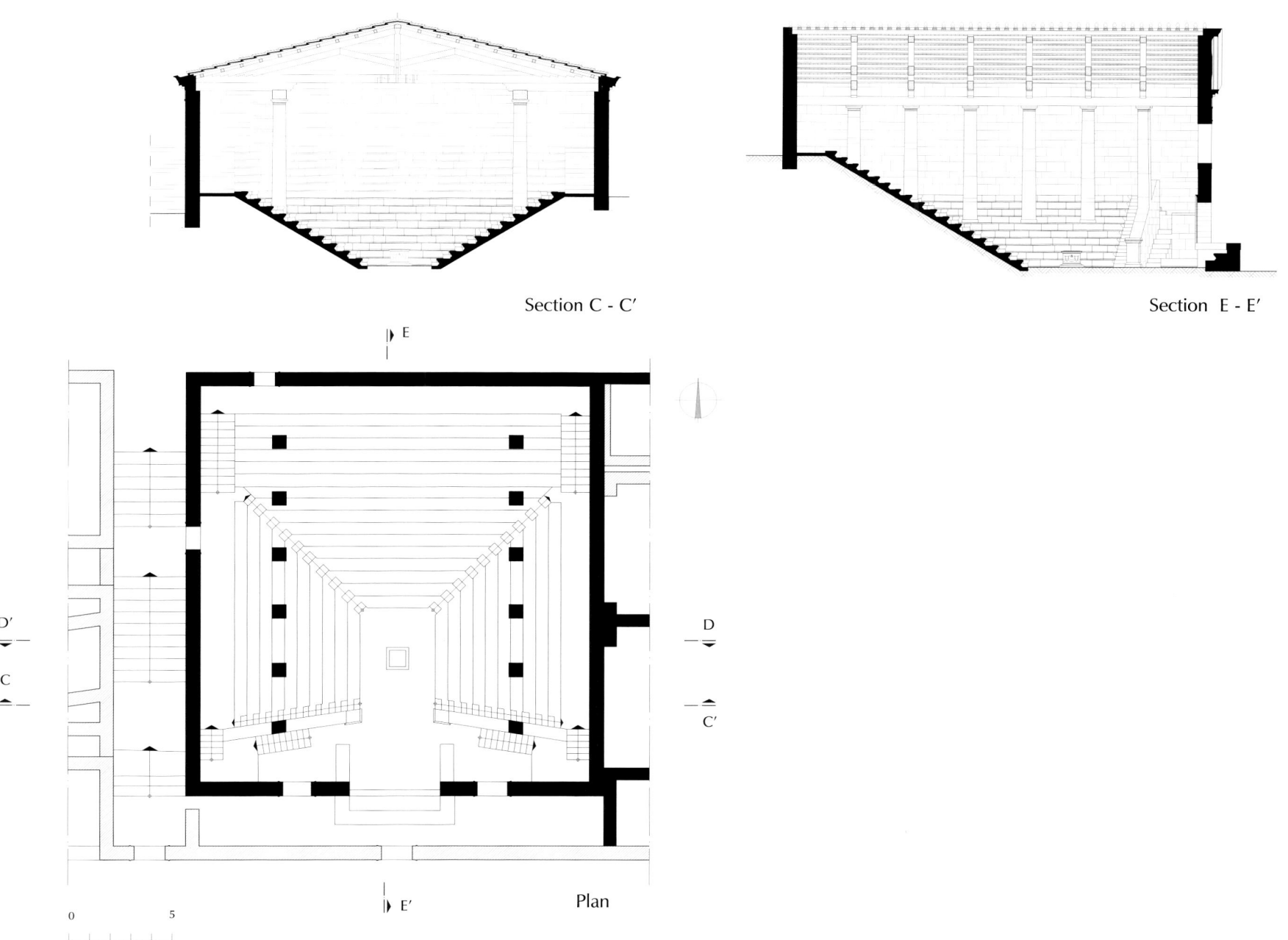

Section C - C'

Section E - E'

Plan

South view

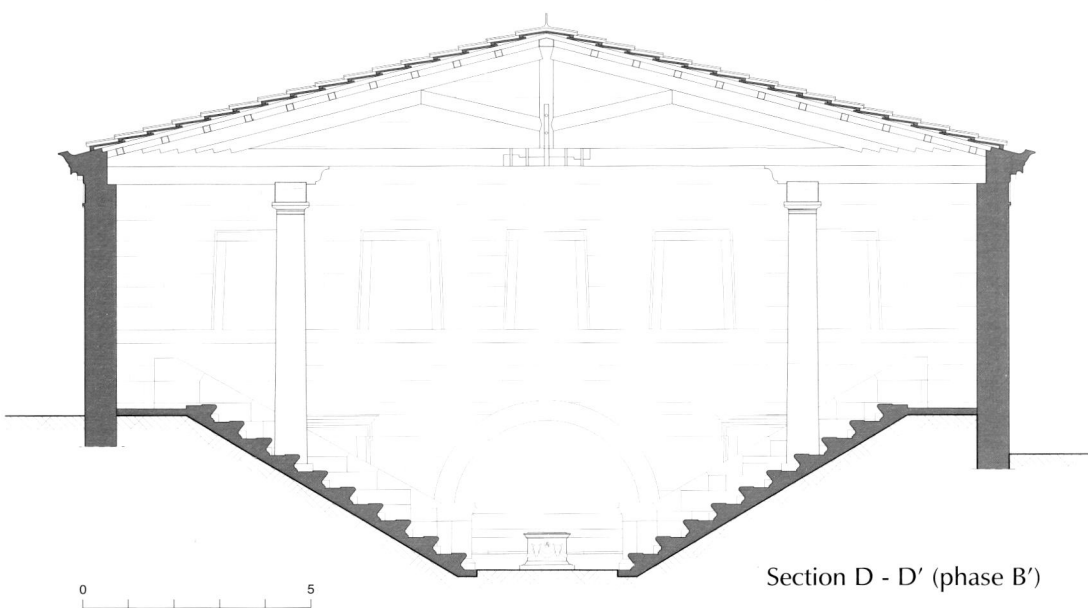

Section D - D' (phase B')

0 5

Perspective of interior space during phase A'

PRYTANEION

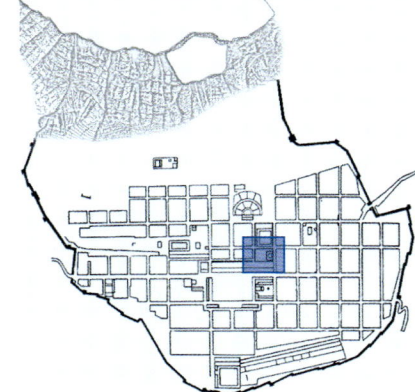

The Prytaneion was a public building having some of the features of a private residence, but often of a monumental structure. It contained the "common hearth" of the city. It was also the place where the epistates resided[1] during their twenty-four-hour duty, where meals were offered to the prytaneis and select citizens, where guests were accommodated and the city's sacrifices were conducted. The weights and measures were kept here as well.

LOCATION: In Priene it is thought likely that the Prytaneion was the building whose ruins have been found to the east of the Ekklesiasterion. To the north of the building there is a street leading to the Temple of Athena, while to the east there is an uphill road that starts at the Agora. Here also the ground slopes considerably. Thus, the floor of the building, which is at the same level as that of the Sacred Stoa, is 2.5m lower than the road to the north of the Prytaneion.

The Prytaneion was built after the Ekklesiasterion-Bouleuterion. It seems, however, that its construction had been planned in advance, since the exterior of the Ekklesiasterion's eastern wall is not as elaborately built as the western wall[2]. According to Kleiner[3], the Ekklesiasterion and the Prytaneion were probably not planned simultaneously, although they were constructed not too far apart in time.

DESCRIPTION OF THE BUILDING: The Prytaneion in its present form belongs to a later phase of the years of the Roman Empire. Most of the findings that have been recovered can be traced back to this period. It is reasonable, however, to assume that in the later-phase construction the original form was preserved, which means that the original building, like the surviving one, included a peristyle (colonnaded structure); but this is impossible to confirm. It is difficult to reconstruct graphically the Prytaneion in its original form since even the ruins discovered during excavations are in very bad condition[4].

The building was accessible through the Sacred Stoa. By reconstructing the arrangement of the houses in the city one can assume that the building included a peristyle around a courtyard, where there are still the ruins of a cistern (perhaps for collecting rainwater), a basin (possibly as a provision in case the cistern overflowed), and two carved supports of what was presumably a marble altar[5].

---

1. The Prytaneis was a body consisting of the representatives of the phylae (tribes) to which the citizens belonged. The epistates presided over this body for 24 hours. MacDowel, D. M., "Prytaneis" in: Hornblower S., Spawforth A. (ed.), Oxford Classical Dictionary, Oxford: University Press, 1996, p. 1269.

2. Wiegand, Th. – Schrader, H., Priene. Ergebnisse der Ausgrabungen und Untersuchungen von den Jahren 1895-1898. Unter Mitwirkung von G. Krummer, W. Wilberg, H. Winnefeld, R. Zahn. Berlin: Königliche Museen zu Berlin, 1904, p. 233.

3. Kleiner, G., Priene, RE Suppl. IX, 1962, p. 1202.

4. Miller, S. G., The Prytaneion. Its Function and Architectural Form. Berkeley – Los Angeles – London: California Press, 1978, p. 117.

5. Op. cit., p. 120.

View of the Prytaneion from the southeast (1896)
© DAI Istanbul

To the south there were three structures, the central one serving as an entrance. To the west there was a structure accessible only through the courtyard, while to the east there was a similar structure, the entrance to which has not been traced. In the southeast corner of the latter, a rectangular hearth has survived in fairly good condition, possibly belonging to the original phase of the building. The sacred flame of the city burned there. On the basis of findings in the area it is assumed that this hearth was reconstructed several times[6].

To the west there are two more rectangular structures separated by a wall whose date is difficult to determine. At the entrance to the southernmost of these structures, which is 2.5m wide, there are indications that a door was attached. The northern wall was supported by a blind arch built of baked bricks, which must be dated back to Roman times[7]. The narrow walls of the northern chamber were also supported by arches.

On the north side of the Prytaneion there are three more chambers of equal depth but different width, on a level 60-75cm higher than the corridor of the peristyle. It is not easy to draw any conclusions about the purpose of these structures, due to the difference in levels, the lack of benches and the fact that any objects found there have been lost[8].

---

6. *Op. cit., p. 120.*

7. *Next to the door a column has been preserved with an honorific inscription of the late Roman period, referring to one of the arch-prytaneis. The base of the column consists of a Doric capital placed upside down, while its shaft is made of previously-used material.*

8. *Miller, S. G., op. cit., p. 119.*

PRYTANEION

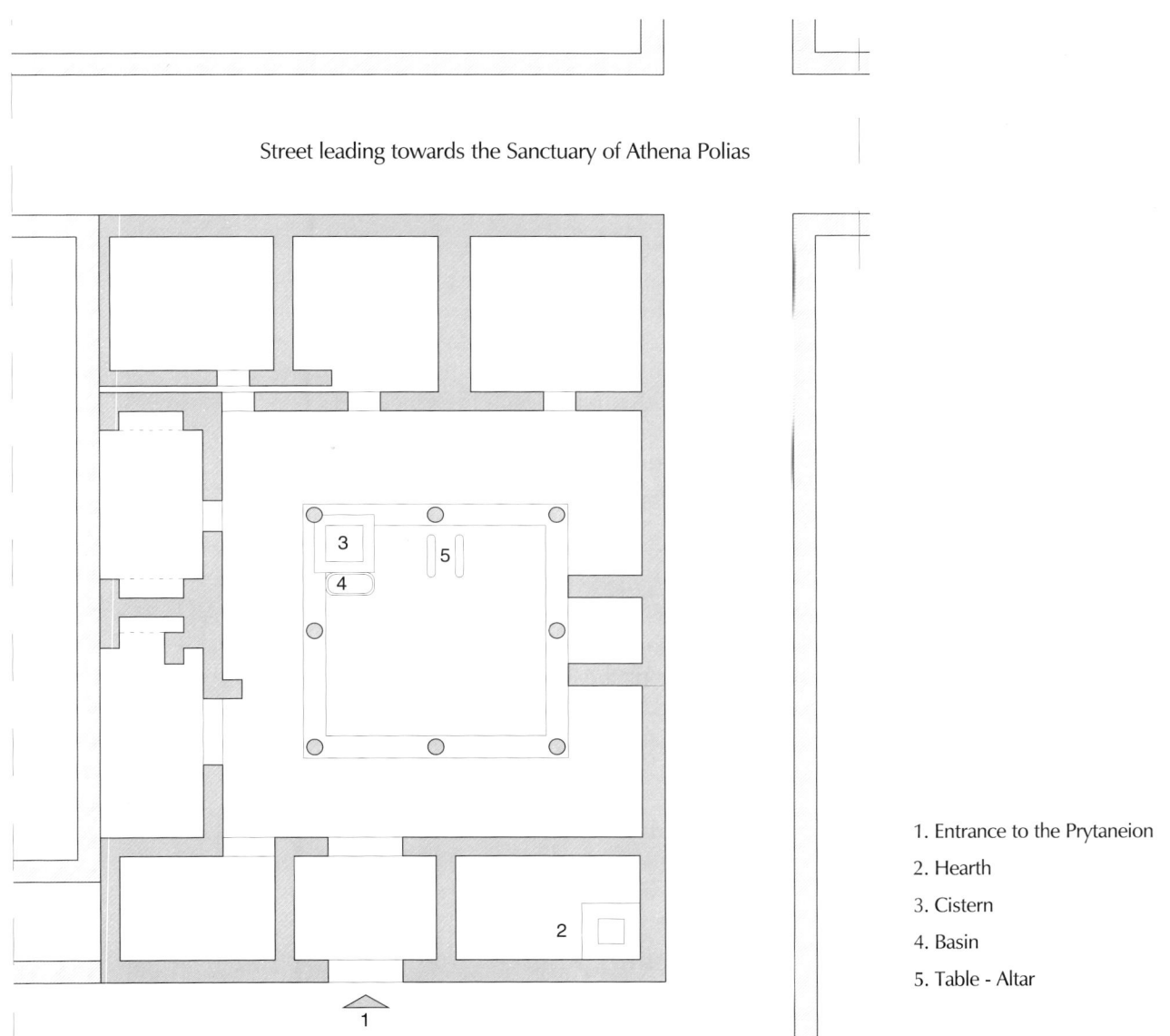

Street leading towards the Sanctuary of Athena Polias

1. Entrance to the Prytaneion
2. Hearth
3. Cistern
4. Basin
5. Table - Altar

SANCTUARY OF ATHENA POLIAS

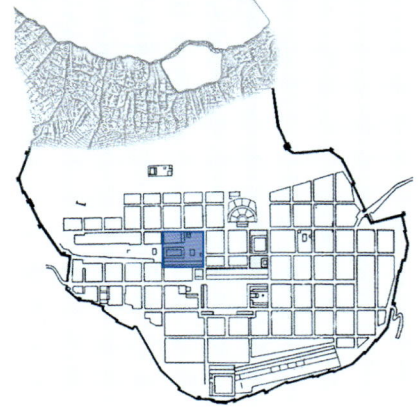

LOCATION: The site selected for the planning of the sanctuary and the construction of the Temple of Athena Polias was a conspicuous location on the northwest side of the Agora, situated on a steep hill, with maximum elevation of 96m above sea level. Due to the slope of the ground and in order to attain an even area of appropriate dimensions, a large terrace was constructed with a strong retaining wall at its south side. When excavations around the end of the 19th century revealed this imposing, carefully constructed wall, some of its parts had been preserved intact up to a height of 7m. The west section of the wall was attached to the temple's foundation in its southwestern corner, and its east corner extended to the propylon, while its east to west axis was not parallel to the temple. The retaining wall was not constructed in a uniform way, which leads to the conclusion that it was probably not built in the same period.

The sanctuary's courtyard occupied exactly two building plots and was distinctly separated from the neighbouring houses. Access was gained from the east through an amphiprostyle propylon with an Ionic prostasis. Apart from the temple, the sanctuary included an altar, a Doric stoa and a treasury. Archaeological findings in the area indicate that it must have taken a long time to construct the temple and the rest of the buildings in the sanctuary.

THE TEMPLE: The Temple of Athena Polias in Priene is one of the most magnificent monuments in the history of Greek architecture. Its construction began shortly after the foundation of the city, around 350 BC. In Roman times it was dedicated to the worship of Augustus.

Already in ancient times the temple was recognised as a model Ionic temple. The architect, Pythius, wrote a monograph describing the principles he followed in designing the temple. Thanks to Vitruvius, who studied Pythius' text, the Temple of Athena, and its morphological details in particular, became a standard reference work and study guide during the Roman period and even later, during the Renaissance and the Neo-Classical revival. It should be noted that before the construction of the Mausoleum at Halicarnassus (around 353 3C), a work also attributed to Pythius, the features of the Ionic order were not yet discernible in Ionia.

The building of the monumental peripteral temple dates back to 350-330 BC. It is known that after his victory at the Granicus River (334 BC), Alexander the Great decided to cover all expenses needed for the completion of the temple, as a gift to the city[1].

---

1. Upon his command, a commemorative inscription, in which he himself was named as the dedicator of the temple, was incised beneath the capital of the south anta. Schede, M., Die Ruinen von Priene. Archäologisches Institut des Deutschen Reiches. Abteilung Istanbul. Berlin und Leipzig: 1. Auflage, 1934.

SANCTUARY OF ATHENA POLIAS

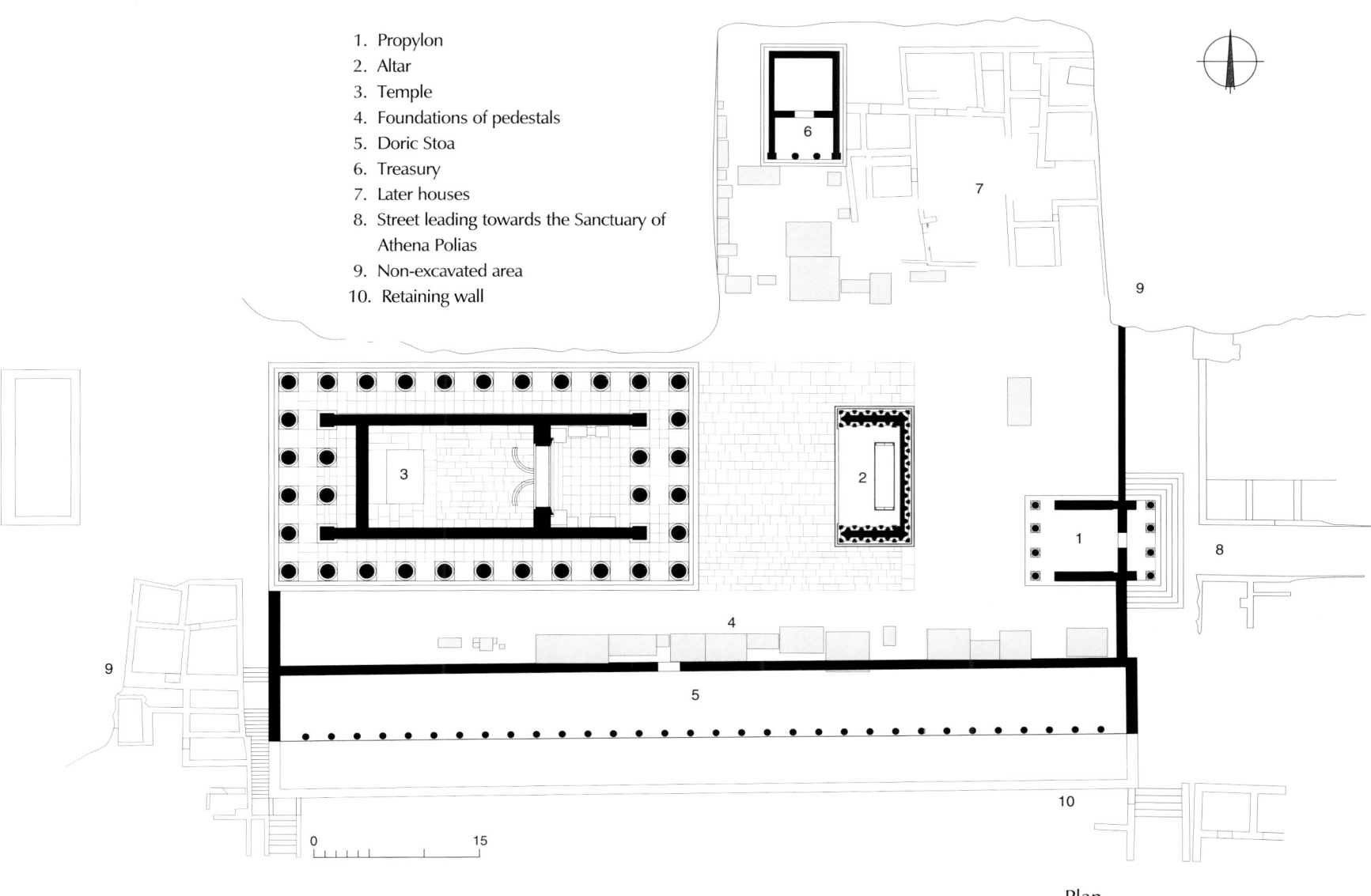

1. Propylon
2. Altar
3. Temple
4. Foundations of pedestals
5. Doric Stoa
6. Treasury
7. Later houses
8. Street leading towards the Sanctuary of Athena Polias
9. Non-excavated area
10. Retaining wall

Plan

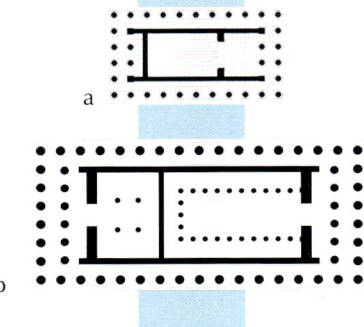

a. Temple of Athena Polias
b. Parthenon

It is reasonable to conclude that, before that time, the building of the temple had reached as far as the construction of the antae, the capitals of which are decorated according to the style of the 4th century BC. In the same period, or a little later, the construction of the east pediment and possibly of half of the east section of the temple must have been completed. The west section remained incomplete for at least 200 years. None of the surviving architectural members of the higher positions of the upper level are dated earlier than the mid-2nd century BC.

It is likely that the architect of the temple aimed at establishing a model typology of the Ionic order combining elements of older periods[2]. He focused on the pure relation of different elements and on creating a structure where all dimensions were integral multiples of a fundamental measurement unit, which was the attic foot[3], the so-called "embates", also adopted by the Romans. The proportions of the temple are harmonious, its dimension ratios being always integral, a feature that characterised the academicism of the late Classical era[4]. Order and mathematical harmony are the central features of the structure and are immediately evident; they are predominant not only in the horizontal plane but also in the temple's façade. Noteworthy is the fact that the temple is perfectly parallel to the east to west axis.

The temple was made of blue and gray limestone from Mount Mykale, a material predominant in most of the buildings of the city, with the exception of their foundations, where occasionally hard breccia stone was employed.

The temple is peripteral, of Ionic order, with eleven columns on the long side and six columns on the narrow side[5]. The temple is "hekatompedos" (100-feet long): the length of the cella is 29.48m, i.e., 100 attic feet, which was exactly the length of the earlier temple of Athena in the Acropolis of Athens, as well as of the Parthenon cella. There are a "pronaos" and an "opisthodomos", a feature appearing for the first time in Asia Minor. Three steps lead from the ground level to the "pronaos". In the ground plan the "pronaos" is almost square (30 x 32 attic feet), in contrast to the "opisthodomos" that has a smaller depth (12 attic feet). A doorway connected the "pronaos" with the cella, where the statue of the goddess stood.

2. Gruben, G., Die Tempel der Griechen, München: Hirmer, 1986, p. 380.

3. The attic foot in Priene was equal to 29.46 cm. Hoepfner, W. – Schwandner, E. L., Haus und Stadt im klassischen Griechenland. Deutsches Archäologisches Institut, Architekturreferat. In Zusammenarbeit mit dem Seminar für Klassische Archäologie der Freien Universität Berlin. München: Deutschen Kunstverlag, 1994, p. 195.

4. As an example the following dimensions (in attic feet) are mentioned: the overall length of the temple 100 feet, the cella 50, the pronaos 30, the height of the temple on the long side 50 (the column 43 and the entablature 7). The height of the column is 10 times its smallest diameter. The diameter of the columns is estimated to 0.30m, their height to 2.70m, whereas their inter axial space to 1.20m. Thus the total external dimensions are: 13.20 x 7.12m.

5. The ground plan of the temple strictly follows a grid system following a unit size of 6 x 6 attic feet.

TEMPLE AND ALTAR OF ATHENA POLIAS

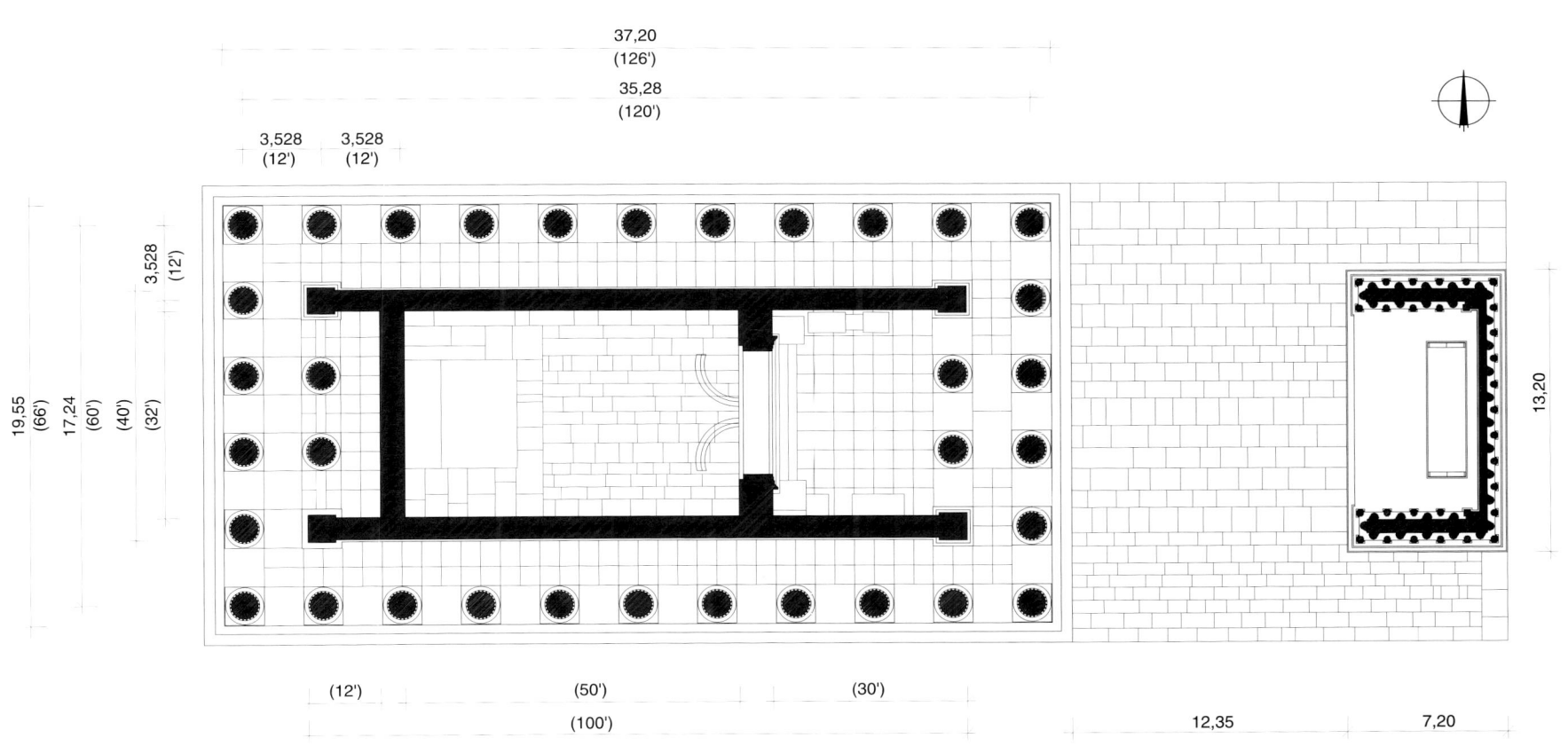

a: Dimensions in metres
(a): Dimensions in attic feet

Plan

The "opisthodomos"[6] is not connected to the cella. When the monument was discovered, one could still see the marks made by the sliding doors on the floor of the cella, which stood three steps above the "pronaos". The division of the temple into a deep "pronaos" and a narrow "opisthodomos", both having a facade with two columns in antis, was to become characteristic of other temples in Asia Minor[7].

The shafts of the columns have 24 flutes, ending in vertical bands. Each column stands on a square plinth, which increases the height of the base of the column and prevents people from moving too close to the column. The base of the column is formed according to the Asia Minor model: it consists of three pairs of fine tori, one on top of the other, having between them a trochilus of the same thickness. A fourth torus, much thicker, is placed on the uppermost pair.

The height of the columns cannot be determined with accuracy. According to studies based on a graphic reconstruction of the south anta, the height of the columns was either 11.60m or 12.90m, the second version being more likely.

The capitals were modelled on those of the archaic Artemisium at Ephesus, but in the Temple of Athena Polias they assume their classical form. The capitals of the external columns are more oblong and decorated mainly on their front side, in contrast to the capitals of the interior columns of the "pronaos" and "opisthodomos" which are more elaborately formed[8]. A basic feature of the capitals is the pair of volutes facing each other and forming pulvini on the sides. Between the volutes and the shaft of the column is the echinus, a circular disc with a section of Ionian moulding that bears relief eggs. The capitals are crowned by a fine abacus, decorated with a Lesbian moulding.

The architrave, along with the crowning decorative band, is of the same height as the cornice (3 1/2 attic feet). It is evident that the proportions of the members are related to those of the whole structure, which contributes to the internal harmony of the monument. The architrave is divided into three successive horizontal bands, each slightly projecting from the previous one. The uppermost band is a little wider than the other two and is decorated with an Ionic moulding with relief eggs.

Ionic capital of the Artemision of Ephesus (Archaic period)

6. *Under Augustus the temple was renovated: three steps were added leading from the pronaos to the cella, while the opisthodomos was closed off with "partitions" and was turned into a treasury, Wiegand, Th. – Schrader, H., Priene. Ergebnisse der Ausgrabungen und Untersuchungen in den Jahren 1895-98, Berlin, 1904, p. 133.*

7. *Such as the Temple of Dionysus in Teos (Antiquities of Ionia IV Tafel XXII), the Temple of Apollo, the Smintheion in Troad and the Temple of Artemis Leucophryene in Magnesia-ad-Maeandrum. Wiegand, Th. – Schrader, H., op.cit. p. 86.*

8. *Gruben, G., op. cit., p. 383.*

TEMPLE OF ATHENA POLIAS

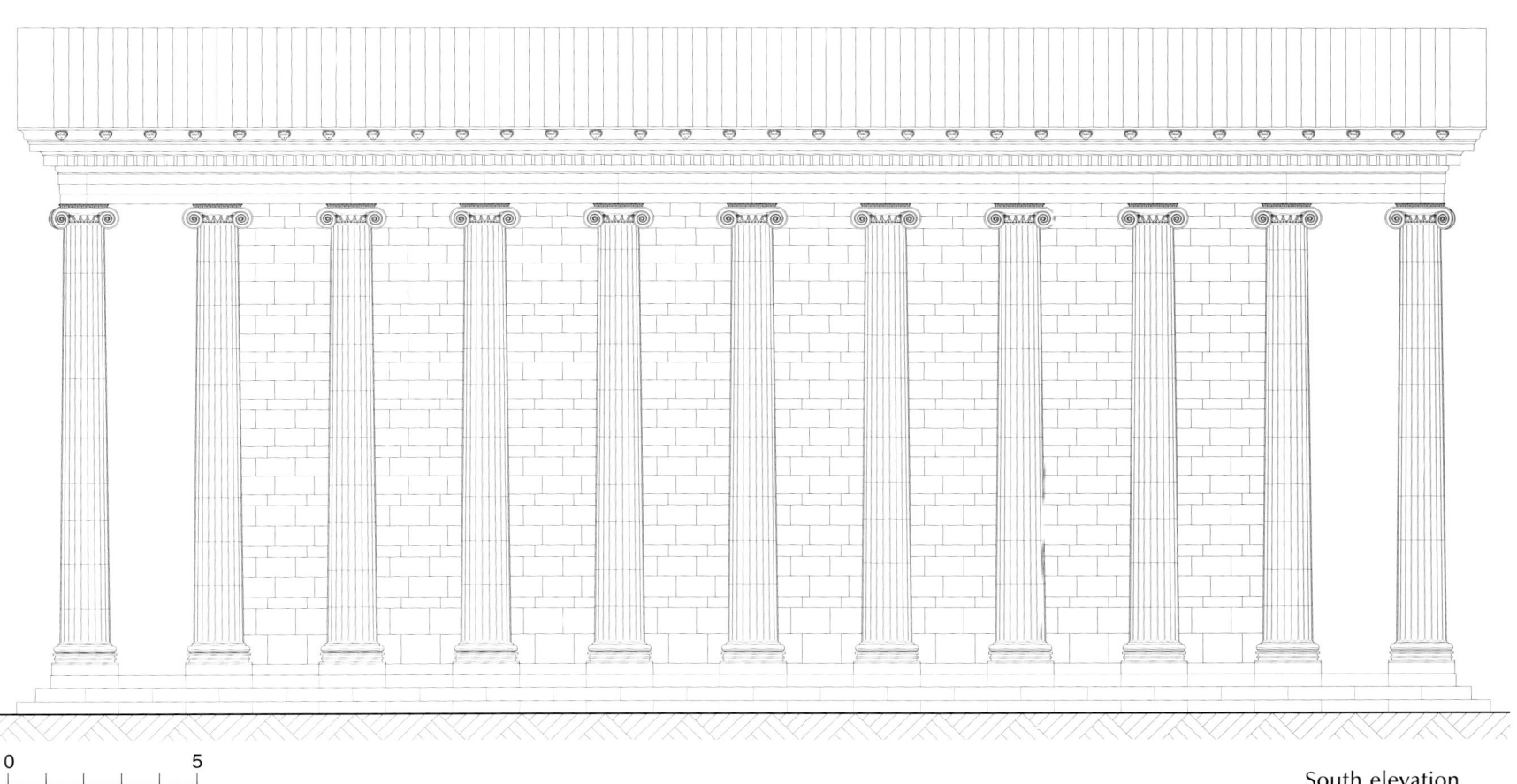

South elevation

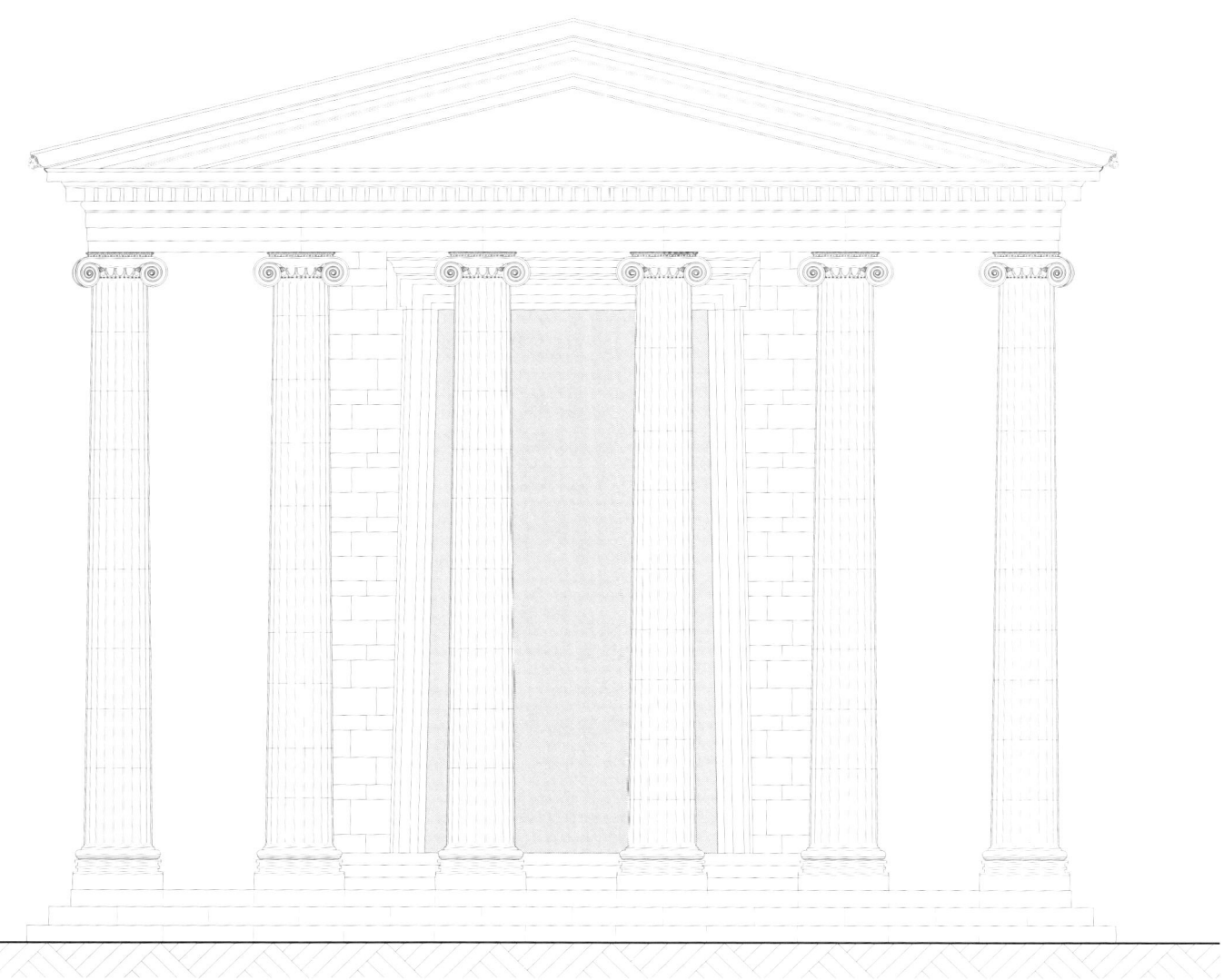

East elevation

TEMPLE OF ATHENA POLIAS

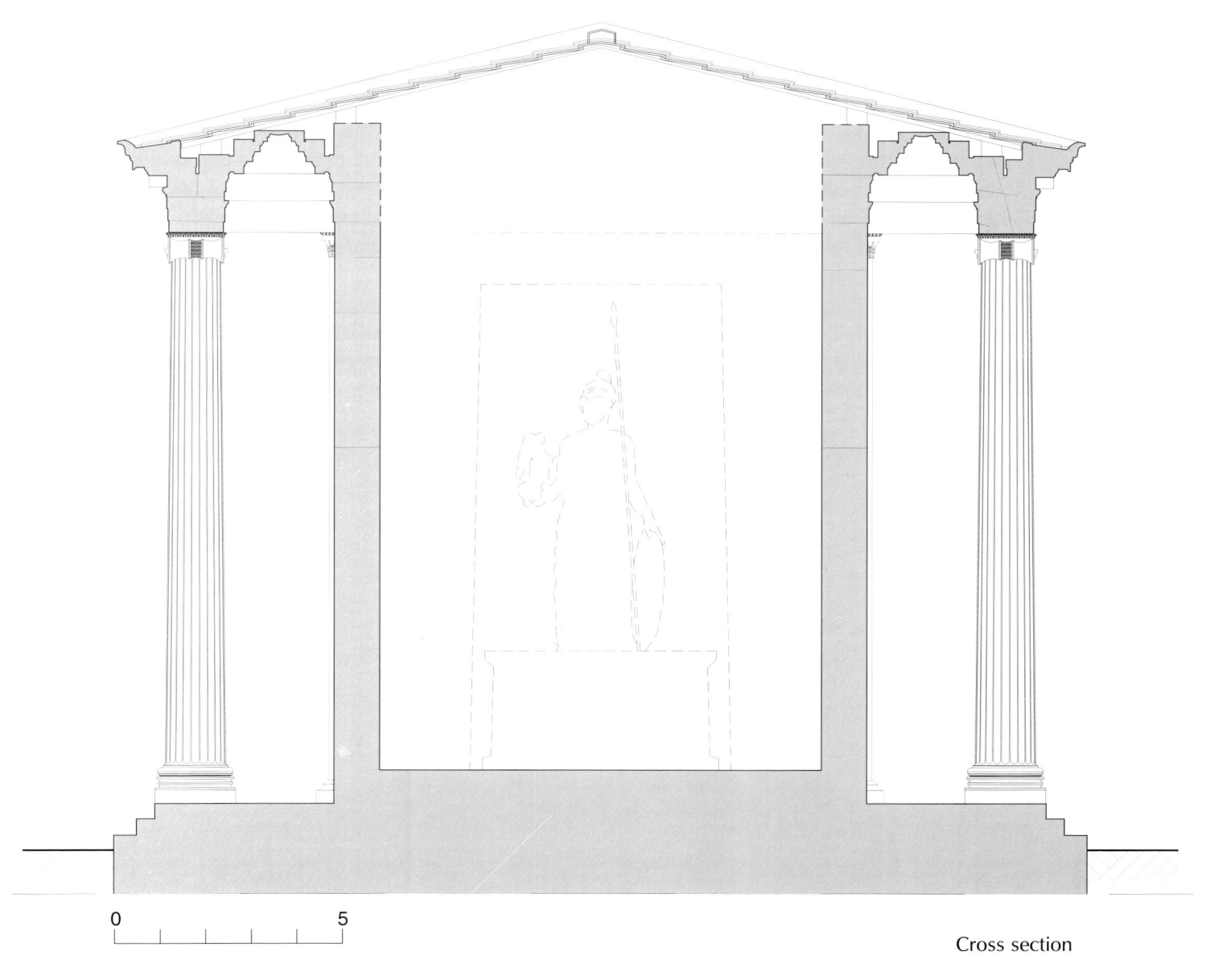

Cross section

TEMPLE OF ATHENA POLIAS

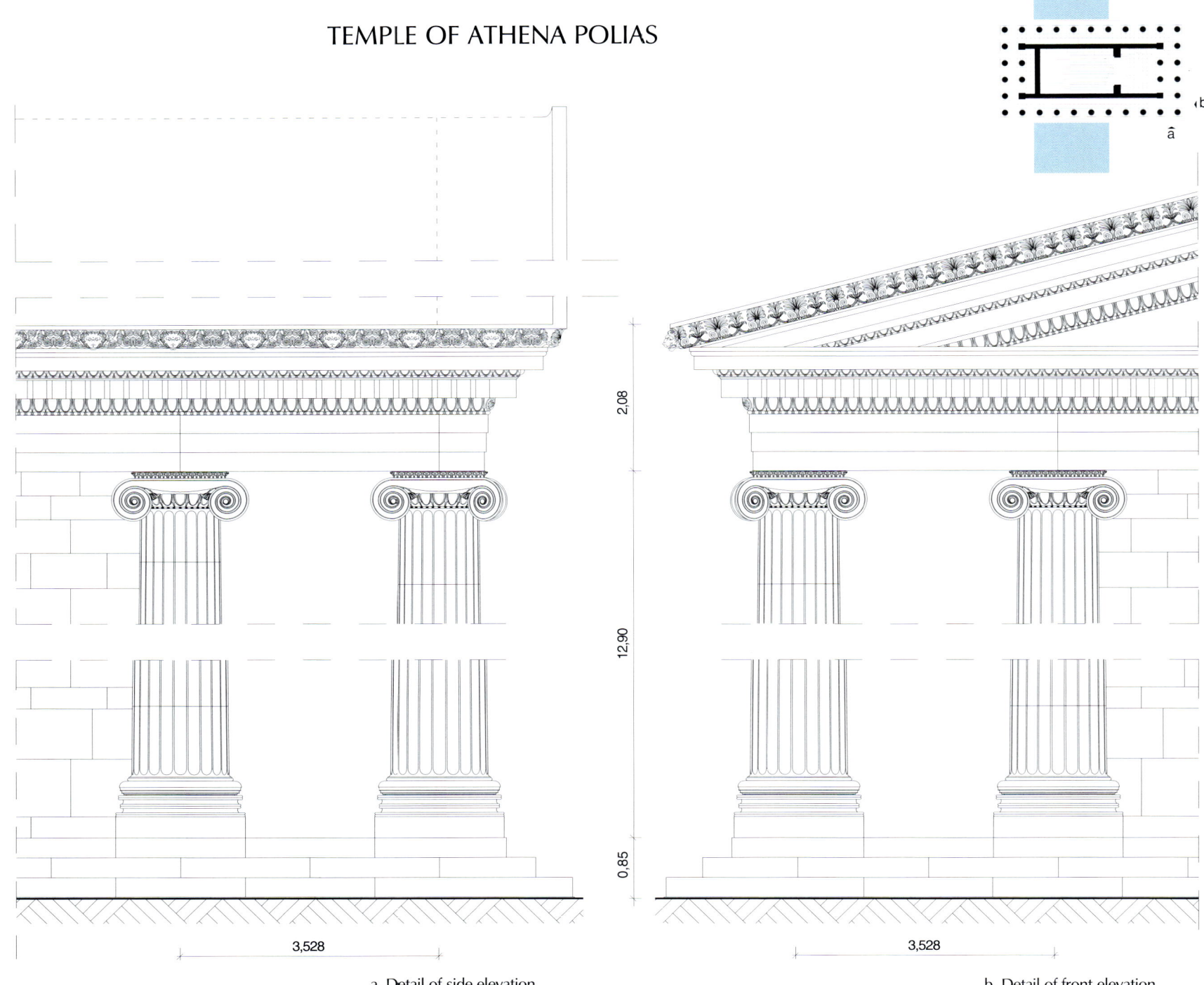

Architectural order

a. Detail of side elevation

b. Detail of front elevation

TEMPLE OF ATHENA POLIAS

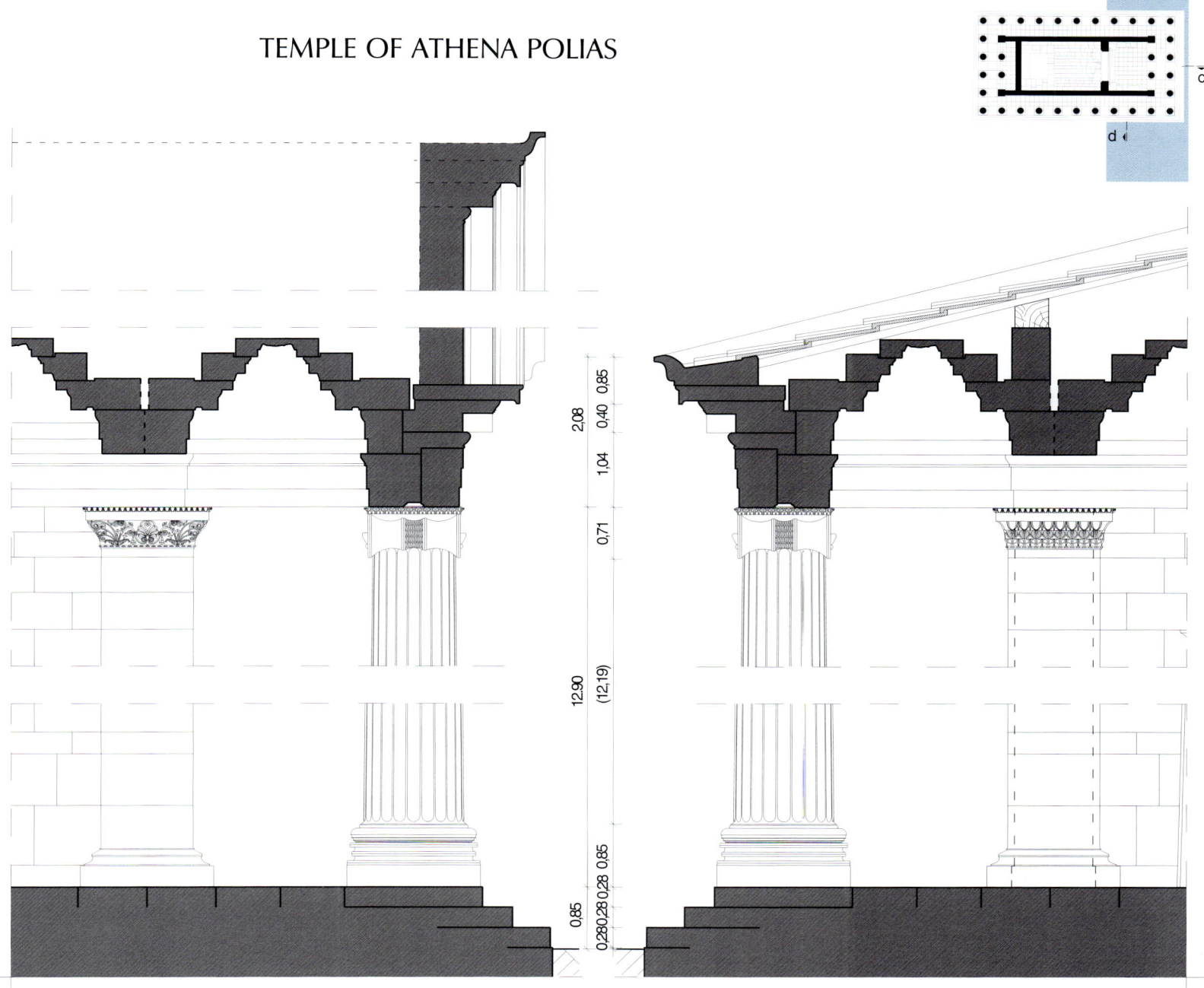

c. Longitudinal section at right angles to the main elevation

d. Cross section parallel to the main elevation

Architectural order

Above the architrave the cornice protrudes sharply, while above the cornice there are ornaments of relief plants[9]. On the long sides of the temple, above the horizontal cornice, there are lion-heads, three in each inter-columnar space, for the draining of rainwater. From the position of the corner stones of the sima and the cornice it can be deduced that the ratio of height to width of the pediment was 1:8.

DECORATION: It is likely that the architect of the Temple of Athena Polias aimed at combining elements of the Ionic tradition, which had until then appeared isolated or in fragmented form in different monuments. One of the basic intentions of the architect seems to have been to emphasise the purity of forms and proportions of the monument. Thus, there were probably no sculpted decorations in the temple.

The pronaos may have been the only exception. On the face of the south anta and the adjacent south wall there are inscriptions constituting a public archive of texts[10]. Along the walls stood votive offerings on pedestals. The side capitals of the Ionic antae were decorated with tendrils facing one another, while the front capitals were decorated with successive series of mouldings and palmettes. The roof of the "pronaos" and the "pteron" (i.e. the surrounding corridor between the columns and the walls of the naos) was panelled and its canopy bore relief scenes. The walls of the naos were not decorated and there were no pedimental sculptures on the tympanum of the pediment.

THE STATUE OF THE GODDESS: The form of the first statue of the goddess Athena remains unknown. In the middle of the 2nd century BC this statue was replaced by a later sculpture, an offering of Orophernes, as indicated by the coins minted at that time[11]. The form of the new statue is known from Roman coins[12]. It was an imitation of the chryselephantine (gold and ivory) statue of Athena Parthenos by Phidias in Athens. The goddess was standing, a calm expression on her face, holding a helmet, a shield and a spear. In her right hand, with the extended arm resting on a column, she held a small deity, probably the goddess Nike (Victory). The statue was 6.5m high, i.e., three times shorter than the original statue in Athens[13].

COLOUR: Thomas[14], a member of the Society of Dilettanti expedition that located the sanctuary (see below), was the first to notice the colours on the architectural elements of the temple. Later, when additional studies were made, some of his observations were corrected.

The statue of the goddess (after Carter)

9. The decoration of the sima follows the arrangement encountered in the Temple of Athena Alea in Tegea. Wiegand, Th. – Schrader, H., op. cit., p. 104.

10. On the upper stone of the south anta there is the dedication to Alexander the Great. Wiegand, Th. – Schrader, H., op. cit., p. 96.

11. They are tetradrachms, some of which have been found in special indentations on the base of the statue as a kind of dedication.

12. Catalogue of Greek coins in the British Museum, Ionia, p. 239, Nos. 55-58.

13. The body of the statue was made of wood, covered with gold, and only the naked limbs were of white marble (Schede, M., op. cit., p. 36). As coins of the Imperial period confirm, the Priene statue is modelled on the chryselephantine (gold and ivory) statue in the Parthenon: the base of the Priene statue was of the same depth as its model but only two thirds of the width. (Wiegand, Th. – Schrader, H., op. cit., p. 110).

14. Op. cit., p. 108.

TEMPLE OF ATHENA POLIAS

View of the "pteron" from below

Thomas discovered that two colours, cinnabar red and copper blue-green, were mainly used as the background to the sculptural decoration. Red was the basic colour of the Ionic eggs and Lesbian moulding, and blue was used as the background of the panels and the abacus of the capitals.

Later, blue was used for the Ionic eggs and Lesbian mouldings, and red for the panels. Red and blue, therefore, were probably the colours that alternated in the panels too.

THE ALTAR: Exactly opposite the east face of the Temple of Athena Polias, at a relatively short distance, was an altar modelled after the famous altar of Zeus at Pergamum. The exact dating is difficult: the sculptural decoration follows the style of the 4th century BC, while the inscriptions point to the time of Augustus. The altar was undoubtedly constructed at a later date than the temple, as is suggested by the different ways in which the two buildings were constructed.

The axis of the altar coincided with that of the temple. Its lowest steps were at a distance of 12.35m from the temple. The altar was rectangular, Π-shaped, and open to the west. It is one of antiquity's monumental podium altars, with an elaborate sculpture or relief decoration. Along with the construction of the altar, the space between the temple and the altar was also paved.

According to the reconstruction made by von Gerkan, the altar was placed on a platform on which stood a Π-shaped podium. The structure above the podium had a full entablature and enclosed the table. The main feature of this structure was a wall with a free colonnade running all around it, except for the internal long side. On the external faces, six columns on each narrow side and eleven on each long one were placed on high pedestals[15]. In the interior faces of the narrow sides stood four more columns. Each pair of columns frames a female figure in relief. The perimetrical, vertical surfaces of the podium were decorated with relief scenes from the Gigantomachy. Between the two branches of the Π-shaped podium, a wide and quite steep staircase led to the table[16]. According to a more recent reconstruction by Carter, there was no podium and the reliefs of the Gigantomachy decorated the canopies of the panels in the temple of Athena Polias. This view is widely accepted today.

15. The diameter of the columns is estimated at 0.30m, their height at 2.70m, whereas their inter-axial space at 1.20m. Thus the total external dimensions are: 13.20 x 7.12m.

16. Dimensions of steps: 0.24m high, 0.25m wide.

ALTAR OF THE SANCTUARY OF ATHENA POLIAS

Main elevation

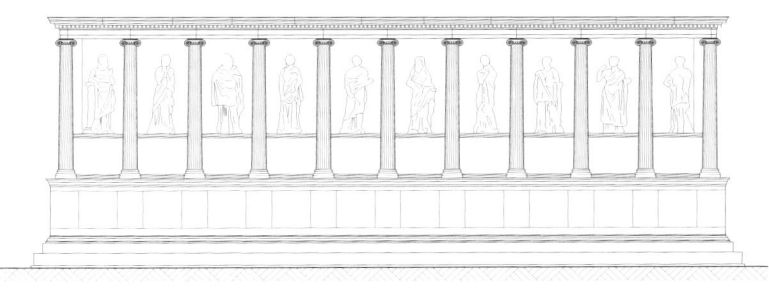

Back elevation

Plan

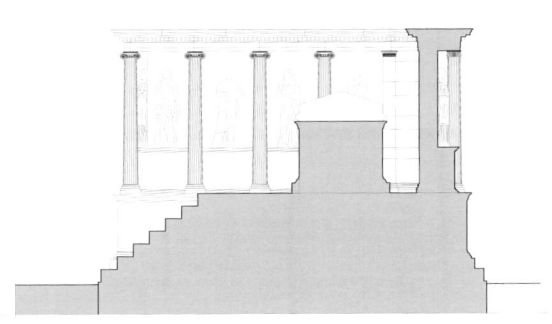

Section

Graphic reconstruction (after von Gerkan)

ALTAR OF THE SANCTUARY OF ATHENA POLIAS

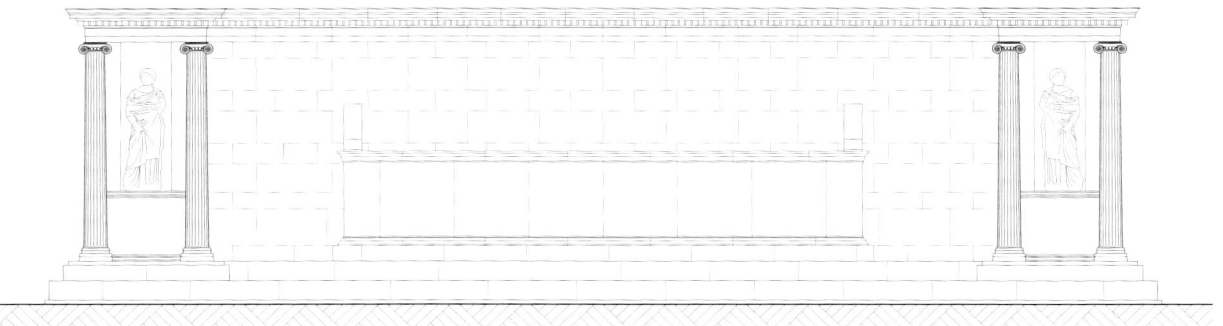

Main elevation

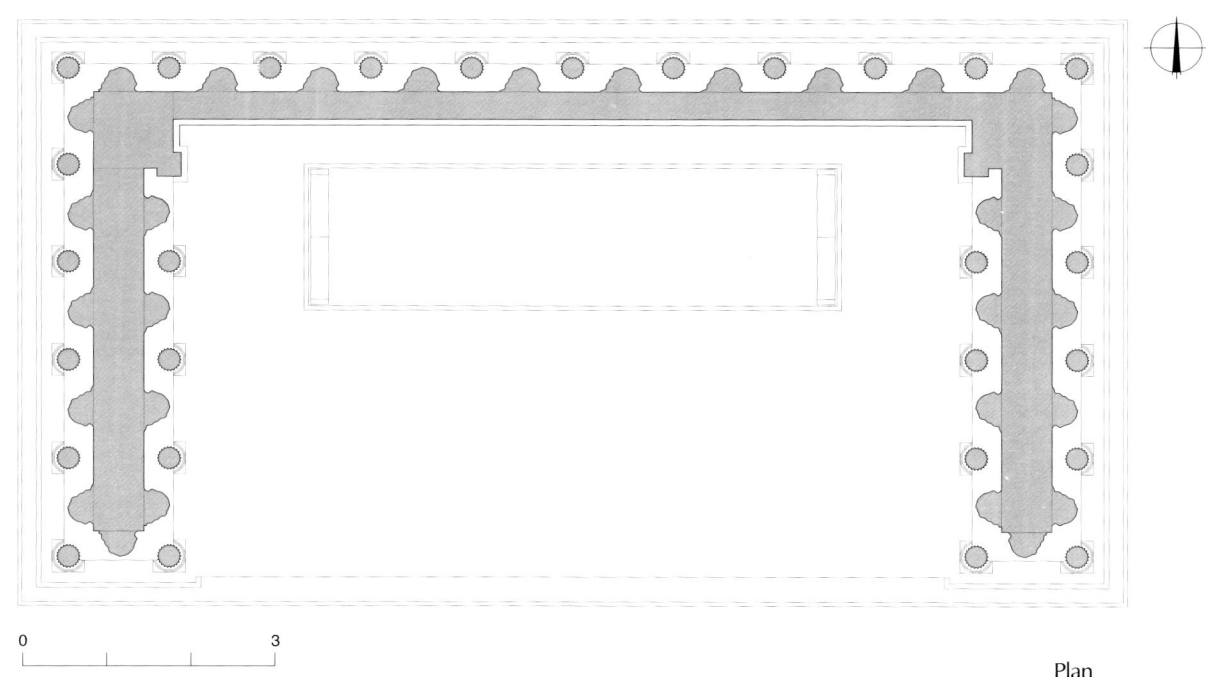

Plan

Graphic reconstruction
(after Carter)

ALTAR OF THE SANCTUARY OF ATHENA POLIAS

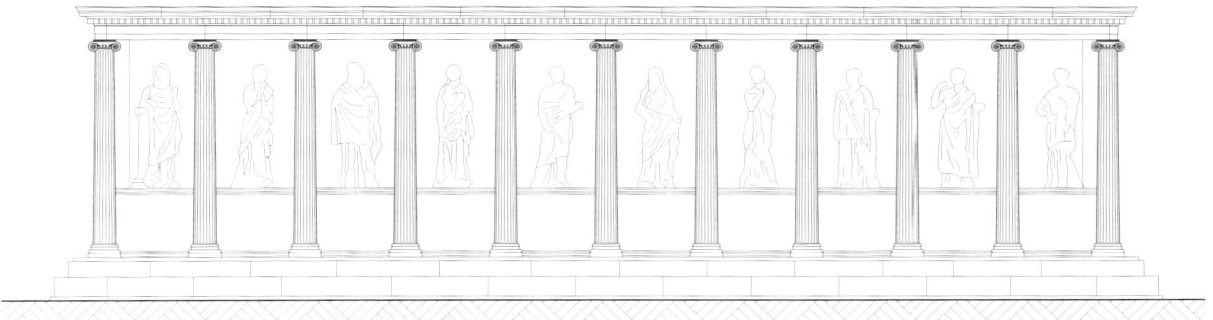

Back elevation

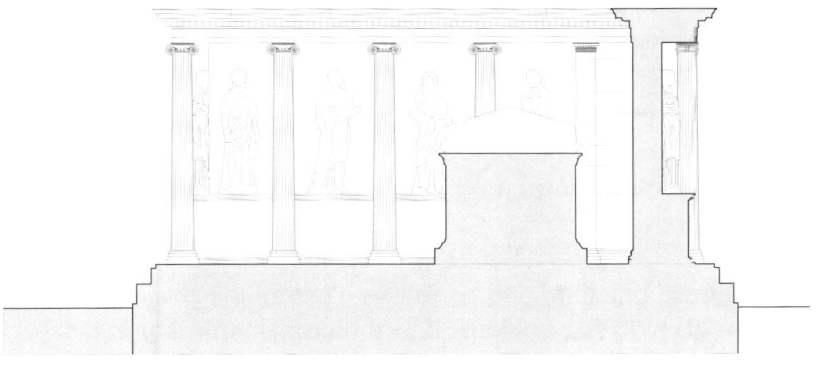

Section

Graphic reconstruction
(after Carter)

The "euthynteria" (aligning-axis) is the only part of the altar surviving in situ; the stones surrounding the central structure were removed during the Christian era. The surviving findings, mainly made of blue Mykale marble, are remarkable for their elaborate form. Surviving fragments of architectural elements, including a few from the entablature and the sculptural decoration, provide valuable information that contributes to the process of reconstructing the monument.

THE FLOOR: The space in front of the temple as far as the altar was lined with marble slabs arranged in parallel zones of unequal width. Half of these slabs were still in place at the time of the German excavations. The length of the slabs was unequal. The floor dates back to the reign of Orophernes. The fact that it was constructed later than the initial phase of construction of the temple and the altar is confirmed by the way the slabs are connected to the euthynteria of the temple. The floor of the temple's cella is paved in a similar way.

THE PROPYLON: Visitors would enter the temple through a propylon. The propylon was parallel to, and as wide as, the road leading to it, while in relation to the axis of the altar it deviated towards the south.

According to archaeological findings, architectural elements and inscriptions, the propylon must have been built between the 2nd century BC and the 1st century AD, probably during the reign of Augustus (27 BC - 14 AD). Its construction was never completed. It was a monumental amphiprostyle building with a pitched roof and pediments. A staircase of six steps led from the street, situated at a lower level, to the level of the propylon's "stylobate". The four columns of the eastern external face were of Ionic order. In contrast to the columns of the western face, those of the east side had flutes. Both faces bore an Ionic entablature with a frieze and dentils. No capitals survive intact.

Two antae of Corinthian order, a fragment of a third one, as well as a part of the abacus of a similar capital, all found nearby, are likely to have belonged to the propylon. It is unclear where these architectural members of Corinthian order actually came from, and the only reason they are now related to the propylon, is because they were discovered close to it[17].

View to the west from the door wall of the Propylon

17. Wiegand, Th. – Schrader, H., op. cit., p. 132.

View of the sanctuary as it appears today, looking to the west

Olympia and Delphi.

Around the building there were two steps, the lowest of which is still preserved in situ. From the transversal wall that separated the pronaos from the cella, only the foundations remain. The doorstep was destroyed later, and the enclosing walls have not survived either.

In the area to the north of the altar, a relatively large part of the west side of the wall enclosing the sanctuary has been preserved. This wall was made of rubble masonry with mortar. In the same place a number of foundations of podiums, probably for offerings, have been found. The north and east parts of the enclosing wall were covered later by houses or were totally demolished. As a result, the boundary of the area is the outline of the street.

THE DISCOVERY OF THE TEMPLE: As with most of the buildings of the Classical era, the Temple of Athena Polias had remained intact until the Christian era. This is confirmed by engraved crosses on the steps of the building. Nevertheless, it was probably never used as a Christian church. Early Christians perhaps only destroyed the "idols" inside the temple, as assumed by Wiegand[23], and burned the roof. There are also indications that in the middle of the 7th century AD, the temple collapsed, possibly because of an earthquake. Fragments of architectural members have been found in the area. The traveller R. P. Pullan discovered layers of ashes on the floor of the cella and Newton found traces of fire in the remains of the statue of Athena[24].

In 1765 Chandler discovered the temple during an expedition of the Society of Dilettanti. Stuart and Revett depicted it in the first volume of Ionian Antiquities[25]. It is evident that at first researchers tried to describe and register the architectural members rather than reconstruct the entire temple.

In 1812, a second, better organised expedition of the Society of Dilettanti, headed by Gell, managed to work out the basic plan of the temple. An attempt was also made to reconstruct its façade[26].

With the financial support of European art-lovers, excavations continued. In the winter of 1868-69 excavations during a new expedition of the Society of Dilettanti, under R. P. Pullan, uncovered the temple[27].

---

23. Wiegand, Th. – Schrader, H., op. cit., p. 83.

24. Op. cit.

25. Op. cit.

26. Op. cit.

27. Op. cit., p. 84.

View of the cella of the Temple of Athena Polias, looking to the west (Copperplate by Pullan, 1868-69)
© DAI Istanbul

It was then that the "crepidoma" with the three steps, the walls of the cella and the two columns of the "opisthodomos" were discovered. The result is depicted on copper engravings of the time, which accompanied publications of the survey.

Four years later, Rayet and Thomas found the temple abandoned. Rayet[28] vividly describes the desolation of the temple that had begun with the looting of the architectural material. In April 1870 villagers of the area had come across silver coins on the base of the statue of Athena. Looking for more coins, they damaged the ruins by destroying the plinths of the wall and the drums of the columns and by removing the floor of the cella. Later, the area was used as a marble quarry; as a result, the monument was gradually covered by heaped fragments of marble. The looting of the ruins by the villagers stopped when excavations were carried out by the Department of Antiquities of the Berlin Museums (1896), as was mentioned in the introductory note.

Today, part of the "crepidoma" survives in situ, as well as a part of the "orthostate" of the wall. Architectural elements of columns, walls and the entablature are scattered around the area. Four columns of the north "pteron" have been restored. The temple is, to the last detail, a unique specimen of a Classical peripteral temple in Asia Minor. Architectural elements of the temple can be found in London (British Museum) and Berlin (Pergamon Museum), where one can also see a lifesize reconstruction of a pair of columns with their entablature.

As with all the other buildings of Priene, so far there is no exhaustive study of the Temple of Athena Polias, a study based on the systematic measurements of the whole of the extant architectural material.

The corner cornice of the pediment of the temple

28. *Milet et le golfe latmique*, Teil 2, p. 3, in Wiegand, Th. – Schrader, H., op. cit., p. 84.

Southeast corner of the Temple of Athena Polias with the altar, looking eastwards (drawing after Krischen, altar after Carter)

The retaining wall of the terrace of the Sanctuary of Athena Polias

View of the cella looking to the east

ASCLEPIEION OR SANCTUARY OF ZEUS

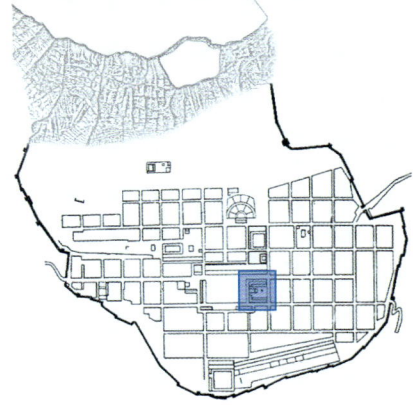

PROBLEMS OF IDENTIFICATION: The Sanctuary was initially dedicated to Asclepius, but in later years it was referred to as the Sanctuary of Olympian Zeus. Hera was another deity worshipped here. Clear evidence that the shrine was dedicated to Asclepius was provided by an inscription on two stones of a small anta found in the temple. From representations of Asclepius on some of the city's coins it is deduced that the god was one of the important deities worshipped in Priene, a fact that justifies the central position of the sanctuary.

After Athena, the second most important deity in Priene was Zeus. The person most involved in the worship of Zeus was the supreme official of the city, the "stephanephoros" (wreath-bearer), who also gave his name to each new year of his rule[1].

LOCATION: The Asclepieion or Sancuary of Zeus is situated on the eastern side of the Agora and occupies an area approximately square in shape[2] that takes up one building plot. The temple is situated at the west end, while the entrance to the sanctuary is from the east. The central position of the Sanctuary of Zeus suggests that it was included in the initial planning of the town. This view is supported by the observation that the axis of the temple deviates by approximately 0.50m to the north, compared to the axis of the shrine itself. This deviation is not incidental; on the contrary, its purpose is to align the axis of the temple with that of the Agora complex. The parallel orientation of the temple and the Agora created a harmonious relationship, probably involving the presence of the god as well as the overall geometric arrangement of the temples of the city. However, it must be noted that during the last phase of the Agora there was neither direct access nor visual contact between the two areas.

DESCRIPTION OF THE SANCTUARY: The sanctuary was rectangular in shape, enclosed by buildings and a wall. In the middle of the west side was the temple, and both the north and south sides were enclosed by a stoa, while on the east side the enclosing wall was interrupted by a unadorned propylon which allowed access from the side street up three steps. The area of the sanctuary has not been fully excavated because its northeastern section

---

1. The stephanephoros had mainly ritual responsibilities. He was responsible for carrying out large sacrifices and he was charged with the expenses for the meals of the citizens involved in the above rites. His characteristic emblem, the wreath, is related to Zeus. At the end of his term of office he had to dedicate a precious cup to the Temple of Zeus. Due to the considerable cost, more than one person would share this honorific post. Schede, M., Die Ruinen von Priene. Archäologisches Institut des Deutschen Reiches. Abteilung Istanbul, 1964, p. 58.

2. From north to south 30m, whereas from east to west 29.67m.

The Temple of Olympian Zeus as it appears today, looking to the west

was later covered by a Byzantine fortification structure. The surviving parts of the structures are mainly the foundations, while from the external wall, which was interrupted by the propylon and ended at the Agora Gate, three layers of masonry stones have survived in their original positions. Neither the east nor the west walls of the sanctuary showed any particular decoration.

THE TEMPLE: The Temple of Zeus was built, without interruption, during the 3rd century BC. The archaeologists who conducted the excavations concluded that the temple was constructed in the era of Alexander the Great because of its similarity to the Temple of Athena. A closer look at the two temples shows that the east face of the Temple of Zeus is, to the last detail, a miniature of the Temple of Athena, while it is interesting to compare the dimensions of the two buildings: in most architectural members the ratio 2:1 was preserved. It is likely that the temple of Athena, being more important, was built first, and was later used as a model for the construction of the smaller Temple of Zeus.

The Temple of Zeus was a simple temple of the Ionic order with a façade of four columns or, according to recent data, a temple in antis[3]. The building ran through the back wall of the chambers in the east wing of the Agora's South Stoa. There was a deep "pronaos" with extending antae, and there was no provision for an "opisthodomos". The Ionic entablature is of the Asia Minor type without a frieze and can be fully reconstructed in a drawing. It is identical to the entablature of the Temple of Athena. The temple had a pitched roof.

The statues of the gods were placed inside the cella. A large marble cube, found 4-5m to the southeast of the temple, is probably one half of their base. The width of this base indicates that it probably carried two statues. Data from worship inscriptions confirm that Hera was also worshipped in the Temple of Zeus. In front of the temple there is a square marble altar, of which only the rectangular base has survived.

The main surviving part of the temple is the "euthynteria" (aligning axis) of the east side.

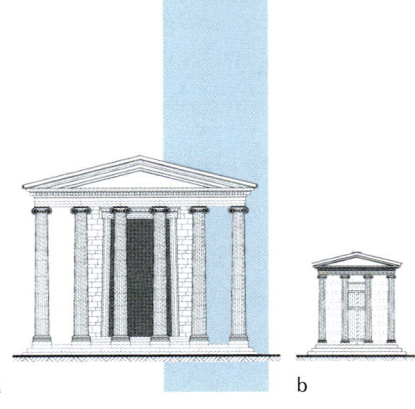

a. Temple of Athena Polias
b. Temple of Olympian Zeus

3. Bankel, H., Abteilung Istanbul, Ausgrabungen und Untersuchungen, in Jahresbericht 1988 des Deutschen Archäologischen Instituts. A.A., 1989, p. 684.

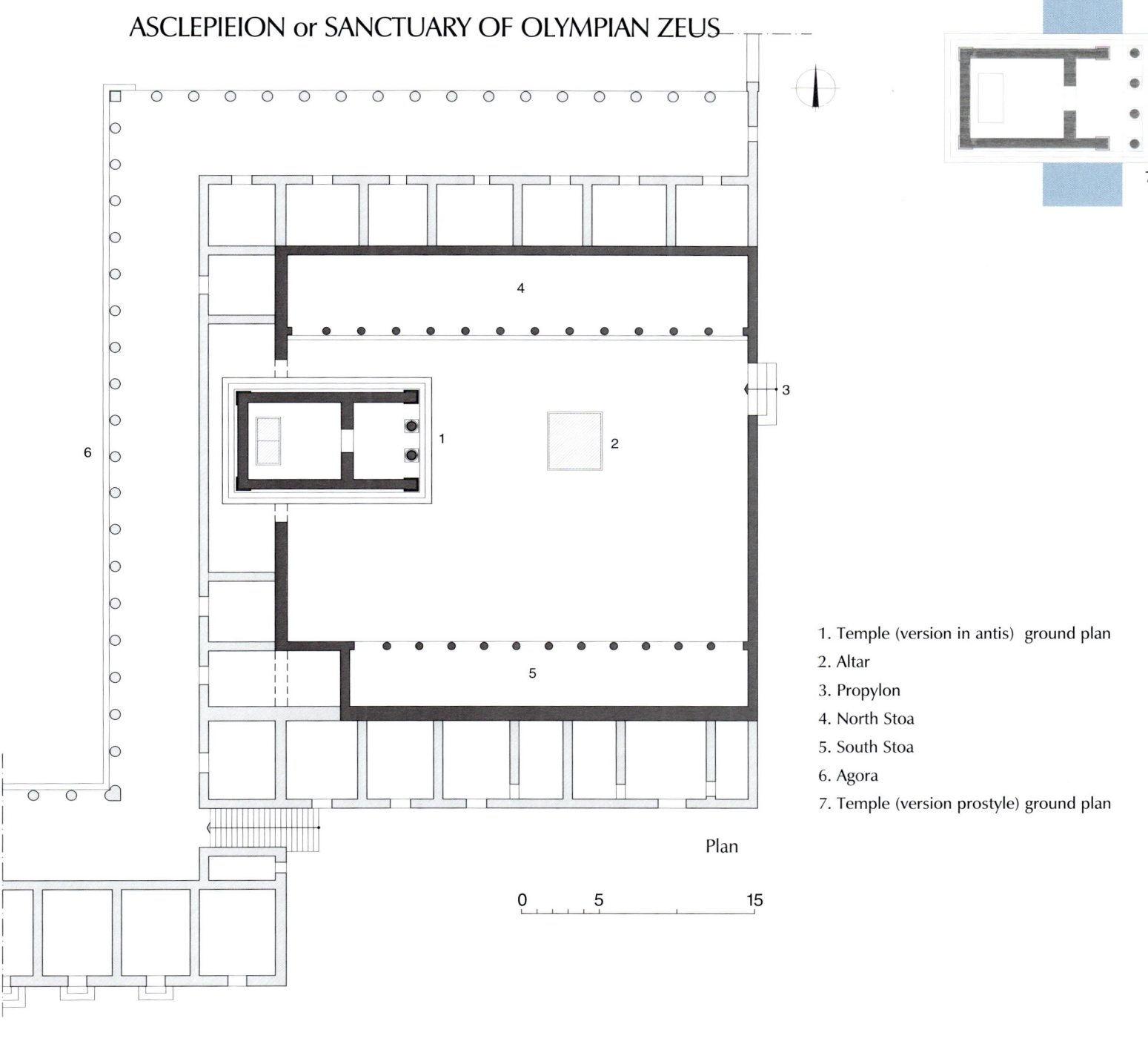

TEMPLE OF OLYMPIAN ZEUS

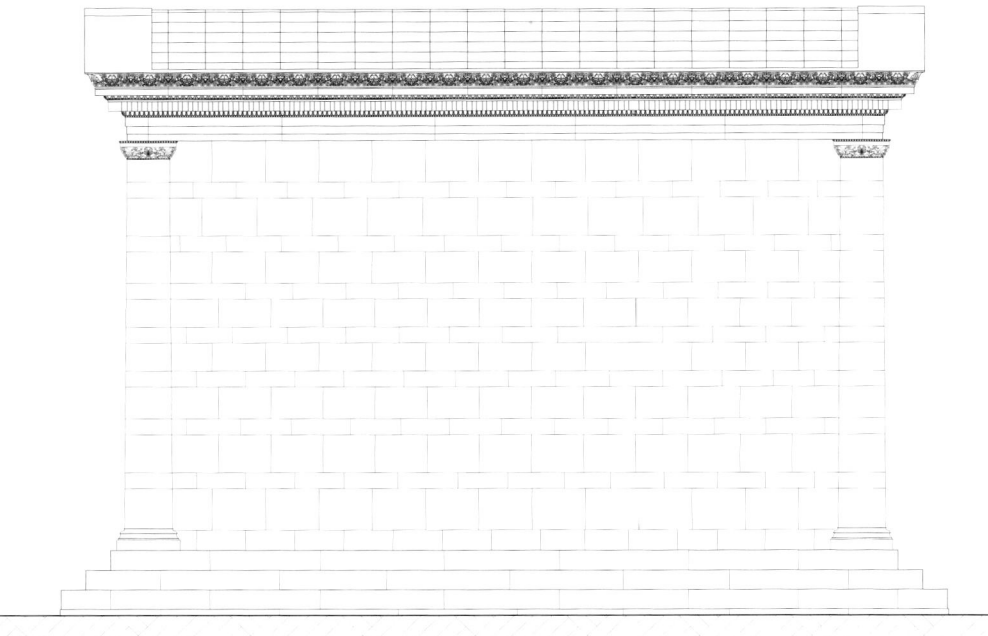

Side elevation

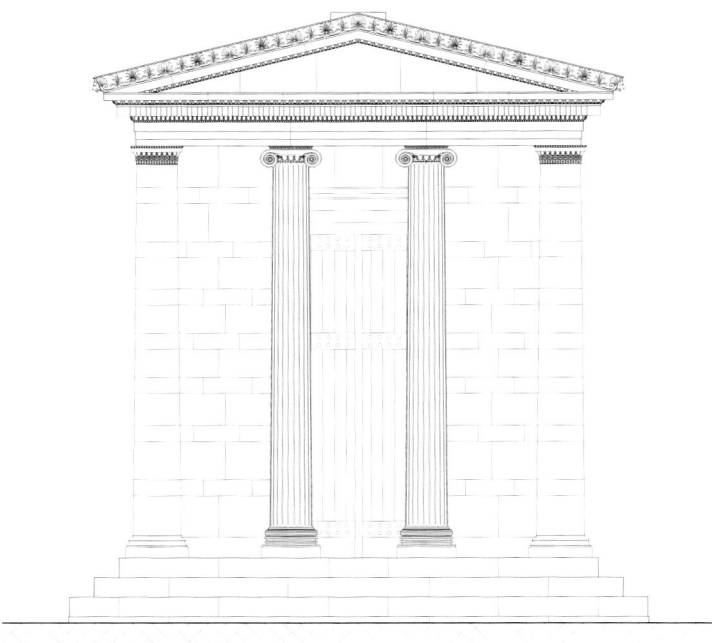

Main elevation

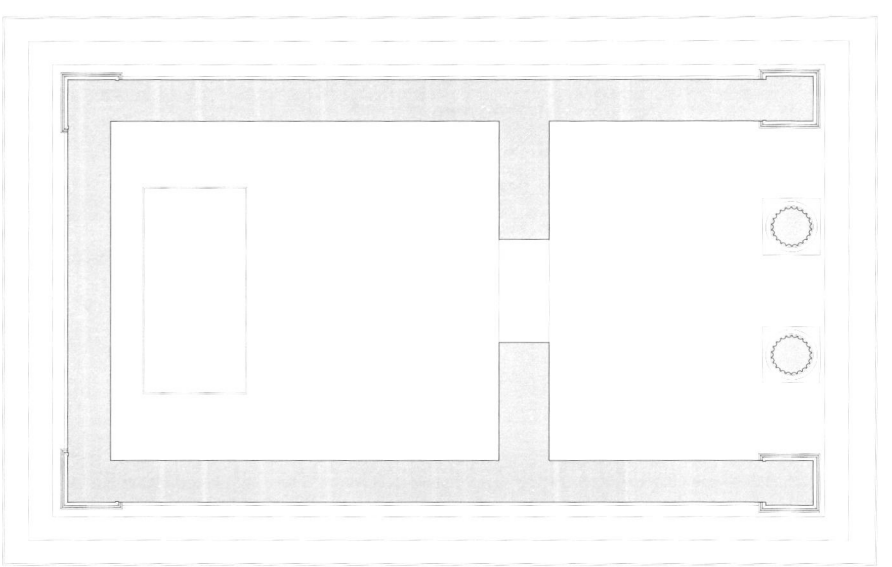

Plan

Version of the temple in antis

0   5

TEMPLE OF OLYMPIAN ZEUS

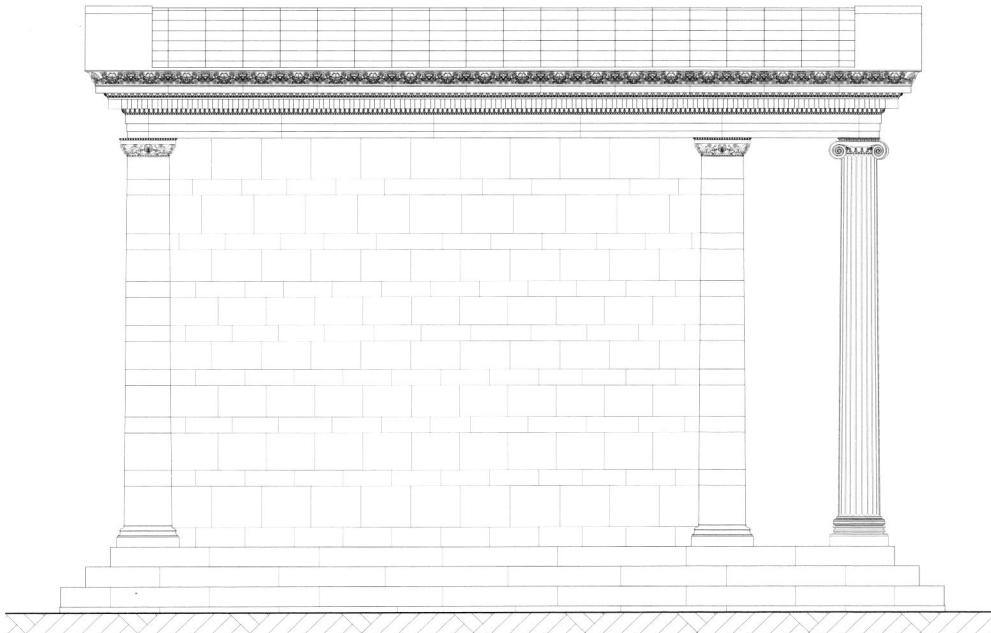

Side elevation

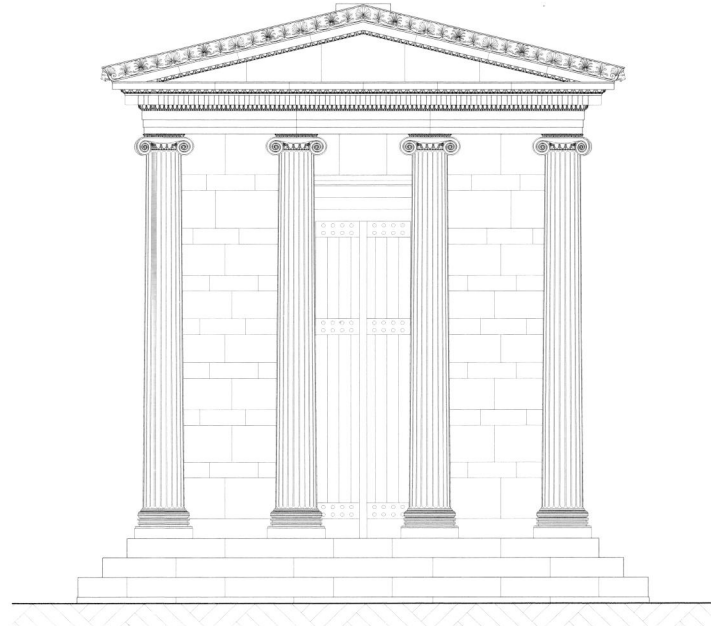

Main elevation

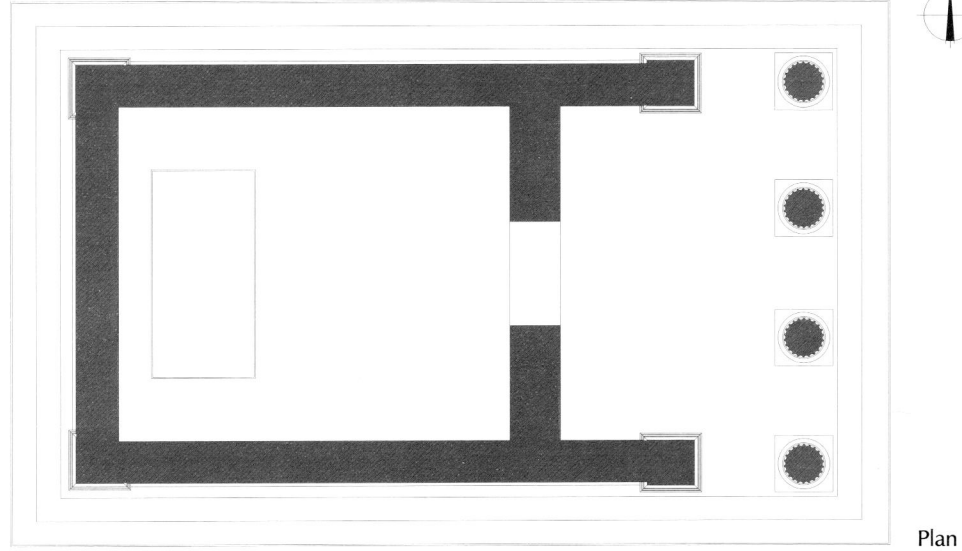

Plan

Version of prostyle temple

Fragment of the entablature (side view)

THE STOAS: The sanctuary also contained two oblong stoas without chambers, extending along its north and south sides. The existence of a stoa on the north side is confirmed by its lowest step that has been retrieved in relatively good condition. The marble steps of the north stoa were placed directly on the rock without an intervening "euthynteria". No remains of the upper step and the columns exist. Some of the architectural elements of the stoa's entablature were later incorporated in a neighbouring Byzantine wall, revealing that the entablature was constructed in an elaborate version of Doric order. Each stone of the frieze of the north stoa consists of four triglyphs and three "metopes". The upper surface of the cornice is horizontal. This indicates that the stoa was probably not covered by a monopitched roof, but supported a flat, functional attic.

The existence of a stoa on the south side of the temple is indicated by traces of the foundation. Some architectural elements of an entablature have been found, having dimensions similar to those of the entablature of the stoa on the north side of the temple but with different decorative details. These elements are similar to those belonging to the South Stoa extending to the Agora Gate. Wiegand believes that they are elements of the stoa situated on the south side of the temple.

Since their elements are evidently not uniform, it is concluded that the two stoas were not constructed in the same period. According to inscriptions of the 3rd century BC, the stoa on the south side of the temple was constructed first, while the stoa on the north side followed, during a later construction phase in the 2nd century BC.

TEMPLE OF OLYMPIAN ZEUS

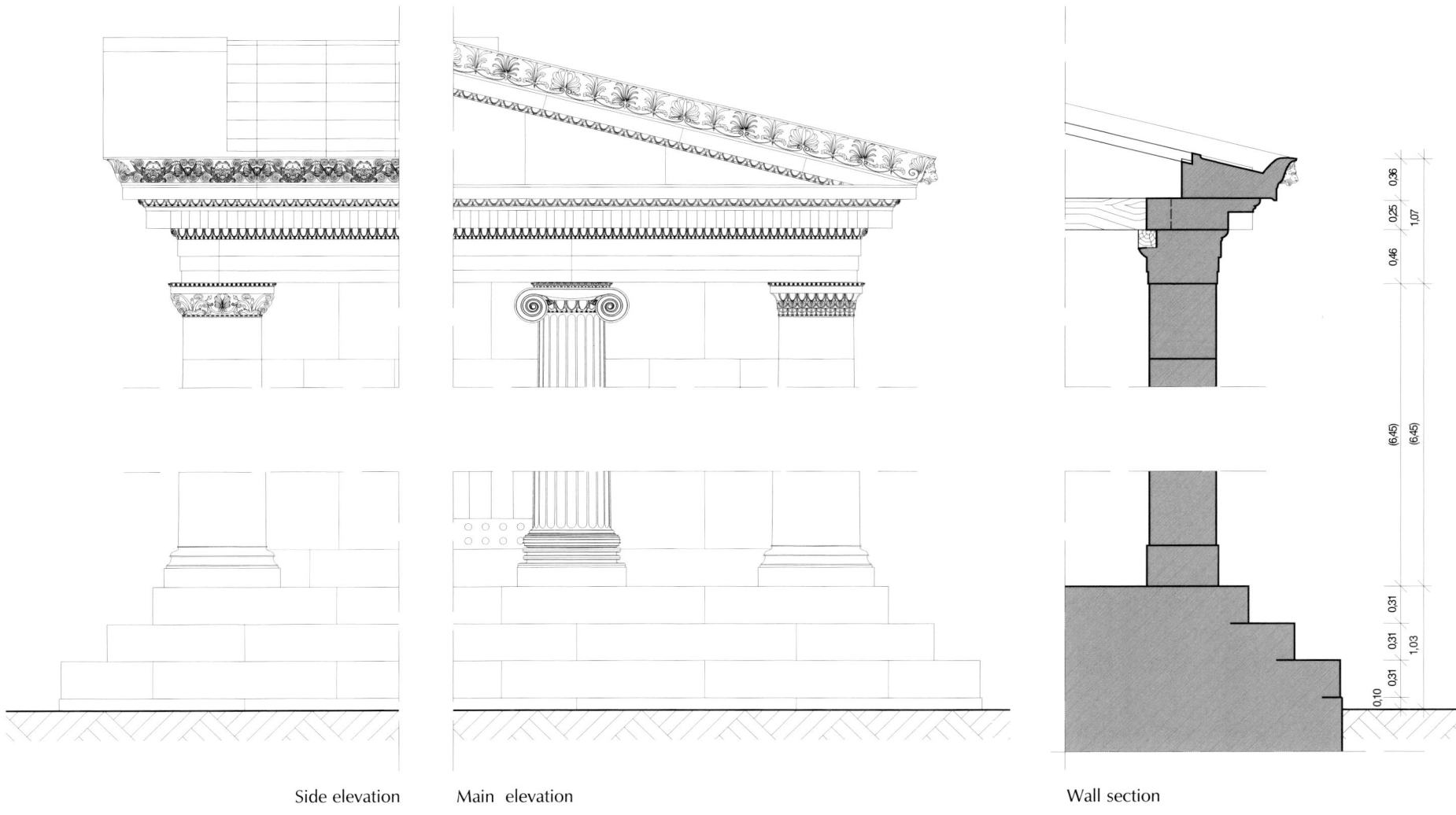

Side elevation   Main elevation   Wall section

Architectural order

AN INSCRIBED ANTA FROM THE TEMPLE OF ASCLEPIUS

by I. Arvanitis

The guards of Teloneia, the fort on the acropolis of Priene, requested the "Demos" of Priene to have an inscription engraved (containing the resolution they had issued in honour of their garrison commander, Elikon, son of Leomedon), on the anta of the stoa standing on the right side of the entrance to the sanctuary of Asclepius. The shaft of the excavated anta was later incorporated into the church of the Byzantine fort that was built on the west side of the ancient Agora. For almost a century it had been kept in the storehouse of the Pergamon Museum at Berlin, along with other inscribed architectural elements, including columns from Priene and other cities of Ionia. There is no reference to the inscriptions in previous publications[1].

The marble anta consists of two parts of different height, 1.72m and 0.892m. The two parts are connected together with two lead joints. On three of its sides, the upper surface bares an anathyrosis about 10cm wide, while in its centre there is a disk-shaped cavity for the embolium of the capital.

The section of the anta is square, and its surface decreases toward the top (side of lower base 50.5cm, side of upper base 43.5cm). The carving on the three visible sides is quite elaborate. The invisible back side of the anta has only been carved with a needle, a fact which suggests that it was in contact with a plastered wall. The coating had also been applied on the equally unrefined, slanting surfaces at the two edges of the invisible side of the anta; that is to say, the wall was as thick as the anta.

The significance of the anta in relation to the planning and development of the Agora of Priene lies in the inscription engraved on its front face. This inscription shows that the anta belonged to the stoa of the Temple of Asclepius (line 45 ff). The names of the persons mentioned in the inscription, combined with persons quoted in other inscriptions in the city, provide important information about the dating of the stoa where the anta belonged and, therefore, about the dating of the entire sanctuary.

---

1. The last publication of the inscription was made by F. Hiller von Gaertringen in Inschriften von Priene, 1906, no. 19.

Photograph of the marble anta
© Antikensammlung
Preussischer Kulturbesitz

The person honoured by the inscription is Elikon, son of Leomedon, who was elected garrison commander of Teloneia when Protarchos served as stephanephoros (wreath-bearer). According to some researchers[2], his ancestors included many distinguished men. His great-grandfather, Laomedon, son of Larichos from Mytilene, was an officer of Alexander the Great and subsequently governor of Syria and Phoenicia until 321 BC, when, driven away by Ptolemy I, he fled to Caria, seeking help from Alketas, brother of Perdikkas. His grandfather Larichos had fought on the side of Seleucus and Antiochus, and was honoured by the Demos of Priene with three different decrees for his remarkable services to the city[3]. His father Leomedon had been neopoios (ship-builder) and stephanephoros, as it is indicated on other inscriptions of Priene[4].

According to the information derived from the inscription, the dating can be established to around the middle of the 3rd century BC[5], which is consistent with the dating based on the assumption that Elikon descended from Laomedon, son of Larichos.

Researchers have not yet reached a definite conclusion as to whether the sanctuary of the Agora corresponds to the Sanctuary of Asclepius of the inscription, although this seems most likely[6]. However, since the view still prevailing is that the sanctuary of the Agora should be identified with the Sanctuary of Asclepius of this inscription, one must use this assumption in order to explain discrepancies with recent dating based on architectural and stylistic data. According to the latter information, the sanctuary cannot have been built before the middle of the 2nd century BC[7].

---

2. Cf. Hiller von Gaertringen, F., op. cit., 15 and 27 comments on inscription no. 18.

3. Op. cit., 26 ff., inscription no. 18.

4. Op. cit., 27, inscription nos. 18. 32 and 30, inscription no. 22.2.

5. These conclusions are based on data resulting from the comparative study of various inscriptions of Priene. Their inclusion here would be beyond the scope of this book.

6. Cf. Koenigs, W., Planung und Ausbau der Agora von Priene, Ist. Mitt. 43, 1993, p. 385.

7. Cf. Rumscheid, F., Untersuchungen zur kleinasiatischen Bauornamentik des Hellenismus, 1994, p. 193 ff. and Koenigs, W., Planung und Ausbau der Agora von Priene, Ist. Mitt. 43, 1993, p. 385 ff. and 394.

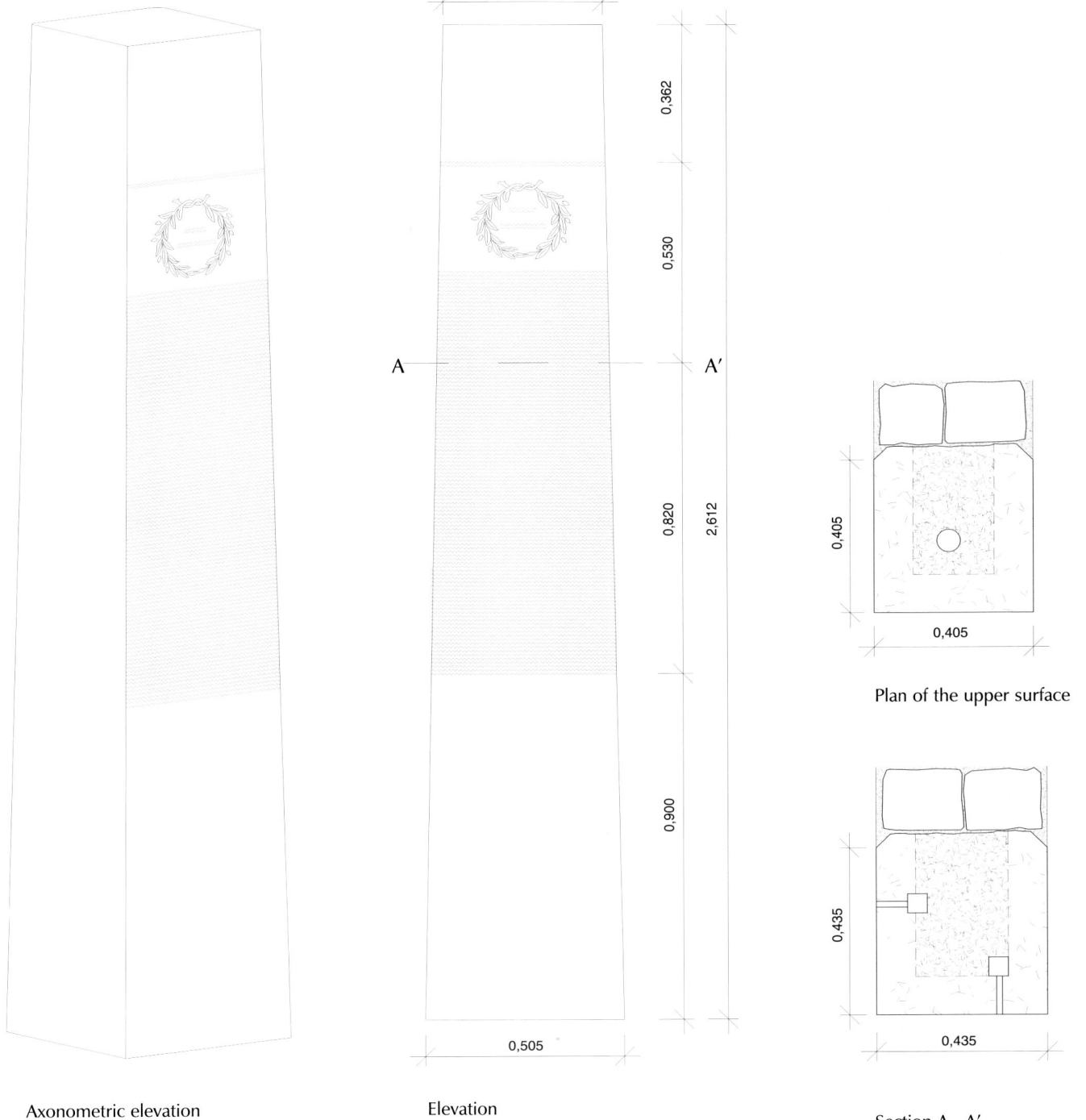

Axonometric elevation

Elevation

Plan of the upper surface

Section A - A'

Perspective version of prostyle temple (after Krischen)

View of the Sanctuary looking to the southwest

SANCTUARY OF DEMETER AND KORE

Immediately after the city was founded, the worship of two other goddesses was established besides the patroness Athena: the goddesses of earth and fertility, Demeter and Persephone. These deities had been honoured since ancient times and every Greek city had sanctuaries dedicated to them. The ear of corn, their symbol, appears on the first coins of Priene. Reference to the two goddesses is made in the oldest inscription found so far in the city, on the Spring Gate of around 350 BC.

LOCATION: The sanctuary is not reflected in the city's road system. It is situated on the north, outside the inhabited area of the city and at its highest point, near the acropolis. The plateau on which it is built stands 35m higher than the one of the Temple of Athena (i.e. 135m above sea-level), offering a unique view of the town and fields. The planning of the sanctuary is similar to that of the Shrine of Demeter at Cnidus.

THE TEMPLE: The area of the sanctuary was accessible through an entrance on the east side of the precinct. The centre was occupied by the courtyard, where rites were performed, and the temple was situated to the west. The length of the sacred area from east to west was approximately equal to the length of one building plot, its width exceeding half a plot[1].

The temple was close to the enclosing wall and occupied approximately 1/3 of the area of the sanctuary. Its plan was unusual: it consisted of a prostasis facing to the east, the main cella[2] and two smaller halls to the north. A wall enclosed the whole area of the sanctuary. Between the precinct and the temple there was a narrow corridor[3].

The "prostasis" consisted of two unfluted Doric columns in antis and extended almost up to the middle of the cella. The door of the cella was not placed between the columns of the "prostasis", but towards the south. The section of the cella to the south of the "prostasis" was 1.50m narrower than the rest of the cella. A sacrificial pit was situated in the remaining free space. It was accessible through a narrow door built in the south wall of the "prostasis". The "crepidoma" of the prostasis had two steps. Most of the drums of the two Doric columns were found in front of the "prostasis". Only on one surviving

---

1. The dimensions of the space are 46.45 x 19.35m, whereas those of a block are 47 x 35m. Wiegand, Th. – Schrader, H., Priene. Ergebnisse der Ausgrabungen und Untersuchungen von den Jahren 1895-1898. Unter Mitwirkung von G. Krummer, W. Wilberg, H. Winnefeld, R. Zahn. Berlin: Köenigliche Museen zu Berlin, 1904, p. 149.

2. With dimensions 11.72 x 6.45m, op. cit., p. 151.

3. 1.15m wide, op. cit., p. 151.

SANCTUARY OF DEMETER AND KORE

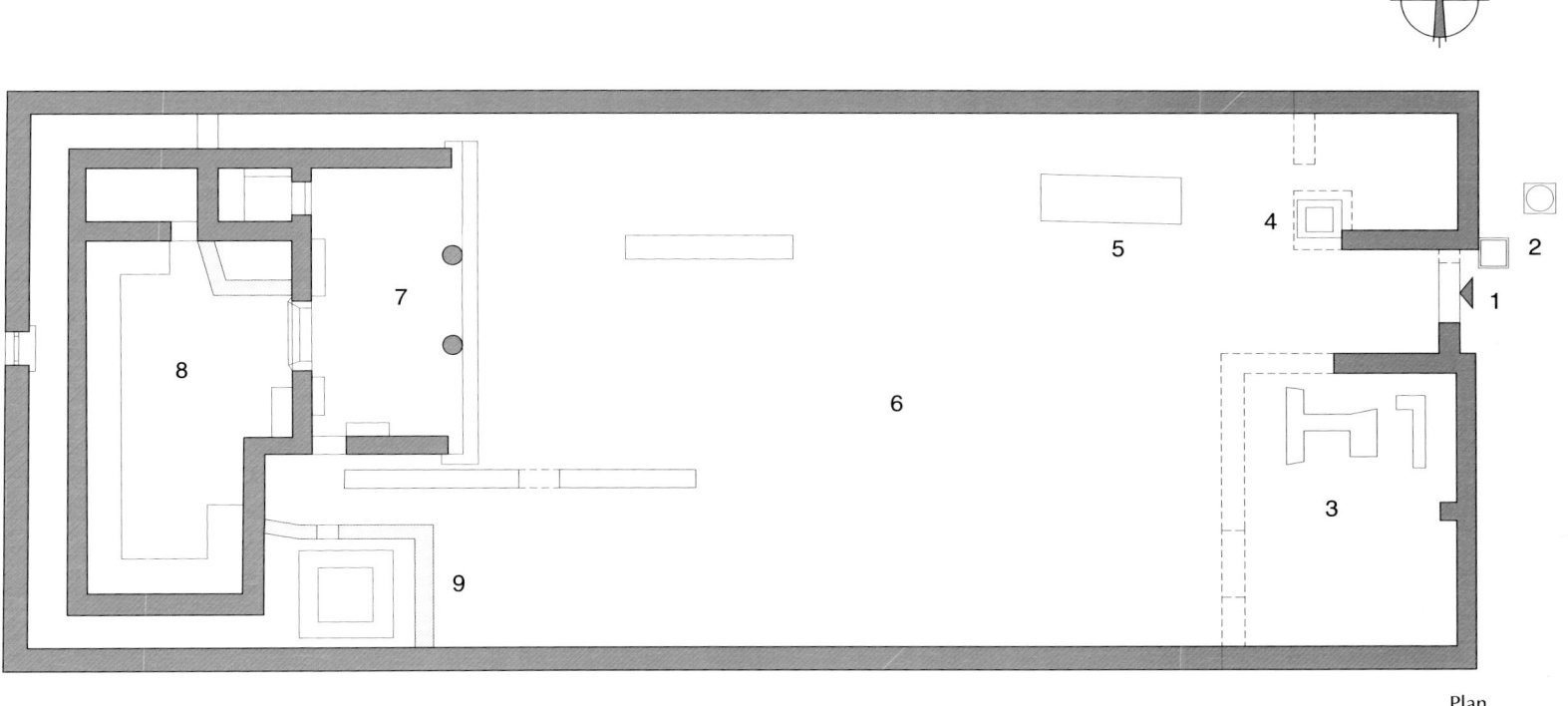

Plan

1. Entrance to sanctuary
2. Bases of statues
3. Houses of priestesses
4. Marble cistern
5. Altar
6. Courtyard
7. Prostasis
8. Cella
9. Sacrificial pit (bothros)

- Surviving traces of sanctuary
- Later constructions
- Conjectural restored plans

capital one can make out traces of 20 flutes. The capital was similar in form to those of the South Stoa of the Agora, but less elaborate. No elements of the entablature have been found.

Inside the temple and along the west side there was an imposing marble pedestal, preserved in quite good condition. One can still make out three cavities, suggesting that statues were placed there. The main purpose of the pedestal was probably to accommodate votive offerings. The walls were not very elaborately made but were covered on both sides with a layer of fine marble-powder to simulate the appearance of orthostates.

There were two marble tables, probably used during sacrifices, opposite the door of the cella and in contact with the pedestal. The table of the northwest corner has collapsed, but the one opposite the door has been preserved almost intact[4]. The floor of the cella was of tamped earth with inlaid smaller stones.

Of the two chambers on the north side of the temple, only the larger one to the west was in direct contact with the cella. Its door had no threshold and was probably closed by a plain cloth curtain. The smaller room had a door on the east facing the prostasis. On the west wall, opposite the door, there was a pedestal, and on the north wall there was a bench. The wall separating the two rooms is 1.80m high and extends as far as the external precinct of the sanctuary.

PIT: The sacrificial square pit (bothros) on the southeast side of the cella was used for animal sacrifices to the deities of the underworld. The pit was on a much lower level, and the ends of the walls formed a kind of pediment that protruded from the ground. The central stone, which supported the boards that prevented the odours of the sacrifices from spreading, was similar in form. The quality of construction of the 0.50m-thick walls is remarkable: one can still make out the continuous joints reaching a depth of 2m in the rock. In later years, a thin wall with a door was constructed around the pit, of which the plain antae have survived.

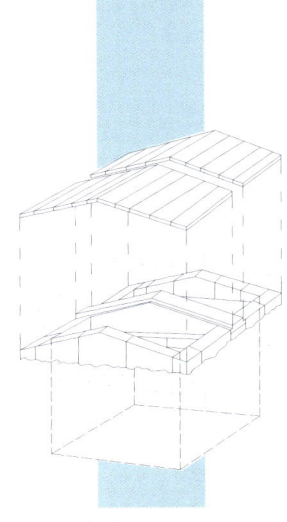

Sacrificial pit (Bothros)

[4]. It has an overall height of 0.85m. The feet are simple slabs, vertically placed, bearing 4 flutings on their narrow, vertical front. At the two ends of the front of the covering slab (1.15m long and 0.62m wide) there are shallow relief capitals with volutes. The upper surface ends in a rim, the aim of which was to prevent the overflowing of libation liquids. Op. cit., p. 153.

Perspective of the temple (after Krischen)

SANCTUARY OF DEMETER AND KORE

HOUSES: The ruins of walls to the left of the sanctuary entrance formed part of the simple dwellings of the priestesses. Opposite and to the right of the entrance was a square marble water reservoir. An altar, which was constructed later, during Roman times, has also survived.

STATUES: Two statue bases have been discovered near the roofed propylon of the entrance. One of them belonged to the bronze statue of Timonassa. Next to it was the marble statue of the priestess Nikesso, which has been found almost intact and is today in the Museum of Pergamon, in Berlin. The statue dates back to the early 3rd century BC and is a remarkable example of the art of that period[5]. Later the Christians carved a cross on the back of the statue.

A large number of baked clay statuettes[6], some small vases, as well as various peculiar clay figures, probably representing female fertility demons, have been discovered near the pit and between the prostasis and a wall constructed later.

---

5. *The priestess is depicted in a ritual posture with her right hand raised. Her dress drapes the body and the folds are rendered in great detail. Her hair, falling on her shoulders, forms braids. The care with which the detail of the folds have been rendered is characteristic, probably to suggest the texture of the cloth (linen or cotton) on the basis of a ritual model. The face of the figure is conjectured from a marble head, and the posture of the body from a small clay female figure with a vase. Both were found in the area of the sanctuary. Op. cit., p. 151 and Schede, M., Die Ruinen von Priene. Archäologisches Institut des Deutschen Reiches. Abteilung Istanbul, 1964, p. 90.*

6. *These terracottas form, as a whole, a special class of figurines found in Priene. They represent female figures, as befits the character of the sanctuary: chiefly adult women, girls and children, probably the goddesses themselves and also their priestesses. Op. cit., p. 157.*

Statue of Nikesso
found in the area of the Sanctuary

© DAI Istanbul

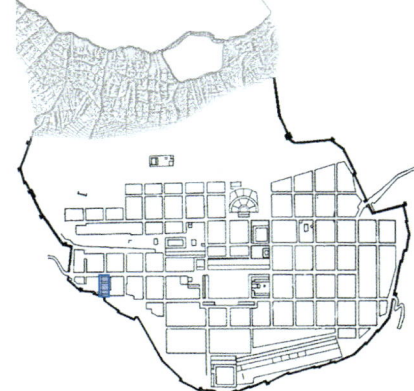

OTHER SHRINES

SACRED HOUSE: Close to the West Gate of the city, on the third block to the south of the central road counting from the east, were two buildings of different purpose: the east and larger section of the block was taken up by House No. 23, and on its west there was an unusual shrine. This was constructed after the original one (which was used as living quarters). The deity to whom this shrine was dedicated[1] remains unknown.

The shrine occupied a rectangular surface 20.50m wide and 35.40m long. The south section was irregular. The area was accessible through a covered gate on the narrow road to the west. The covered areas were arranged on the north, east and south sides, around an open-air courtyard. This arrangement is unusual in Greek shrines: the general planning leads to the conclusion that this was not a single temple but belonged to a complex, something which is supported by evidence on an inscription found in situ. The main area, an oblong two-aisle hall accessible through the long side, was on the north section and bears no resemblance to a temple[2]. It was accessible from the south through a small "prostasis". Later, when the main hall was divided into two spaces by a wall, a second entrance was created towards the west. Constructional details clearly indicate that the dividing wall was not made during the initial construction phase of the building. Three columns divided the hall into two aisles. On the eastern wall a pedestal was later constructed, extending along the north wall. Perpendicular to its long side were two staircases and a third one was constructed on its south section. Between the two staircases was a marble table, the legs of which were decorated with flutes and ended in lion-paws. Wiegand and Schede argue as to the kind of offerings (bloody or bloodless) placed on the table, interpreting in different ways the cleft on the ground.

Of the three rooms on the east side, the last one to the north was accessible through the prostasis to the main hall. In the centre of the room a sacrificial table has been discovered, similar to that of the main hall but with an additional rim around its edge, exactly like the two tables of the Shrine of Demeter, which may indicate performance of bloody sacrifices. The mosaic floor of this hall was one step higher (30cm) than the "prostasis".

---

1. Schede, M., (Die Ruinen von Priene. Archäologisches Institut des Deutschen Reiches. Abteilung Istanbul, 1964, p. 106) claims that, as a manifestation of gratitude, after the alleged visit and stay of Alexander the Great in the city in 334 BC, the citizens of Priene turned this house into a place of worship. A sculpture representing the Macedonian king found among the ruins leads to the conclusion that it was in this place that the cult of Alexander was housed. A relevant inscription mentions the existence of a sanctuary dedicated to Alexander and places the year of construction at 130 BC. The cost of 1,000 drachmas was covered through the sponsorship (choregia) of wealthy citizens.

2. Internal dimensions: 19m long and 9.20m wide. Wiegand, Th. – Schrader, H., Priene. Ergebnisse der Ausgrabungen und Untersuchungen von den Jahren 1895-1898. Unter Mitwirkung von G. Kummer, W. Wilberg, H. Winnefeld, R. Zahn. Berlin: Königliche Museen zu Berlin 1904, p. 173.

SACRED HOUSE

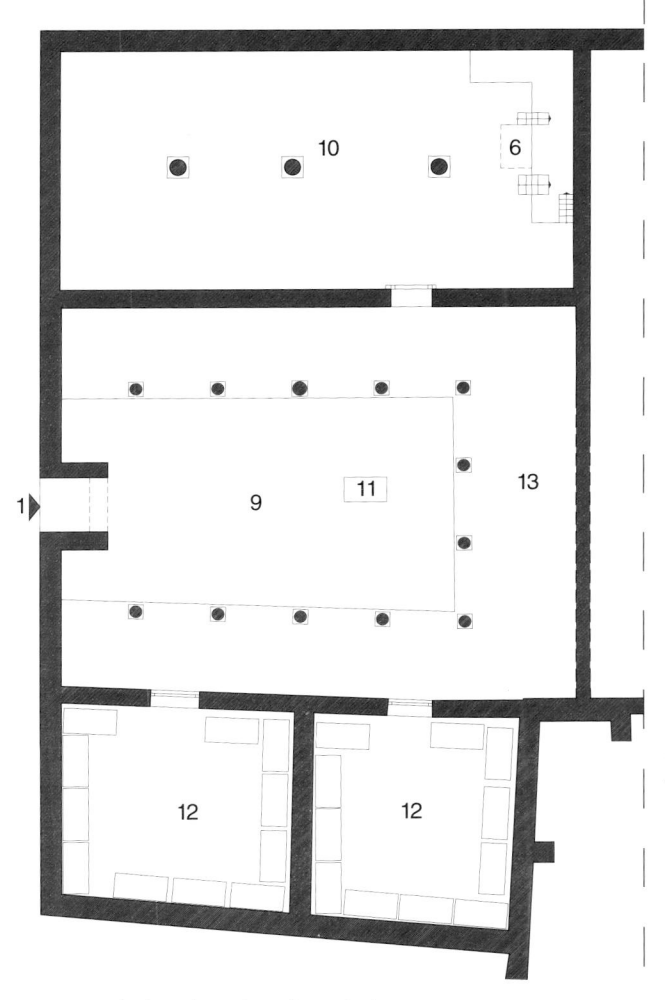

Restored plan of previous form, 3rd century BC

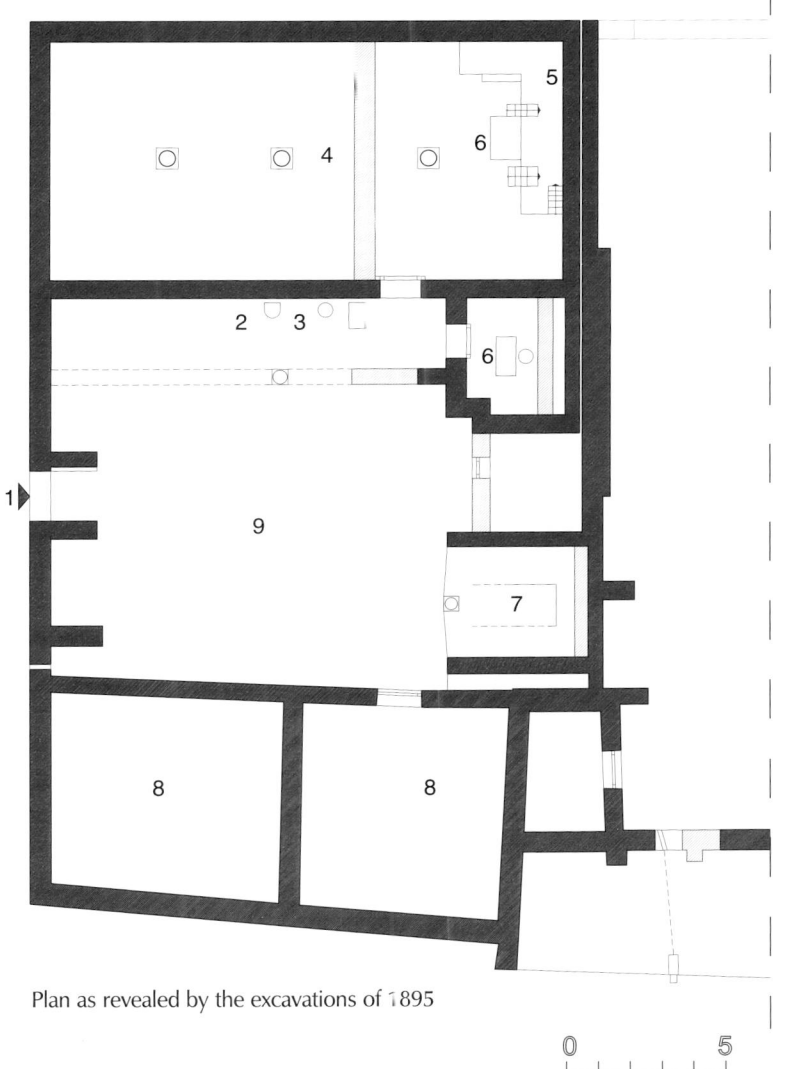

Plan as revealed by the excavations of 1895

1. Entrance of shrine
2. Prostasis
3. Pedestals of statues
4. Sacred House
5. Radial bench
6. Sacrificial table
7. Triclinium
8. Two-storey rooms
9. Courtyard
10. Meeting Room
11. Presumed Altar
12. Symposia Hall
13. Peristyle

- Surviving traces of shrine
- Later constructions
- Conjectural restored plans

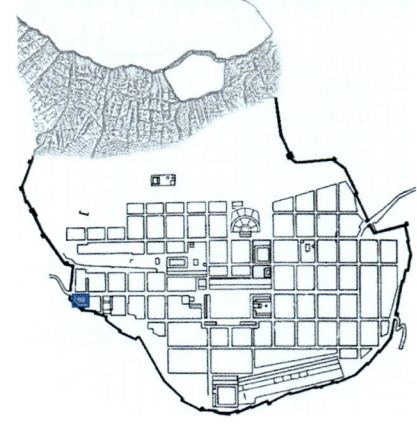

OTHER SHRINES

The central room of the east side was accessible through the courtyard, its floor elevated by 75cm.

The last room to the south was open to the courtyard. A slim column, whose base is still in position, supported the roof beam. This base consisted of a cube and a cylinder cut from a single piece of stone. The top side had a cavity in order to support a thin stone column. The back wall of the room is reinforced, and traces of red are still visible on it. Around the walls ran a low bench, probably a triclinium, similar to that of Pompeii.

The two rooms on the south side of the building also had access to the courtyard. Due to the slope of the ground they were built on two levels. The lower level has mainly survived. More extensive reference to the Sacred House is made in Professor Hoepfner's introduction.

THE SHRINE OF CYBELE: On the first plot, east of the West Gate on the central street, stood the shrine of Cybele. Similar shrines, though less important, stood by the other gates of the city. The assumption that this particular shrine was dedicated to Cybele is based on the discovery in situ of a marble statue of the goddess on a throne[3]. The cult of Cybele as mother-goddess has its roots in Asia Minor. The humble and plain shrine, as well as the small clay and stone statuettes found in different locations of the city, indicate that Cybele was a particularly popular deity, especially among the lower classes.

The area of the shrine was defined to the south by the walls, to the north by the central street of the city, and to the east by an ascending street. From this street one could enter the shrine through a small door. In the west section of the open space there was only a square pit[4], intended for animal sacrifices, its four corners pointing exactly towards the four points of the compass. The east and south sides were cut in the rock, while the west and the north ones were defined by marble slabs placed on a higher level.

---

3. The head and arms of the statue are missing. On top of the chiton the goddess wears a peplos with many fine folds girdled beneath the breast, while an additional himation covers the knees. Her feet rest on a lion. Thick braids cover the shoulders. The throne is schematically depicted. To the east, at a very short distance from the sanctuary, a second, similar statue has been found. The head, breast and arms are missing. The height is 0.80m. The feet of the enthroned goddess rest on a richly decorated footstool. Although the lion is missing, it is obvious that the statue belongs to the sanctuary. Wiegand, Th. – Schrader, H., op.cit., p. 171.

4. The dimensions are 1.50 x 1.50m and 1m deep. Op. cit., p. 171.

SHRINE OF CYBELE

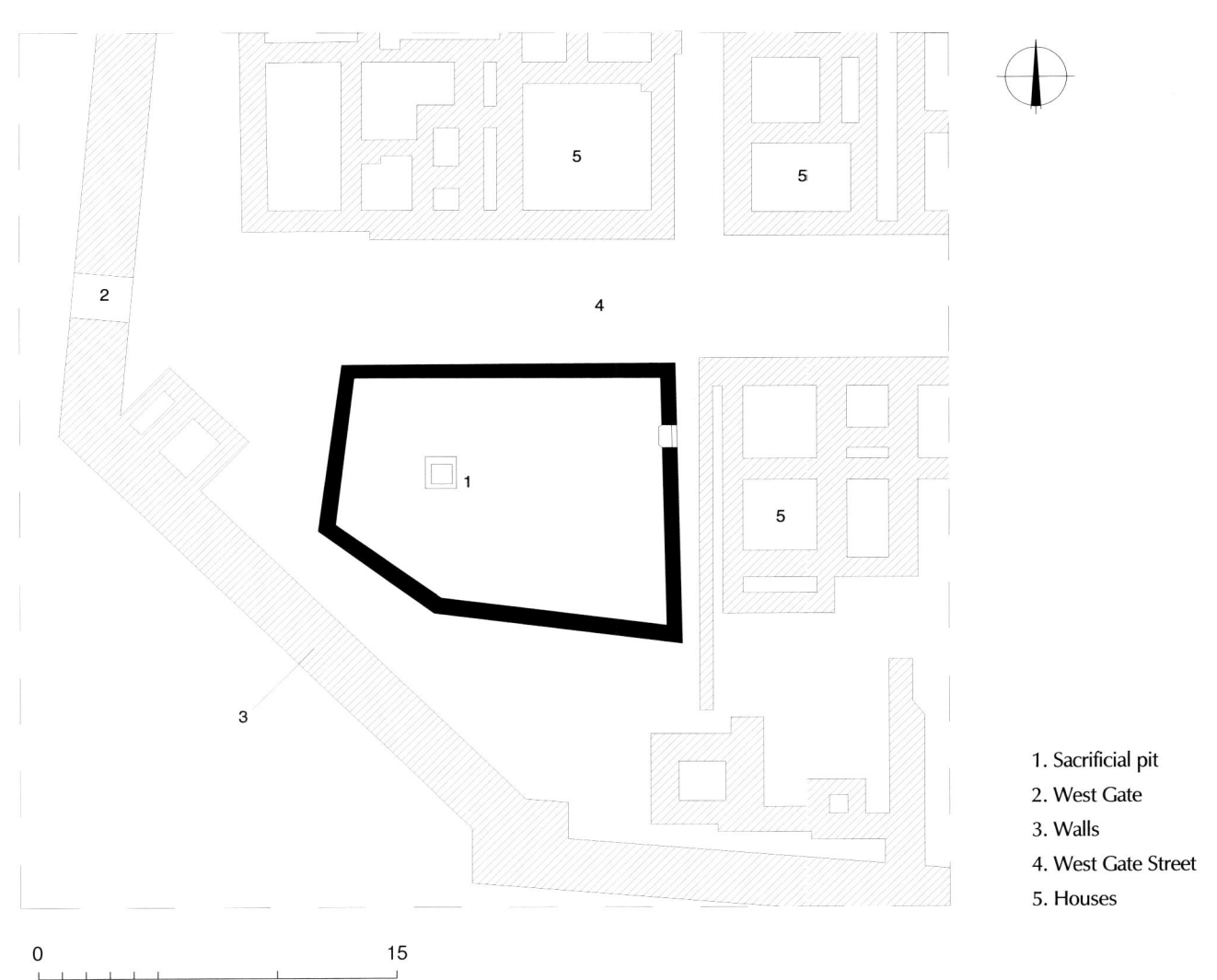

1. Sacrificial pit
2. West Gate
3. Walls
4. West Gate Street
5. Houses

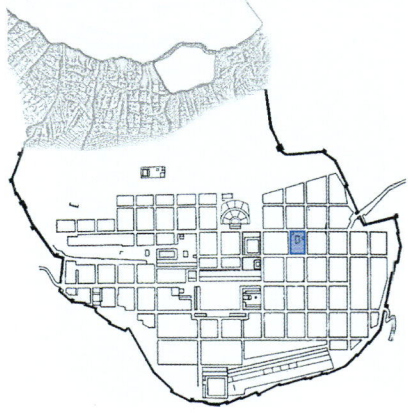

THE SHRINE OF THE EGYPTIAN GODS: The Shrine of the Egyptian Gods stands northeast of the Agora and occupies one plot[5]. It is defined on its northern side by the street leading to the theatre and to the south by the street leading to the Temple of Athena Polias.

From an inscription on a small altar ("Of Isis Sarapis/Anubis"[6]) it is concluded that the Shrine was dedicated to Egyptian Gods. Its form suggests that it was built during the era of the Ptolemies, in the 3rd century BC.

Initially, the area included a precinct and a covered gate on the east side, but no temple. The enclosing high wall was of rusticated masonry. Only the foundations have survived.

The most important element of the area was a large rectangular altar, with proportions 1:2[7], and aligned with the north-south axis. It stood in the centre of the precinct, at an equal distance from the side walls. On its south side there was an ascending staircase with seven steps leading to the higher level[8]. It is not known whether there was a hearth.

In later years a second entrance was made on the north side, near the northwest corner. This entrance was in fact a propylon constructed later than the precinct. Its door was not aligned with the precinct, but it was in the middle of the construction. The propylon is related to a colonnade, constructed after the altar and probably extending along the west side of the shrine.

SHRINES AT THE GATES: On the east and west gates of the city, just before the end of the ascending street leading to the acropolis, there were smaller shrines, dedicated to heroes.

The shrines by the two gates were in the form of an alcove built in the walls. On the south wall of a tower standing to the north of the "Spring Gate", an inscription[9] by Philius from Cyprus has survived, stating that the hero Naulochus was depicted in the alcove. Naulochus was the patron of the eponymous seaside city. The lintel, 3m long, was embedded in the wall, which means that the alcove was an original feature (see introduction by Dr. W. Hoepfner).

---

5. *The external dimensions of which are 47 x 31 m, op. cit, p. 166.*

6. *Op. cit., p. 165.*

7. *14.6 x 7.31m, op. cit., p. 166.*

8. *It was 5m wide and 2.10m deep. Op. cit., p. 168.*

9. *It dates from the fourth century BC. Wiegand, Th. – Schrader, H., op. cit., p. 182.*

SHRINE OF THE EGYPTIAN GODS

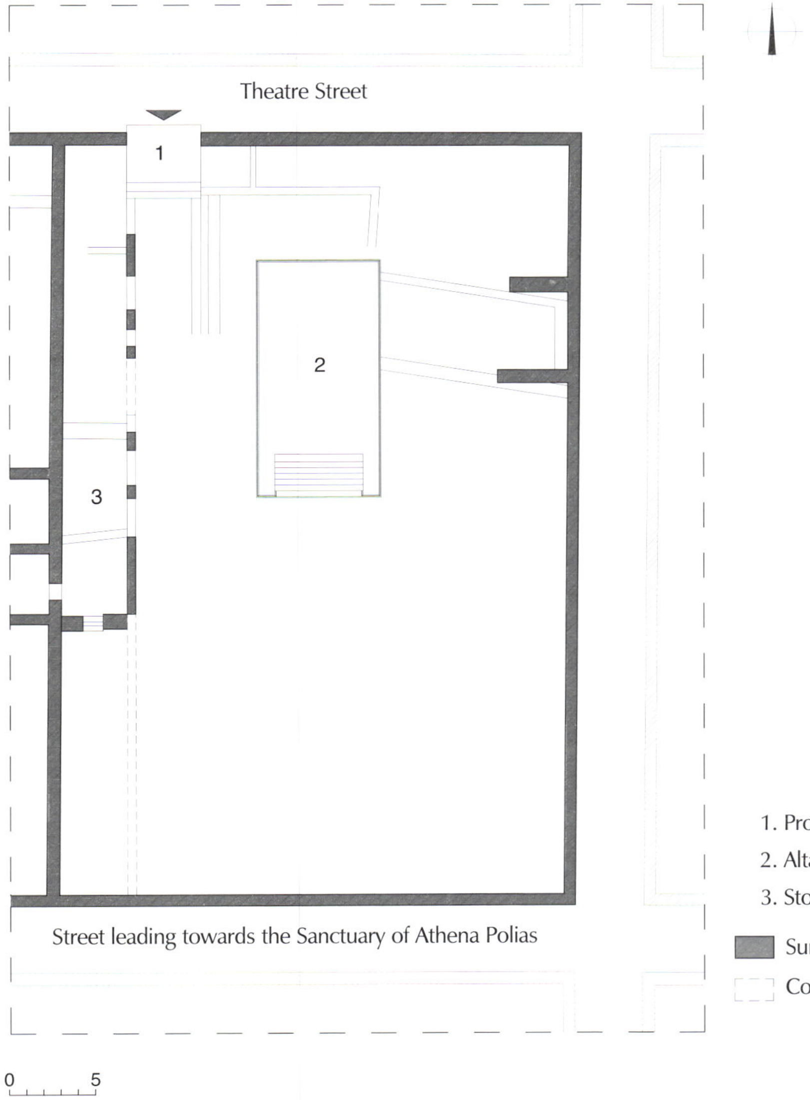

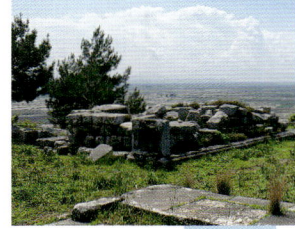

Theatre Street
1
2
3
Street leading towards the Sanctuary of Athena Polias
0
5

The altar today

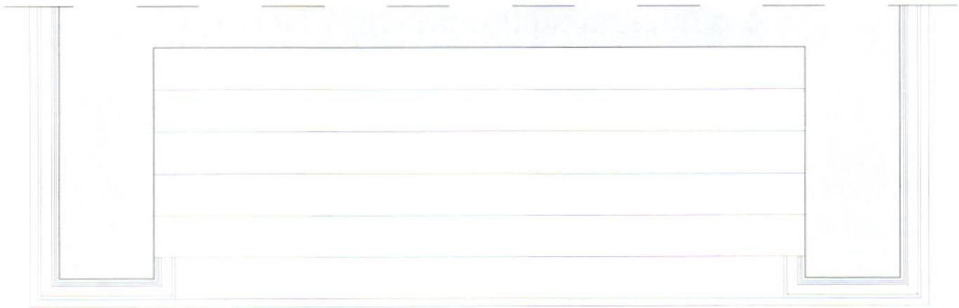

Plan of the altar

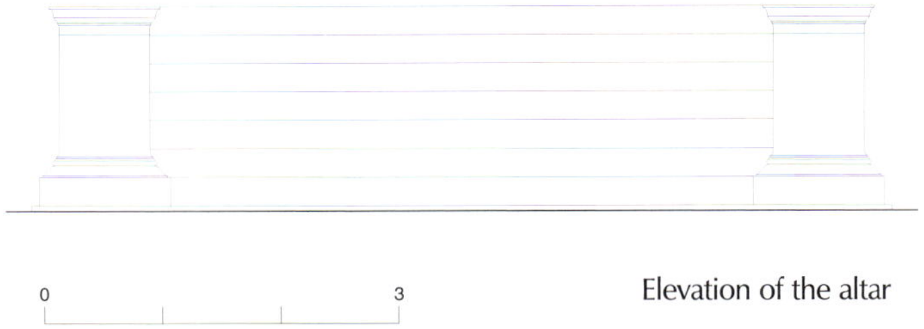

0
3

Elevation of the altar

1. Propylon
2. Altar
3. Stoa

Surviving traces of shrine

Conjectural restored plans

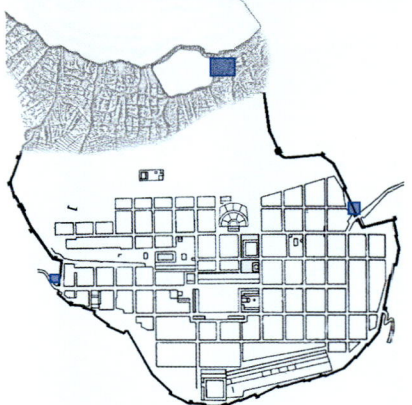

A similar alcove, half-destroyed, has survived on a tower on the west side of the city, near the street leading to the theatre, at a point where there was probably a gate in the walls.

There are no data available about the East and West Gates because they are severely damaged. It is conjectured that there were similar alcoves on these gates as well.

SHRINE OF TELON: At an altitude of 280m above sea-level, a few metres from the final steps leading to the acropolis of Priene, there is an artificial plateau, 12m long and 5m wide, where Wiegand has identified the site of a shrine. There is a special system for the draining of rainwater on its west side.

Two step-like surfaces facing south have survived on the east side, cut in the rock. They were probably bases for statues. Behind them, on the vertically carved rock, one can still see traces of a damaged stele related to Hermes.

On the west side of the plateau there are three alcoves, carved in the rock, in which reliefs related to worship have survived.

It remains unknown to which deity the shrine was dedicated. Given the name of the acropolis, it is possible that the hero Telon was worshipped here.

OTHER SHRINES

View of "Teloneia"

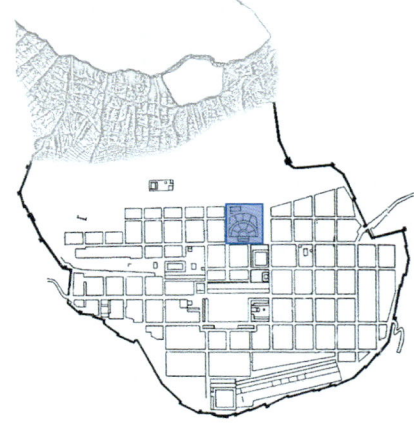

THEATRE

According to the sources[1], tragedies were performed in the Theatre of Priene in the 4th and 3rd centuries BC; in later years reference is made to flute contests for young people as well as to pantomime contests. Apart from its educational and recreational functions, the theatre also served a religious purpose.

LOCATION: The Theatre of Priene is one of the oldest in Asia Minor and displays the basic features of a 3rd-century BC theatre. It is situated north of the Upper Gymnasium, takes up two building plots, and is integrated into the Hippodamian planning system of the city. It extends towards the south, to make use of the slope of the hillside. As a result, spectators sitting on the higher seats had an unobstructed view of the city and the plains. Before the construction of the Ekklesiasterion, the theatre also served as a place of assembly of the citizens.

HISTORY: The auditorium was built first, followed by the stage and the "proscenium" in the 3rd century BC. Around the 2nd century BC the marble seats were added, and a little later, the altar that has survived to this day. There are three major construction phases, related to the way the theatre operated, which are evident mainly in the proscenium and the stage building.

In the early years performances took place in the orchestra. The façade of the "proscenium" was formed by doors alternating with wooden panels covered with painted decorations in the inter-columnar spaces: these constituted the stage set.

Later, when the place of action was moved to the roof of the "proscenium", the façade of the upper level of the stage became more important and was restructured accordingly. This change made it necessary to transfer the officials' seats to a higher position, since the view from their former seats in the first row was now limited. From the new, elevated row of seats, officials could once more enjoy the full view of the "proscenium".

During the 2nd century AD the stage was radically reconstructed. The façade of the stage was demolished and rebuilt deeper to the south. This new façade was built in the Roman style.

---

1. A. von Gerkan (Das Theater von Priene als Einzelanlage und in seiner Bedeutung für das hellenistische Buhnenwesen, München, Verlag für praktische Kunstwissenschaft. F. Schmidt / Kommanditgesellschaft, 1921, p. 61) mentions that the first inscription dates from 332/1 BC. However, according to a more recent dating of the oldest inscription found, the theatre must have been founded in the beginning of the 3rd century. Crowther, C. V., Priene 8 and the History of Priene in the Early Hellenistic Period. Chiron 26, 1996, p. 217.

The Theatre: view to the south

THEATRE

EARLY HELLENISTIC PERIOD: The basic elements of the theatre are the orchestra, the auditorium, and the stage. The orchestra of the theatre of Priene was U-shaped and was covered with tamped earth. There is no evidence that there was a floor or any wooden structure. The area of the orchestra was defined by a perimetric step made of stone, on which were placed benches with backs for the use of officials. One can still see five marble thrones, the proedriae, or seats of honour, intended for prominent citizens. Wiegand[2] assumes that originally these seats were one long backless bench placed at the centre of the structure. Later, after these seats were replaced by an altar dedicated to Dionysus, thrones were constructed around the orchestra with equally detailed decorations on all sides, although some of them were not visible. There was an inscription at the front of each seat, as well as a typical moulding in a recess; the backs, made of different stone, were sloping. The bases bore ornamental lion-paws, and the sides were decorated with ivy leaves. The armrests were slightly curved. Behind the officials' seats, at a slightly lower level, there was a surrounding corridor, approximately 1.8m wide. This corridor, paved with irregular slates, facilitated the movements of spectators; it also served as draining system for the rainwater coming from the auditorium by directing it through underground pipes outside the theatre. At the east end of a corridor, there is a circular base of a bronze statue. At the west end is the pedestal of a klepsydra (hourglass) that was used for the timing of public speeches when the theatre accommodated the sessions of the "Ekklesia of Demos".

In the middle of the row of proedriae, the marble thrones and seats of honour reserved for prominent citizens, stood an altar dedicated to Dionysus, the god honoured by the theatre performances[3]. On either side of the altar there were two narrow entrance points from the surrounding corridor to the orchestra, blocked by a railing. The gap between the two ends of the row of marble seating and the stage was also closed with railings, supported by low pilasters. Thus, the orchestra was totally cut off from the auditorium.

The boundary between the auditorium and the orchestra was the first perimetrical step in front of the lower seats, which was also the external boundary of the corridor behind the proedriae. The auditorium made use of the natural slope of the ground and extended towards the north by way of artificial terraces supported by imposing retaining walls. These walls enclose the whole structure of the theatre in a trapezium, the larger base of which lies on

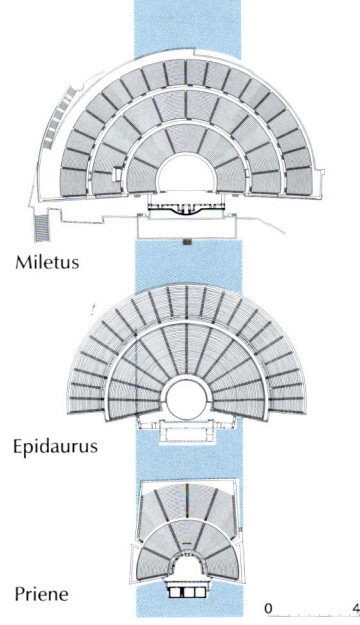

Miletus

Epidaurus

Priene

0   45

2. Wiegand, Th. – Schrader, H., Priene. Ergebnisse der Ausgrabungen und Untersuchungen von den Jahren 1895-1898. Unter Mitwirkung von G. Kummer, W. Wilberg, H. Winnefeld, R. Zahn. Berlin: Königliche Museen zu Berlin, 1904, p. 243.

3. Wiegand found sections of the upper part of the altar in the orchestra and proceeded to reconstruct it. Upon the lowest step stood a low base which has not survived. Upon the base there was the altar proper, which, towards the side of the orchestra, bore an inscription of the early second century BC. The covering slab had an elaborate decoration of Ionic order. On the narrow and the long sides facing the spectators there was an additional upright slab in the form of a frieze. Op. cit., p. 241.

THEATRE

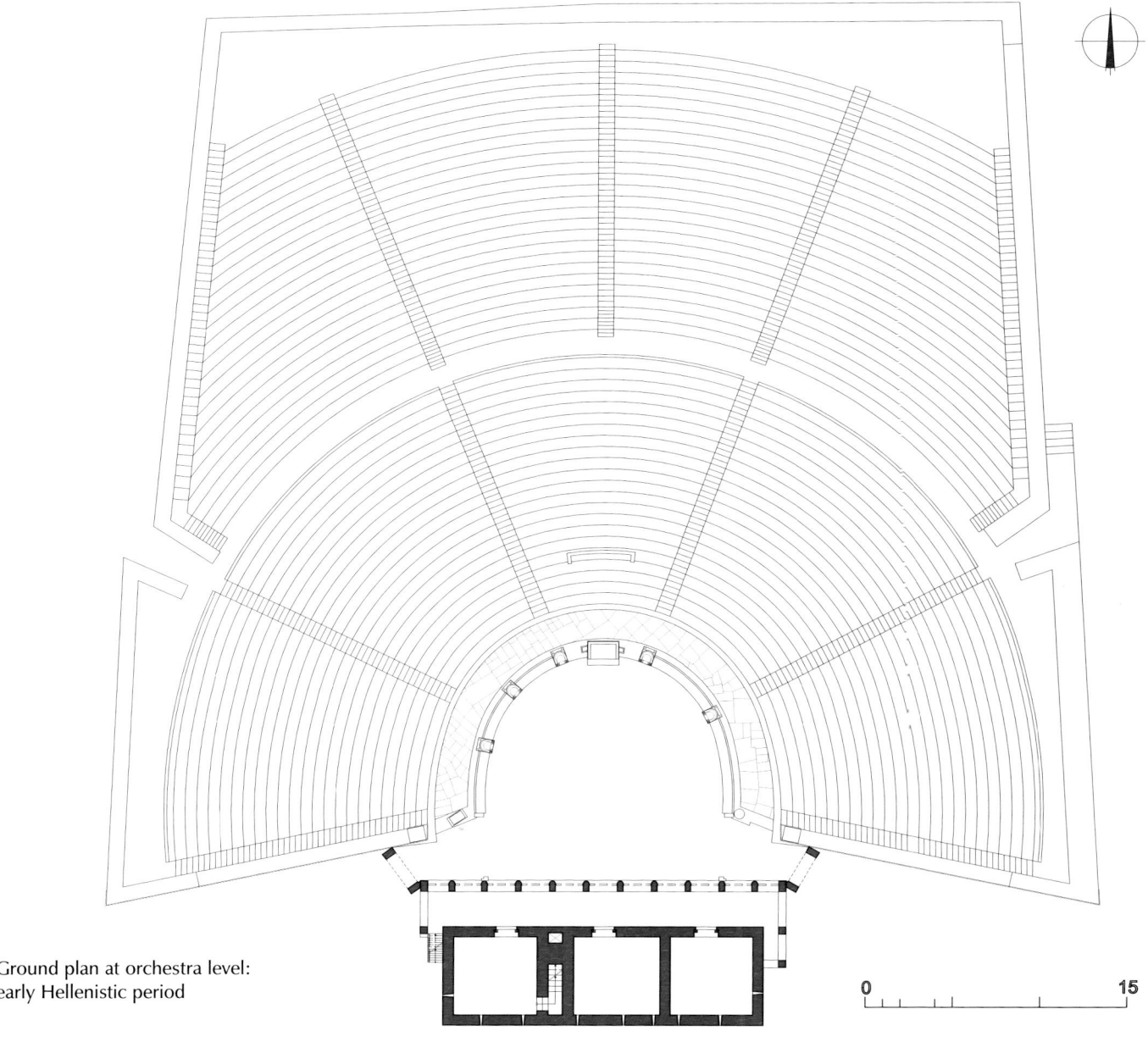

Ground plan at orchestra level: early Hellenistic period

0 — 15

the side of the stage. The enclosing walls are interrupted only by the two side entrances, at the ends of the corridors, between the upper and the lower "diazomata" (landings). The partial collapse of the side retaining walls at a later period resulted in the destruction of the upper part of the auditorium.

The general layout of the auditorium is not circular, as was the rule, but semi-elliptical. The extension of the auditorium beyond the semicircle, typical of Greek theatres, is achieved through the construction of an arc with more than one centre. It is estimated that there were 50 rows of seats, with a seating capacity of 5,000 people, i.e., the total of Priene's population.

At the south front of the auditorium, between the retaining walls and the stage, there were two minor passageways. The retaining walls were lined with stones all along the auditorium reaching the level of the orchestra, where they formed large pilasters on which statues were placed, offerings of "stephanephoros" Kleandros "To Olympian Zeus and the demos"[4]. Each minor passageway had a plain inlet gate. One pilaster of each gate has been retrieved in situ. The gates were blocked by an iron railing.

The masonry of the enclosing walls and minor passageways is rusticated, that is, the face of each stone is curved and projects markedly from the wall. The external wall of the east side of the auditorium has been preserved in good condition. On this wall, between the two minor passageways, one can still see one of the two openings through which the public could enter directly to the corridor.

Access to the seats was gained through six staircases, dividing the auditorium into five sections. Two steps corresponded to each row, which was 0.40m high. The rows consisted of distinct structural members: horizontal slabs and vertical supporting elements. Almost no slabs have been preserved today. In the centre of the fifth row there is a more recent "proedria" (mid-2nd century BC), which, as mentioned earlier, was constructed when the enactment of the drama was moved from the orchestra to the roof of the "proscenium".

Throne

4. Op. cit., p. 238. From the existing evidence it is concluded that the statues were made of bronze with one leg extending, thus expressing motion. Also, Schede, M., Die Ruinen von Priene. Archäologisches Institut des Deutschen Reiches, Abteilung Istanbul, 1964, p. 75.

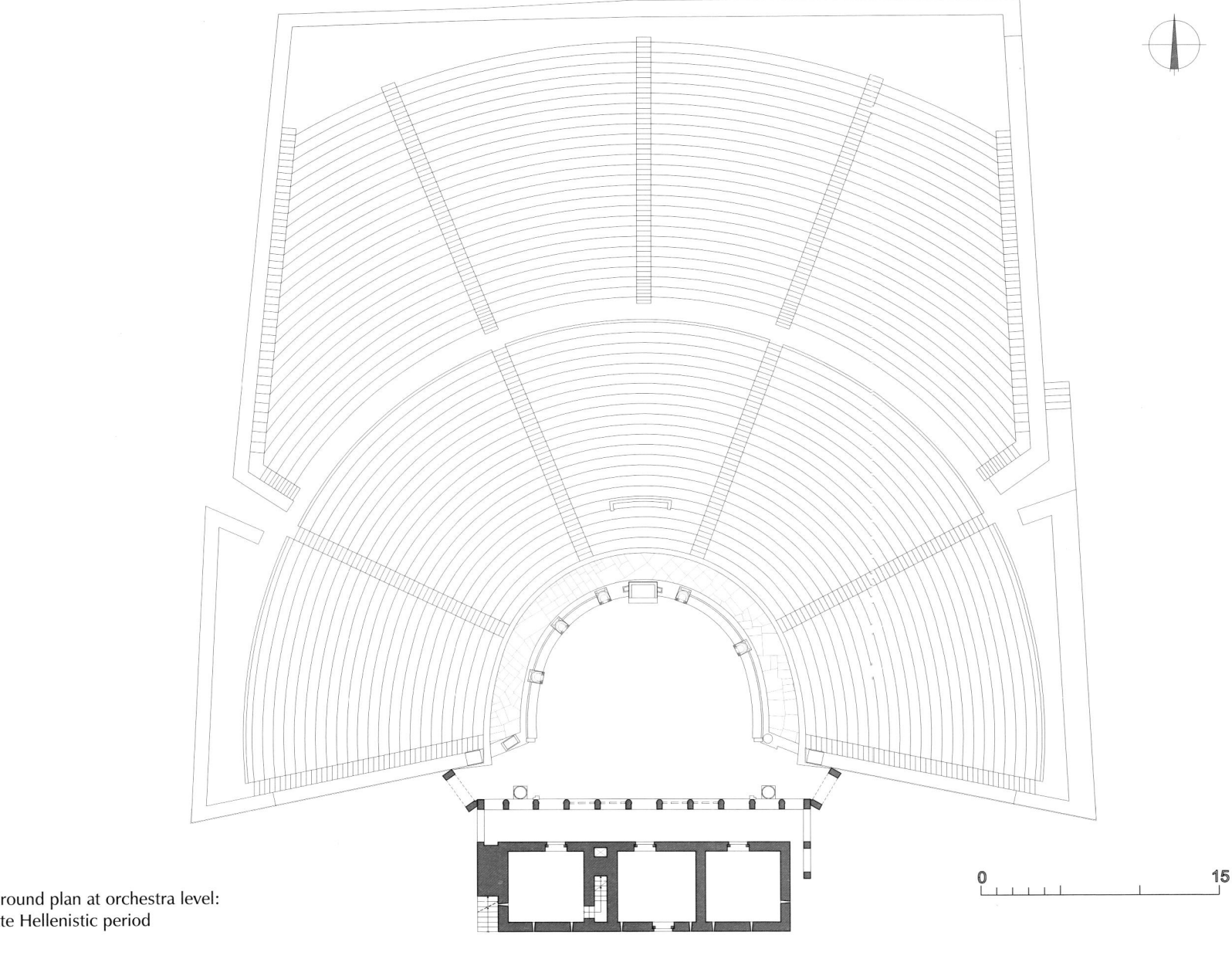

THEATRE

Ground plan at orchestra level: late Hellenistic period

0   15

The view of the auditorium from a room within the stage

The square holes found almost all over the auditorium were, possibly, apertures for the installation of poles supporting a shelter from sun and rain.

The stage consisted of a covered and enclosed rectangular main building, the "proscenium" and a covered stoa on the side of the orchestra, which has survived in relatively good condition.

An imaginary extension of the circle of the orchestra would be tangential to the sides of the "proscenium". The "proscenium", which according to Gerkan was built in 150 BC[5], was 2.7m high, i.e. 0.20m higher than the "proscenium" of Oropos, the lowest known "proscenium". It was enclosed by 12 half-columns of the Doric order, which ended as pilasters and had a full entablature. Its roof, wooden and accessible, was also the floor on which the actors performed. The original blue colour was preserved on the triglyphs of the frieze –four per pilaster– when they were recovered.

Several columns have survived almost intact: twelve on the side facing the orchestra, two on the east side and one on the west side. However, nine of the capitals are missing. In a large part of the western façade, the whole entablature has survived in situ. During the late Hellenistic period, several grooves covered with lead were embedded in the cornices and it is possible that they served for the attachment of metal hooks for the hanging of carpets, light curtains, garlands etc. Several elements of the construction were later incorporated in neighbouring Byzantine buildings.

The openings between the pilasters of the main face of the "proscenium" were closed off by painted wooden panels. The doors at the 3rd, 5th and 7th inter-columnar spaces were also painted. According to the conventions of the ancient Greek theatre, the central gate led to the palace, the west gate to the countryside, and the east gate to the port. The doors could be dismantled and replaced by panels. The façade's end and side inter-columnar spaces were closed off with iron bars[6].

The roof of the "proscenium" consisted of several stone beams resting on the building of the stage at the one end and on the pilasters at the other. The gap between the beams was

5. Gerkan, A. von, Zum Skenengebäude des Theaters von Priene, Ist. Mitt 9-10, 1959-60, p. 99.

6. The well-preserved columns of the proscenium contribute to the understanding of the supporting panels. Initially there were panels in all the inter-columnar spaces, apart from the three with doors. As Dorpfeld remarked, the panels were removed later (but also during the Hellenistic period) from the two extreme inter-columnar spaces and were replaced by horizontal railings that left deep marks. Most probably, the above modification occurred at the same time as the statues of Thrasybulus and Apollodorus were placed in front of the proscenium, the bases of which have survived. Thus, only four inter-columnar spaces were left free for panels. Finally, from marks on the epistyle and the sill, in the two immediately following inter-columnar spaces of the ends, it has been concluded that railings were placed here as well at a later period. Wiegand, Th. – Schrader, H., op. cit., p. 247.

THEATRE

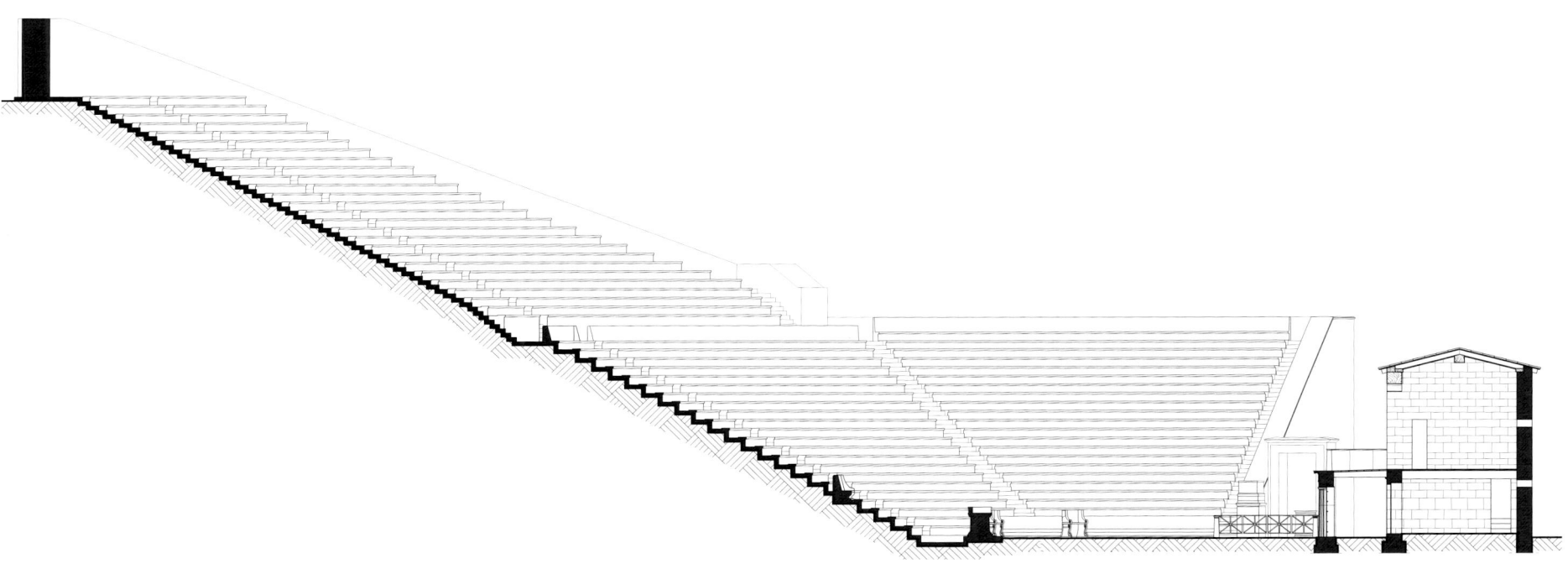

North-south section:
late Hellenistic period:

bridged by planks, which constituted the floor of the stage (logeion). During the early years, this floor served only for the appearance of the "deus ex machina". One could reach the level of the floor from the west side of the stage building, initially via a wooden staircase, although this was replaced by a stone one in the late Hellenistic years. Of the stone parapets enclosing the "logeion" on its short sides, only the west one has survived. The existence of a similar parapet on the east side is considered certain, although none of its parts has been found. However, there are marks from apertures and supports on the northern cornice.

In front of the proscenium was an array of offerings and statues. For the most part, only foundations of their bases have survived. In the second and the penultimate inter-columnar space there are still two bases of bronze statues.

The main stage building is a simple rectangular two-storey building, 18.41 x 5.82m, with three chambers on each floor.

The stage was built in the beginning of the 2nd century BC, when actors still performed in the orchestra, while –as mentioned above– the "logeion", the roof of the "proscenium", was used only for the appearances of the "deus ex machina". Based on the dating of the new "proedria", in the fifth row, it is ascertained that the actors performed to the roof of the "proscenium" from the middle of the 2nd century BC onwards.

On the ground floor there were three rooms open to the "proscenium" without internal communication. The back and the side walls had small windows. Between the central and the west room there was an interior staircase leading to the upper storey, which has not survived. Taking into consideration the slope of the ground at the lowest level and the provision for the draining of rainwater at the base of the staircase, it is concluded that this part was uncovered.

THEATRE

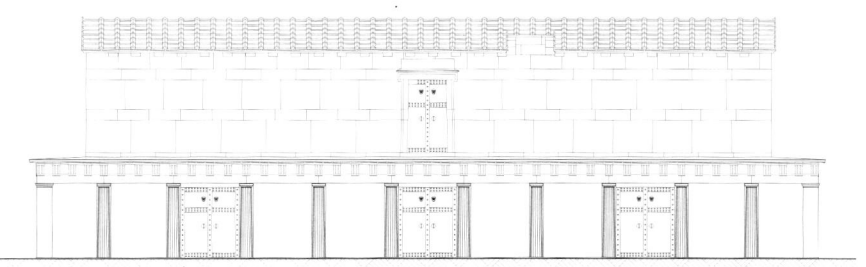

Elevation of stage

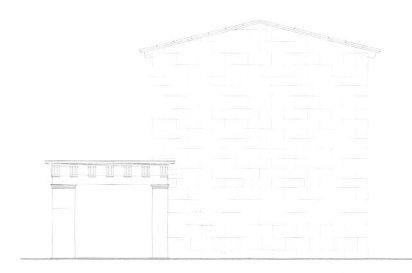

Side elevation

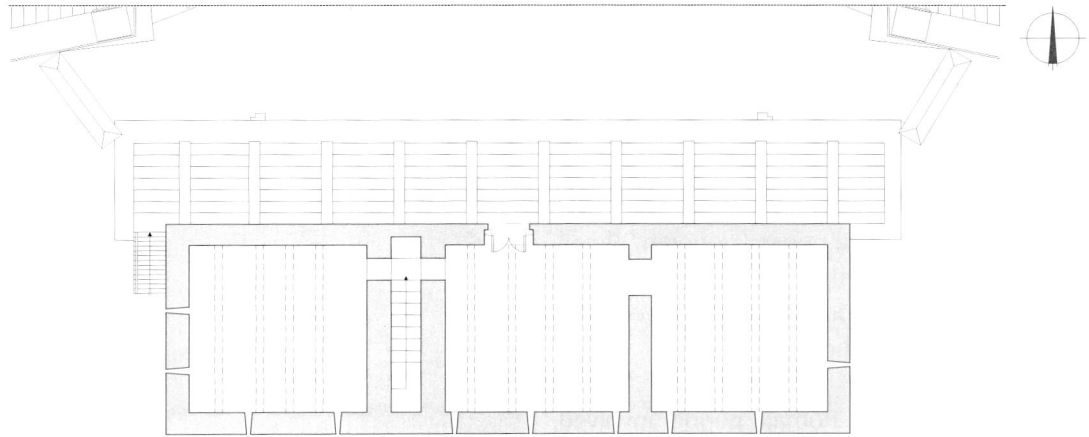

Logeion level-plan

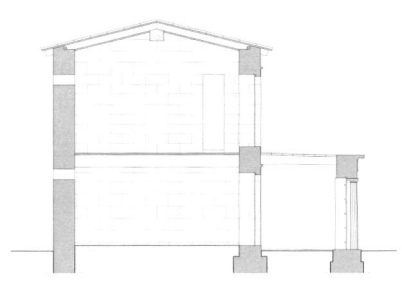

Cross section

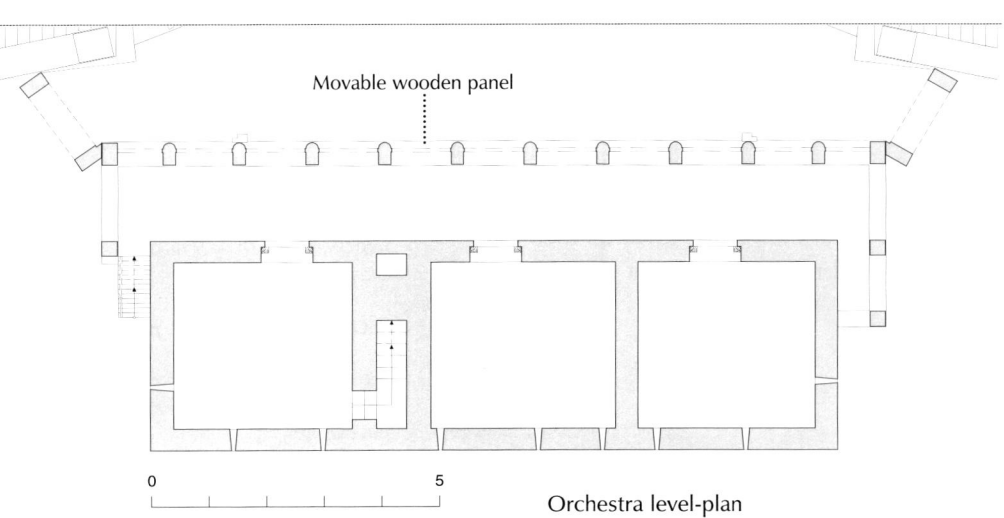

Orchestra level-plan

Stage-proscenium
early Hellenistic period

Opposite the fifth pilaster of the proscenium counting from the west, touching the north wall of the stage, there was a vertical opening with direct access from the staircase, which intersects the two floors and the roof; it probably facilitated the appearance of the "deus ex machina" on the roof of the building, the "theologeion"[7]. This is in fact one of the more interesting features of the Theatre of Priene. The upper level of the building was also divided into three chambers[8].

LATE HELLENISTIC PERIOD: The stage building was the main part of the theatre to be altered during the late Hellenistic period[9]. The original wooden staircase at the west end of the logeion was replaced by a stone one, which was attached to the wall. Confirmation that this staircase was not included in the original plan is provided by the fact that this part of the west wall was now given its final form. Moreover, the corner pilasters and the epistyle were elaborately constructed. All these elements, as well as one of the small openings of the west room, were partly covered by the construction of the staircase[10].

In the same period, at the back (south) part of the middle chamber on the ground floor, a door was opened up in order to facilitate movement. For the same reason doors were opened up on the east and west sides (i.e., the narrow sides) of the upper ("logeion") level, where the most important alterations were made. On the main (north) side, where there was originally only one small opening, three larger ones were opened, which were not symmetrical, while the middle opening was also wider than the others.

ROMAN PERIOD: The transformation of the theatre during the Roman period involved, primarily, the extension of the "proscenium", which made it deeper, and the demolition of the wall of the upper level of the Hellenistic stage, which was rebuilt two metres to the south.

During that period the lower level (orchestra) served only as an auxiliary to the Roman stage. Thus, with the exception of the three doors, all the spaces between the half-columns of the "proscenium" were walled up and the building was painted in a different colour. After the replacement of the portable panels in the inter-columnar spaces of the "proscenium" by thin, coated walls, the background decoration became, in a sense, permanent. A fragment of such a "built-in painting", up to the height of half a metre at the last inter-columnar space towards the west, has survived. It depicts a double door using white, black and red colours on a yellow background.

View of rows of seats

7. Schede, M., Die Ruinen von Priene. Archäologisches Institut des Deutschen Reiches. Abteilung Istanbul, 1964, p. 75.

8. Describing the colours of the last phase, Wiegand mentions the following: "...the band of the epistyle was red, the triglyphs blue. Triglyphs and metopes were crowned by a continuous Ionic moulding with painted eggs of red and blue colour. The mutules of the cornice were blue, whereas the spaces between them (viae) were red. The moulding on the bases of the mutules was red and blue, whereas the underlying vertical surface, as well as the lowest horizontal surface of the cornice, were red". Wiegand, Th. – Schrader, H., Priene, op. cit., pp. 246-247.

9. Gerkan, A. von, op. cit., pp. 68-69.

10. According to Wiegand, op. cit., p. 251, it is not known whether the floor was divided into three rooms.

THEATRE

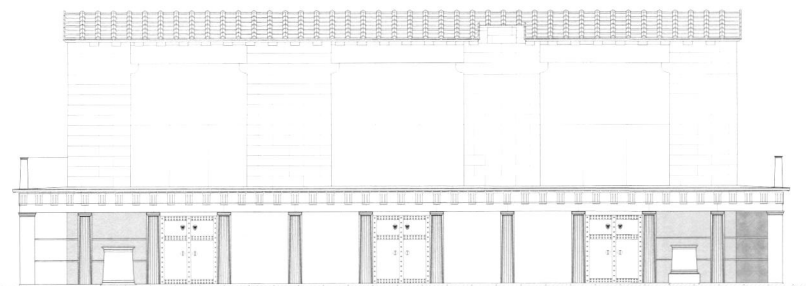

Elevation of stage

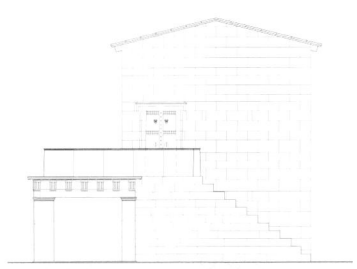

Side elevation

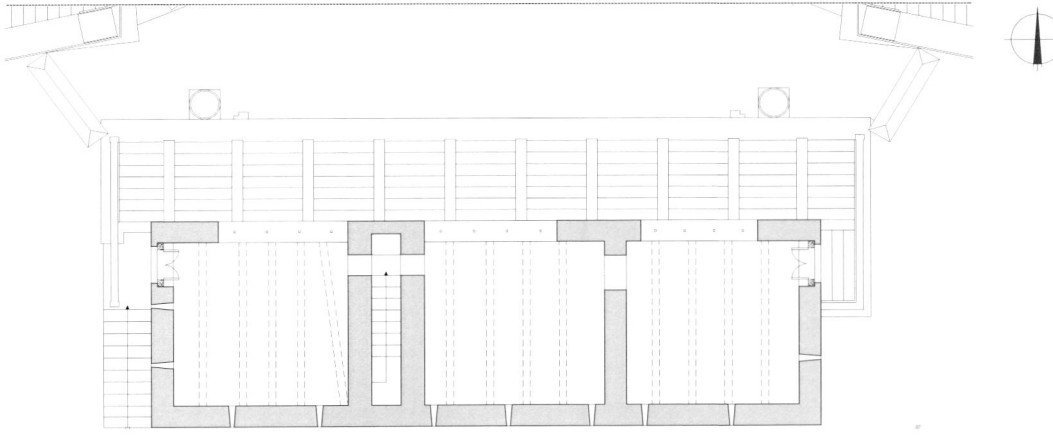

Logeion level-plan

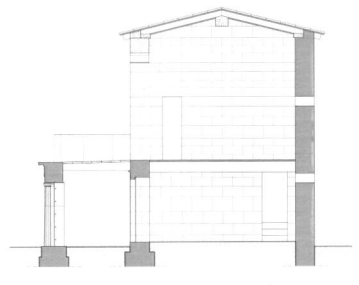

Cross section

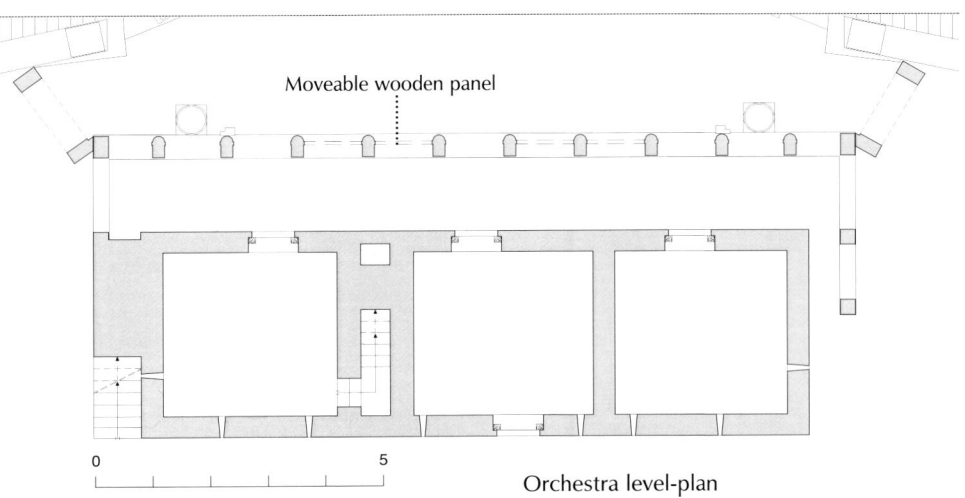

Orchestra level-plan

Moveable wooden panel

0   5

Stage-proscenium
late Hellenistic period

The layout of the new two-storey façade of the stage building was typical of Roman stages, having two alcoves and three doors. In addition, the ceiling of the ground floor was reinforced with the construction of a vault of brick masonry. A pile of loose stones and mortar has been discovered. This probably served as a mixture for the construction of the underlayer of a mosaic floor that has not survived.

Of the imposing new wall of the stage façade, only two fragments of the cornice have survived. They bear a crudely developed moulding, probably plastered. Since no relevant information is available, it is not possible to estimate the height of the new wall or the form of its roof. But it is highly probable that the roof was fairly heavy, which would explain the marks left by supporting pilasters in the southwest and southeast corners.

In Roman times a large water reservoir was constructed at the west passageway, probably related to the nearby "thermae" (public baths) in the area of the Upper Gymnasium[11].

COLOUR: According to Schede[12], the colours of the Theatre differ markedly in the Hellenistic and the Roman periods. Initially, only two colours were used, minium red on certain horizontal elements and deep cobalt blue on the triglyphs. The shafts of the half-columns, the capitals, the "epistyle", the "metopes" and the cornice had no colouring.

During the Roman period the use of colour was much more extensive. All the columns and capitals were painted red[13].

---

11. Gerkan, A. von, op. cit., p. 75.

12. According to Wiegand, op. cit., p. 245, the addition of a staircase should have been decided upon during the construction of the proscenium and the stage. This is probably why the epistyle of the proscenium does not extend to the corner of the stage.

13. Gerkan, A. von, op. cit., p. 83.

THEATRE

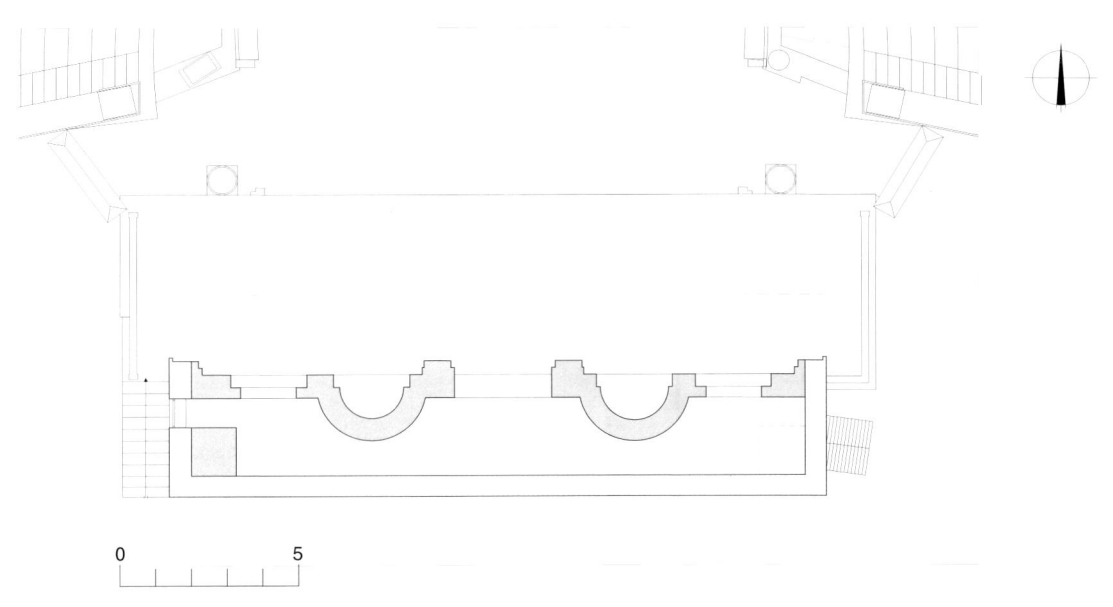

Logeion level-ground plan

▭ Older construction
▭ Imperial Roman period, Older stage boundary

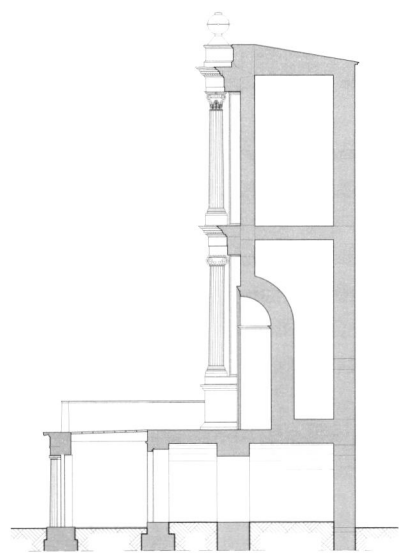

Cross section

Stage
Imperial Roman Period

The proscenium as it appears today

THEATRE: THE PROSCENIUM

Architectural order

Perspective of the auditorium from the east end of the proscenium

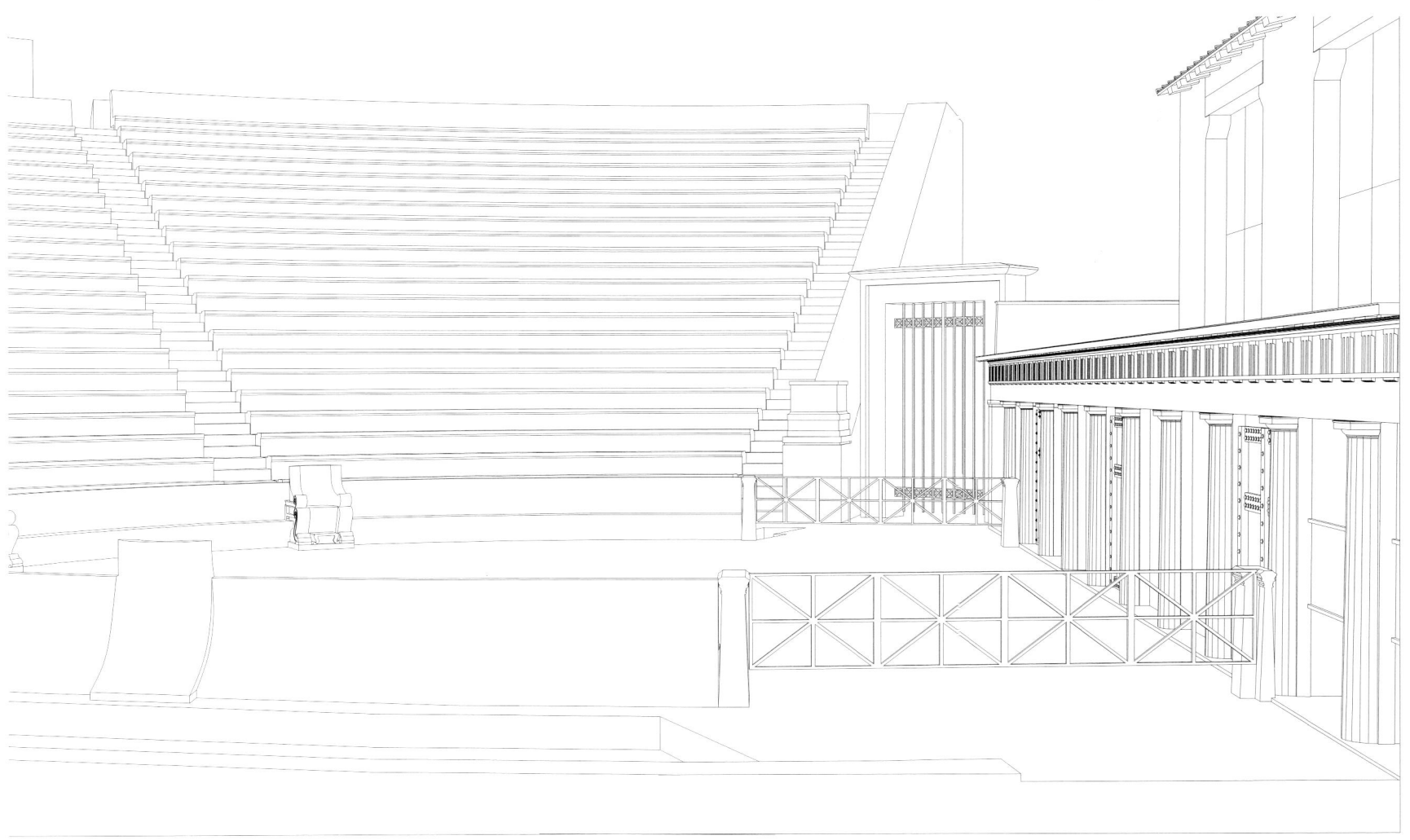

Perspective of the auditorium from the west parodos

Perspective of the late Hellenistic stage overlooking the Temple of Athena Polias and the valley of the River Maeander (drawing after von Gerkan)

Perspective of the west parodos (drawing after Krischen)

GYMNASIA

INTRODUCTION: Gymnasia were public institutions for the education, musical training and athletic practice of the young. Every ancient Greek city had a gymnasium with its own self-contained facilities. Originally they were simply open spaces, situated outside the built-up part of the city or in areas related to the Agora. Later they developed into buildings. The type of gymnasium containing a covered palaestra was developed in the first half of the 4th century BC. According to the Roman architect Vitruvius[1], gymnasia had a square or rectangular plan. They consisted of a central yard with circumference of two stadia ("diaulos") or 1,200 attic feet, with colonnades enclosing the yard on its four sides. On one side, usually the north, was a second colonnade, the "xystos". This colonnade was parallel to the first one and was usually one stadium long and 32 attic feet wide. This is where athletic games took place when the weather was bad[2]. The open-air tracks where the young athletes received training in good weather were called paradromies.

The plan of three of the sides of the courtyard included "exedras", i.e. halls with a bench extending around the walls, where philosophers, teachers of rhetoric and artists assembled and conversed. The largest of these halls was the "Ephebeum" or "exedra" for the "ephebi" (with proportions 3:2, according to Vitruvius), where young pupils were instructed in philosophy and oratory. The rooms around the "Ephebeum" were used as "apodyteria" (dressing rooms) and for bathing and body care. A stadium also included the "konisterion", containing the "konistra", i.e., a deep sandpit with fine sand for "alindisis" (wrestling on the ground)[3], the "korykeion", where the boxers trained with "korykes" (leather bags full of sand) and the "elaiothesion", where athletes rubbed their bodies with oil. Some of the games and sports that took place at the gymnasia, according to the sources, are the "sphairomachia", the "strovilos", the "pentalithos", running, wrestling, discus, boxing etc[4].

According to contemporary teaching systems, students were divided into "ephebi" (adolescents) and young men. In Priene the "ephebi" probably received instruction in the older Upper Gymnasium; the complex of the Lower Gymnasium, built later, was intended for the teaching of young men. Both gymnasia probably had a common supervisor. The citizens of Priene generously donated oil, training equipment and contest awards to the gymnasia, which indicates their importance. In contrast to the Upper Gymnasium, whose initial structure was gradually altered as its functions changed with the passage of time, the Lower Gymnasium preserved its simple layout and its initial character, thus providing clearer information about the function of the Gymnasium.

1. "Pyrsos", Megali Elliniki Engkyklopaideia, Athens, 1929, vol. 8, "Gymnasio", p. 763.

2. Bouras, Ch., Mathimata Istorias tis Architektonikis, vol. A, 1st ed. 1968, 2nd ed. 1980, 3rd ed. Athens: editions Symmetria, 1991, p. 320.

3. Activity in which the athletes rolled on the ground.

4. "Pyrsos", Megali Elliniki Engkyklopaideia, op. cit., p. 763.

The Baths of the Lower Gymnasium at the time of the German excavations
©DAI Istanbul

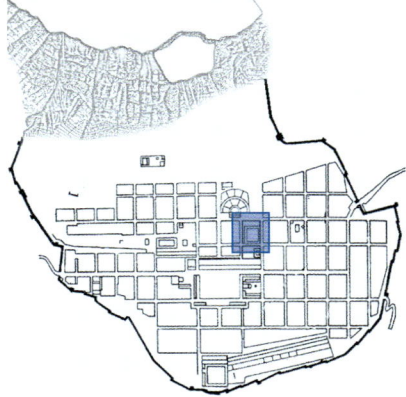

UPPER GYMNASIUM

UPPER GYMNASIUM: The Upper Gymnasium is in the north section of the city, between the Ekklesiasterion and the theatre, and occupies one building plot. On its north side is the street leading to the theatre, on its south side the street leading to the Sanctuary of Athena Polias, and on its east side the ascending street that passes by the West Gate of the Agora and the Temple of Asclepius. Originally, the Gymnasium was accessible through this street. Later the entrance was transferred to the south side, on the street leading to the Sanctuary of Athena Polias, at the point where an ascending street with steps ends, next to the Ekklesiasterion. It is not clear whether the neighbouring block to the west was included in the Gymnasium area.

HELLENISTIC PERIOD: Since the complex underwent many important reconstructions during the Roman and Byzantine eras, very few parts have survived from the initial Hellenistic construction, and they are not well preserved. The initial plan of the Upper Gymnasium dates back to the 3rd century BC and included a large, rectangular peristyle with rooms on the north side. A propylon stood at the entrance on the east side of the yard. Doric columns found in the neighbouring Byzantine Cathedral probably originate from the Upper Gymnasium.

The surviving parts of the Hellenistic building include an elaborately constructed section of the south and east yard, some traces of the propylon on the east and the foundation of a semi-circular exedra in the courtyard. Other findings of the same period include the remains of a carefully constructed foundation, covered by later structures, which provides information about the original boundary of the building to the south. As in the case of the later Lower Gymnasium, the colonnades of the peristyle on the east and south had no rooms at the end.

ROMAN PERIOD: During the Roman era the north section of the Gymnasium was taken up by "thermae" (public baths); this alteration was quite common in Hellenistic gymnasia. The new construction extended to the north towards the street of the Theatre and to the west towards the neighbouring block. As a result, the steep descending street leading from the Agora to the theatre was dispensed with.

The inside of the walls included alcoves and rectangular recesses, and built-in clay heating pipes.

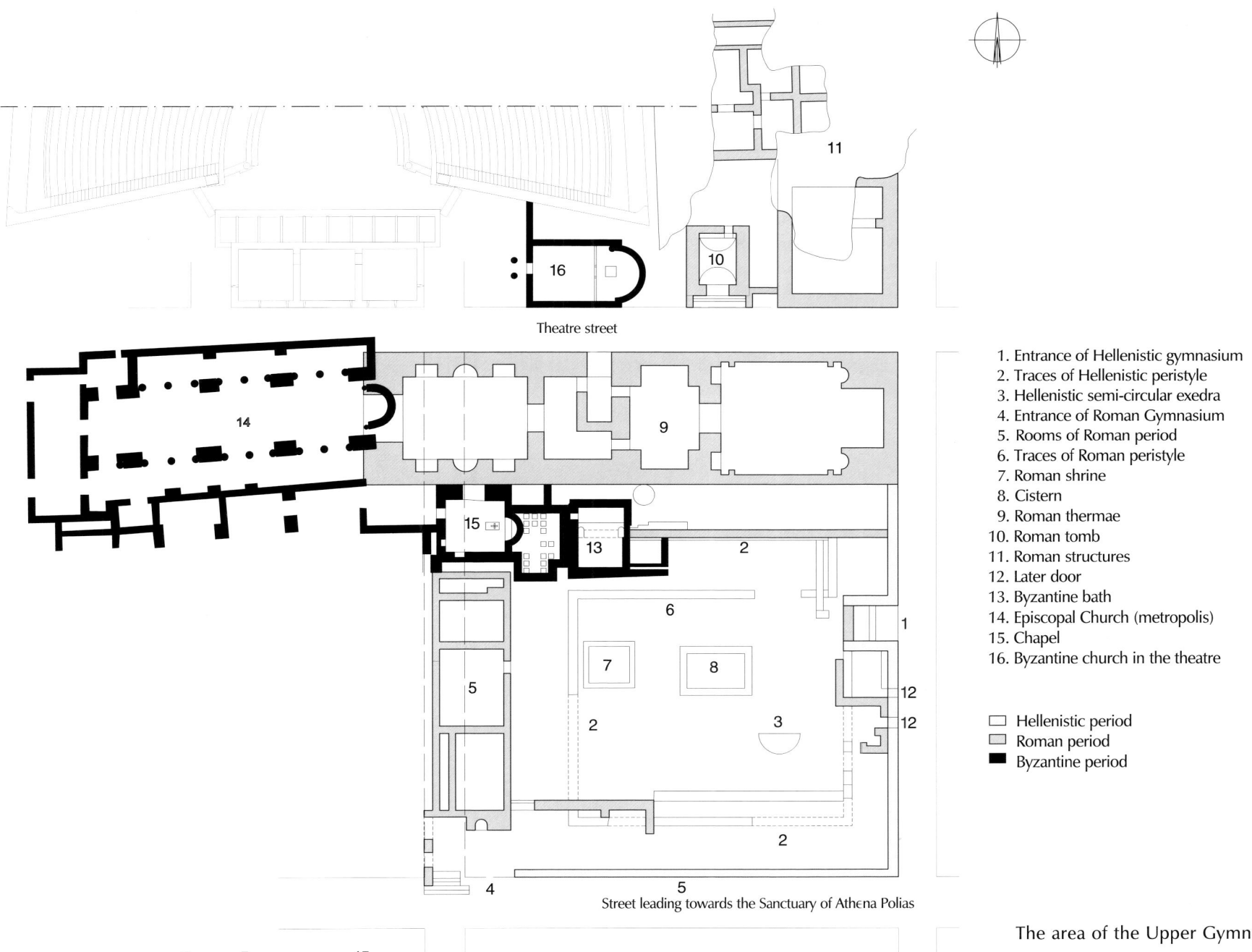

The area of the Upper Gymnasium

UPPER GYMNASIUM

In the late Roman period the west and east colonnades of the Upper Gymnasium were reconstructed by adding several rooms at the end. Rooms were also built in the remaining section of the abandoned passage to the Theatre. A row of columns was constructed on the west side in front of the new rooms. Rooms were also added to the northern stoa, and the row of columns was transferred to the south, towards the courtyard. These columns, as indicated earlier, were later used for the construction of the neighbouring Christian Cathedral. Only their "stylobates" have survived in situ. It is possible that the large cistern, built in the west passageway of the Theatre, also belonged to the same thermae complex.

In the courtyard of the Upper Gymnasium stands a small Roman shrine, probably for the worship of the emperor. The surviving elements of this shrine are the mouldings of the wall base and the antae and part of the marble base in its interior[1].

Trial excavations carried out on the north side of the complex revealed large halls containing many fragments of terra sigillata, i.e., Roman pottery, which almost invariably was coated with a characteristic brown-reddish glaze and bore additional decorative motifs and relief figures. In the same place a Roman vaulted tomb dating back to the Augustan era was discovered. It is the only pre-Christian tomb within the walls. It is constructed of masonry and mortar, and its south front has a marble facing[2].

CHRISTIAN ERA: During the Christian era a plain bath with a deep cistern and hypocausts (i.e., facilities for the heating of water) was constructed at the southwest corner of the Gymnasium's courtyard. The upper part of a column base from the Temple of Athena Polias was used as a table by the bathers. This complex was destroyed by fire. A small chapel was built on its ruins, which was in use at the same time as the large Cathedral nearby. This chapel was accessible from the south aisle of the Cathedral.

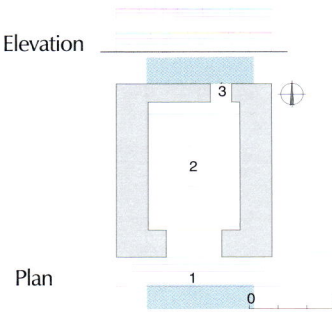

Roman tomb : 1. entrance
2. chamber 3. arched window

1. A coin of emperor Hadrian and a circular statue base with an inscription dedicated to Emperor Domitian has been found in the area of the sanctuary. It is characteristic that the above inscription was removed after the Emperor's death. Schede, M., Die Ruinen von Priene. Archäologisches Institut des Deutschen Reiches. Abteilung Istanbul, 1964, p. 81.

2. Above the chamber of the tomb there is a small square room. On the north side there is a high arched window resting on a parapet with balustrades and is crowned with a lower pediment. The statue of the deceased was probably placed on the sill. In the interior, the room was shaped like a triclinium. On the long sides there were benches. The free space in the centre of the room was a long and narrow corridor 0.70m wide and 2m long. Access was from the north side, through a square opening that closed with a marble slab. The funerary gifts found in it are exhibited in Antiquarium in Berlin. Wiegand, Th. – Schrader, H., Priene. Ergebnisse der Ausgrabungen und Untersuchungen von den Jahren 1895-1898. Unter Mitwirkung von G. Kummer, W. Wilnerg, H. Winnefeld, R. Zahn. Berlin: Königliche Museen zu Berlin, 1904, p. 278.

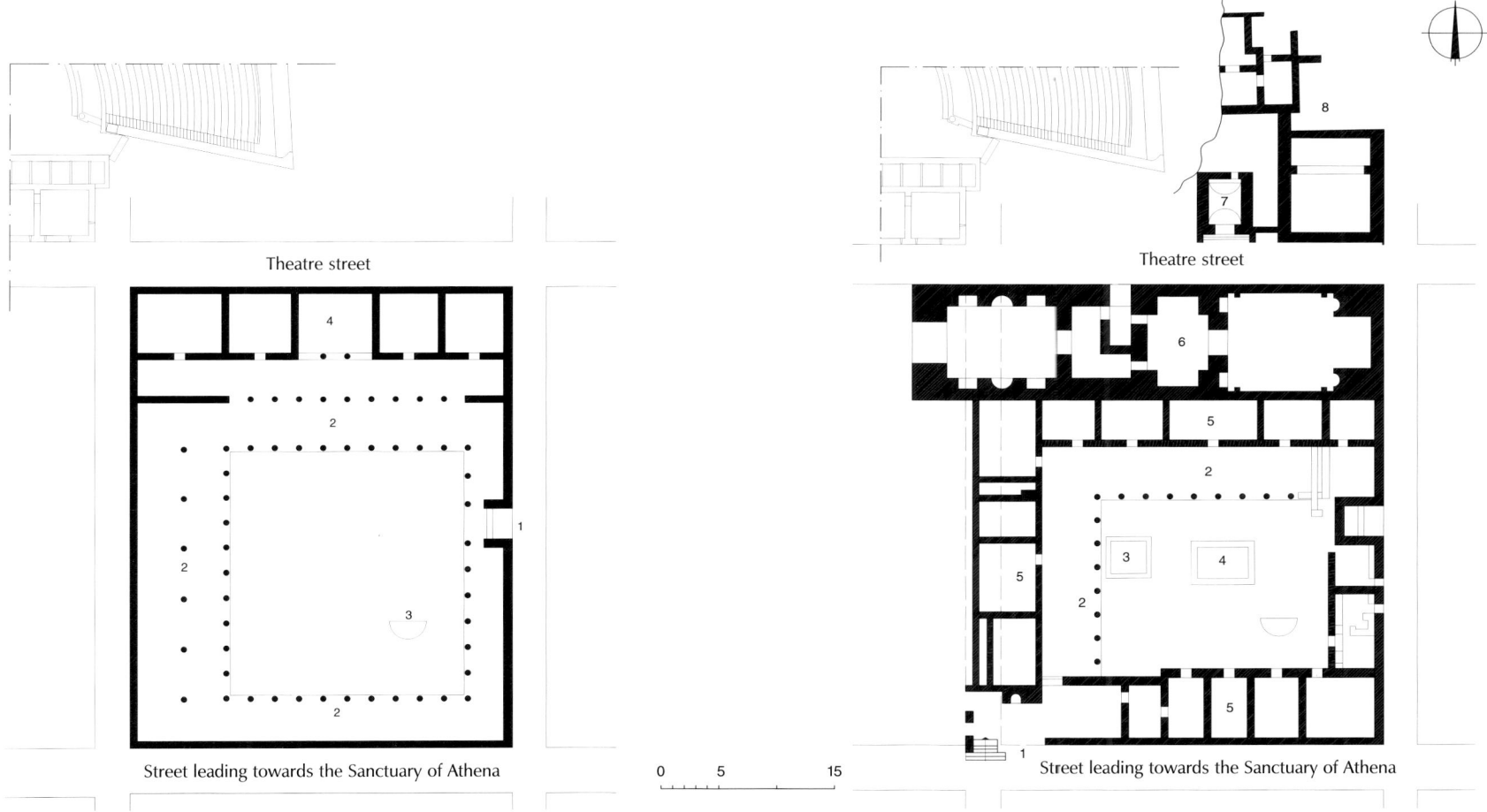

LOWER GYMNASIUM

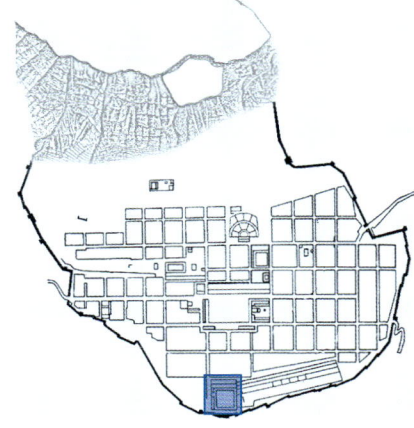

LOWER GYMNASIUM: The Lower Gymnasium and the adjoining Stadium were not included in the initial planning of Priene. Both were built in the late 2nd century BC and stood on the south end of the town, near the walls. In order to save space, the houses on the south side of the street were demolished. The south and west sides of the Gymnasium were enclosed by a strong wall supported by buttresses. The complex was accessible through a steeply sloping street starting from the southwest end of the Agora.

Like other buildings in Priene, the Lower Gymnasium is characterised by the mathematical harmony of its structural units[1]. Its general layout includes a square peristyle courtyard enclosed on all sides by stoas. The north and west sides include rooms behind the stoas. The overall length of the building on the north (and best preserved) side, is 49.3m.

PROPYLON: The entrance to the Gymnasium on its west side is formed by a plain Doric propylon. The foundations of this "propylon" as well as the lower step have survived in situ. Other surviving parts are fragments of the antae, the columns, the cornice, and the "tympanum" of the pediment.

EXEDRA: Adjoining the north wall of the "propylon" is an "exedra", a rectangular hall open to the courtyard, of which only the supports of two columns and the bases of the marble benches running around the interior have survived[2]. The columns were Doric, like those of the "peristyle", but stood on isolated irregular stones instead of on a continuous "stylobate". A marble wall, 0.7m thick, separated the exedra from the oblong room on its side.

PALAESTRA: The palaestra is the centre of the complex. It is a square courtyard with a Doric peristyle standing one step higher than the courtyard. The depth of the "peristyle" is not uniform. Rooms (3.5m deep) exist only on the west side. Along the stylobate of the north side, and more specifically in the space between the northeastern corner and the sixth inter-axial space, runs an open marble water pipe, which develops into a deposit cistern and then extends as far as the Stadium to the east. A door on the east end of the northern stoa also leads to the stadium. The Gymnasium stands 6m higher than the running track of the stadium. Finally, there is a pedestal in front of the middle column of the north side, of which the lower part of the base with a decorative moulding has survived. According to Krischen, the pedestal supported a statue that was found at the "Ephebeum", one of the rooms of the north row.

---

1. The basic unit of measurement is the attic foot (0.2957m). The four sides of the peristyle are arranged in 14 inter-axial spaces, each of them being 8.5 feet long. The height of the column is estimated at 14 feet, whereas that of the entablature at 3. Thus, the overall height of 17 feet is two times that of the inter-axial space: a 2:1 ratio between height and width is observed. In addition, from the analytical calculation of the dimensions, it is estimated that the inter-axial spaces are 8½ feet on average and corner inter-axial spaces a bit larger, 9 feet approximately. In the case of the columns only the lower diameter (0.55m) can be accurately estimated. Taking into account the ratio between the height of the column to the lower diameter 7.5:1, a column height equals to 4.14m results. The corner columns were similar to the rest, i.e., they did not take the form of antae with semi-columns. Also, it is concluded that to each inter-axial space correspond 4 triglyphs and metopes in a 2:3 ratio. Krischen, F., Das hellenistische Gymnasium von Priene JDAI, 1923-1924, p. 136.

2. Wiegand, Th. – Schrader, H., Priene. Ergebnisse der Ausgrabungen und Untersuchungen von den Jahren 1895-1898. Unter Mitwirkung von G. Kummer, W. Wilberg, H. Winnefeld, R. Zahn. Berlin: Königliche Museen zu Berlin, 1904, p. 267.

LOWER GYMNASIUM-STADIUM

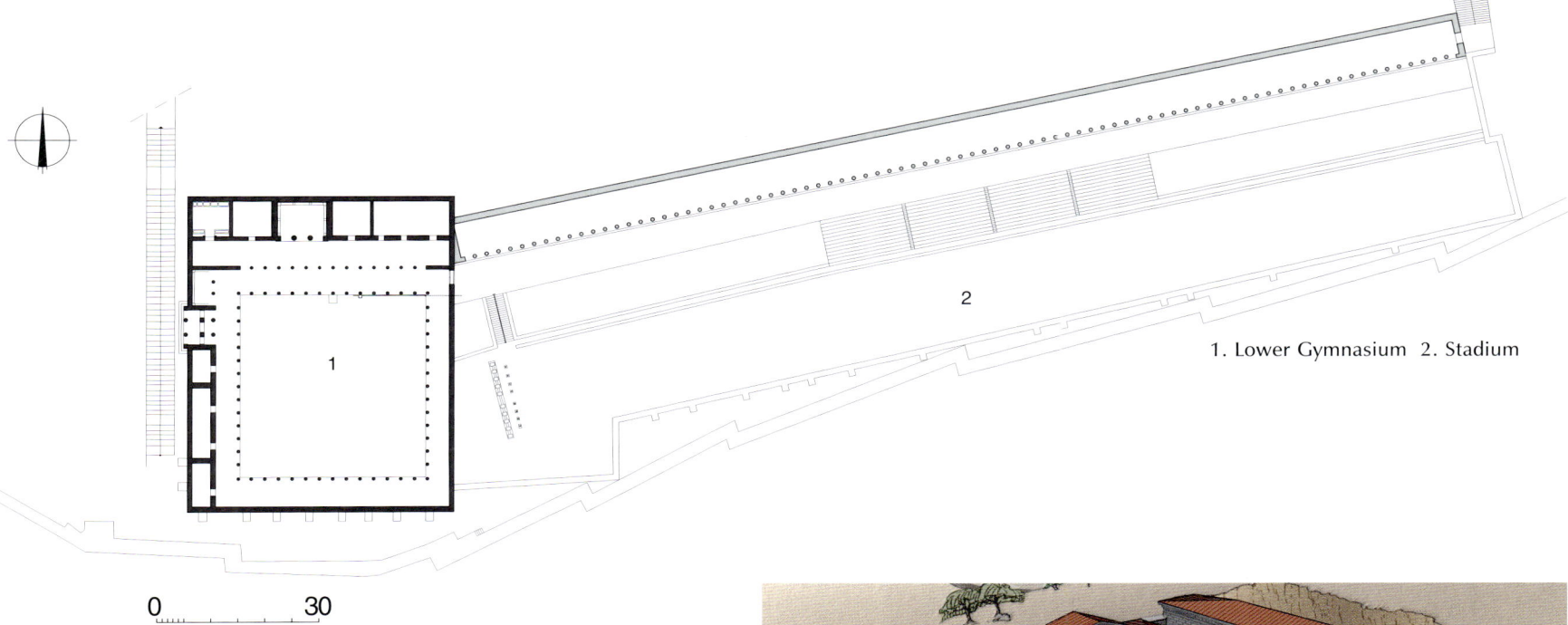

1. Lower Gymnasium 2. Stadium

Perspective of Lower Gymnasium (drawing after Krischen)

LOWER GYMNASIUM

The "stylobate" at the northeast corner of the "peristyle" has been preserved in good condition, and marks from column supports can still be seen in some places. No "epistyles" of the entablature have been found, but several fragments of its triglyphs have survived. Some parts of the cornice have also been found, from which one can deduce that the saddle roof was not very sloped. The south and east stoas are almost totally destroyed because of the collapse of the walls and the plundering of building materials for use in later constructions. Only their foundations have survived in their original position.

Ephebeum: graffiti showing pupils' names

On the north side of the Palaestra there is a second row of columns behind the row of Doric columns. These columns are also of Doric order and have the same arrangement as the columns of the "peristyle". Outside the "peristyle" of the Palaestra, to the east and west, the columns give way to a fully built wall. As in the case of the "exedra", the columns stand on separate "stylobate" stones.

INTERIOR COURTYARD: In the area between the north end of the Palaestra and the row of rooms of the north side of the Gymnasium there was a second, oblong, interior courtyard, 47.61m long and 4.9m wide. It provided ventilation and light to the northern rooms facing south. The façade of the series of rooms of the north side had an entablature of the Ionian order with a frieze decorated with "bucrania" (ox-heads), wreaths and sacrificial vessels. A cornice and sima, of which only fragments have survived, were above the frieze. The roof was monopitched.

EPHEBEUM: The most imposing space, at least among the five spaces of the north side of the complex, is the central hall (9.49 x 6.40m). According to the description of Vitruvius, this hall was the "Ephebeum" or ephebic exedra, where young pupils were taught philosophy and rhetoric. When this room was revealed during excavations it was discovered that the walls and the shafts of the antae were covered with the engraved names of young pupils.

LOWER GYMNASIUM

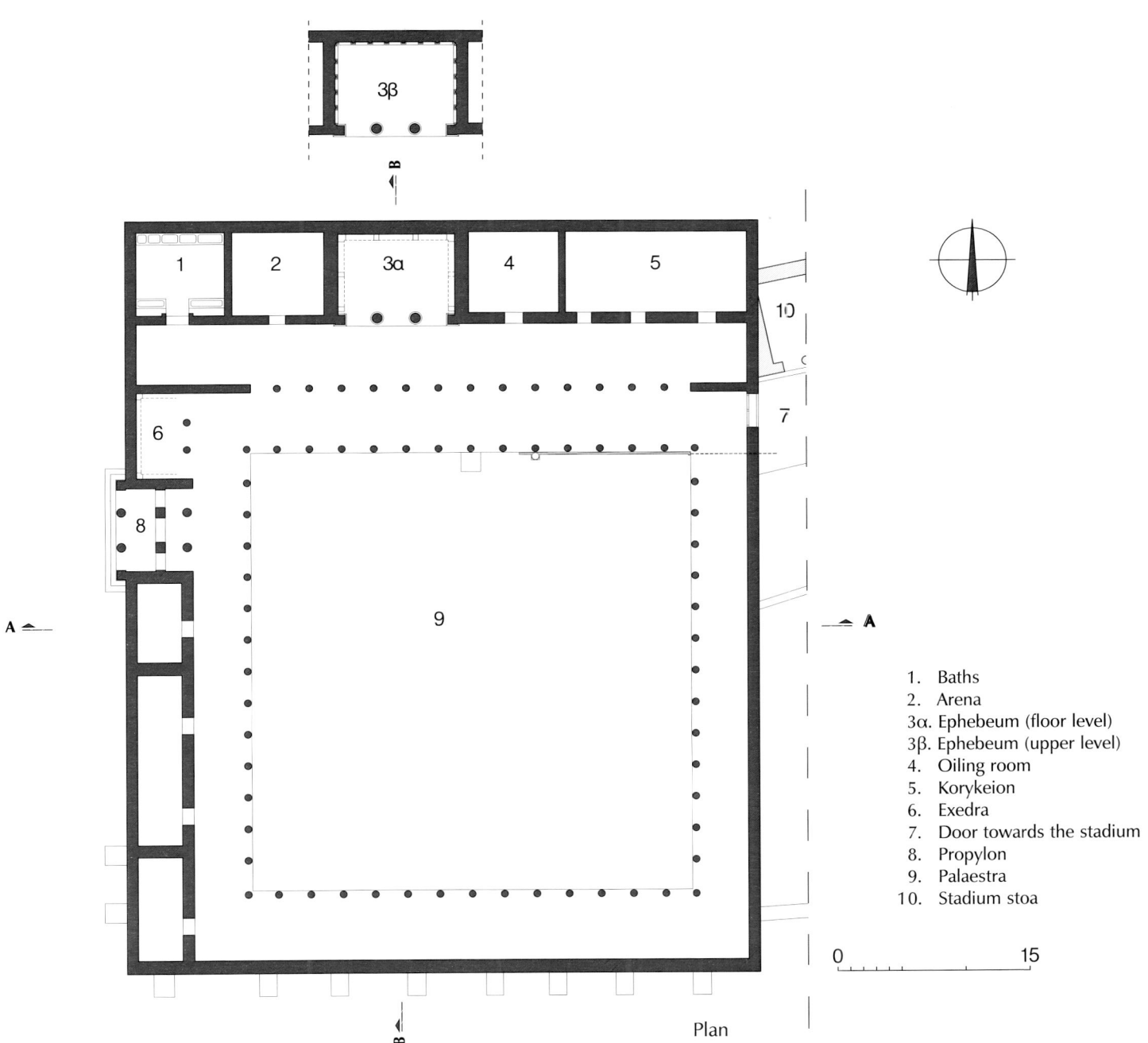

1. Baths
2. Arena
3α. Ephebeum (floor level)
3β. Ephebeum (upper level)
4. Oiling room
5. Korykeion
6. Exedra
7. Door towards the stadium
8. Propylon
9. Palaestra
10. Stadium stoa

Plan

LOWER GYMNASIUM

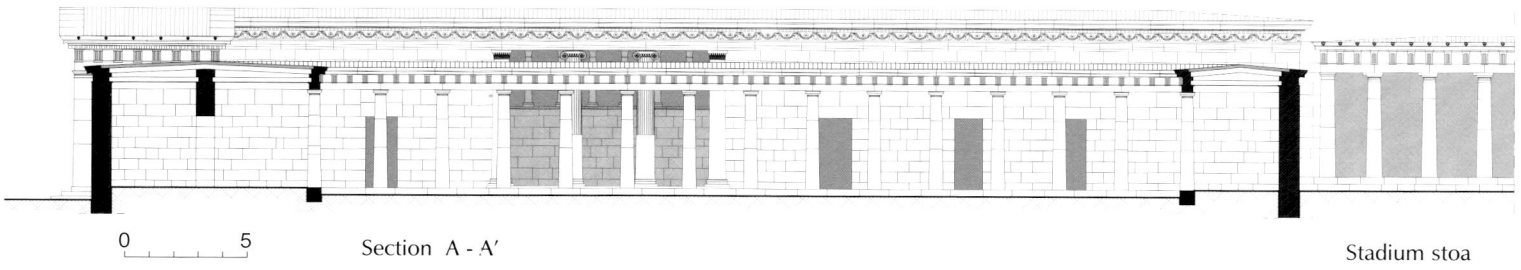

Section A - A'   Stadium stoa

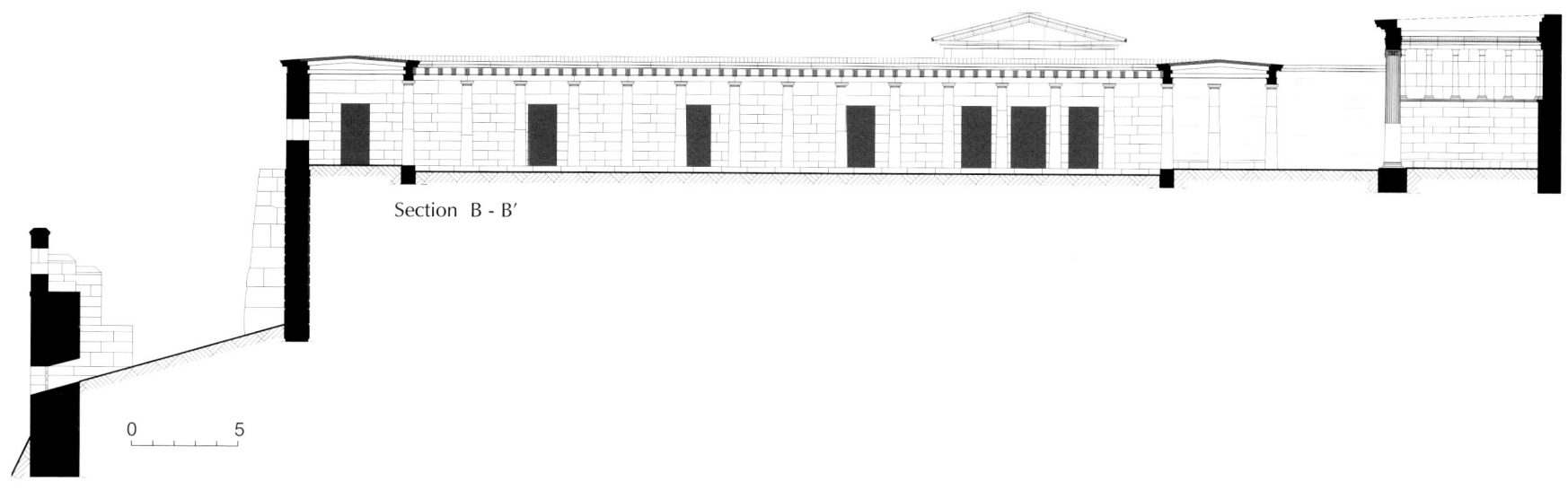

Section B - B'

LOWER GYMNASIUM

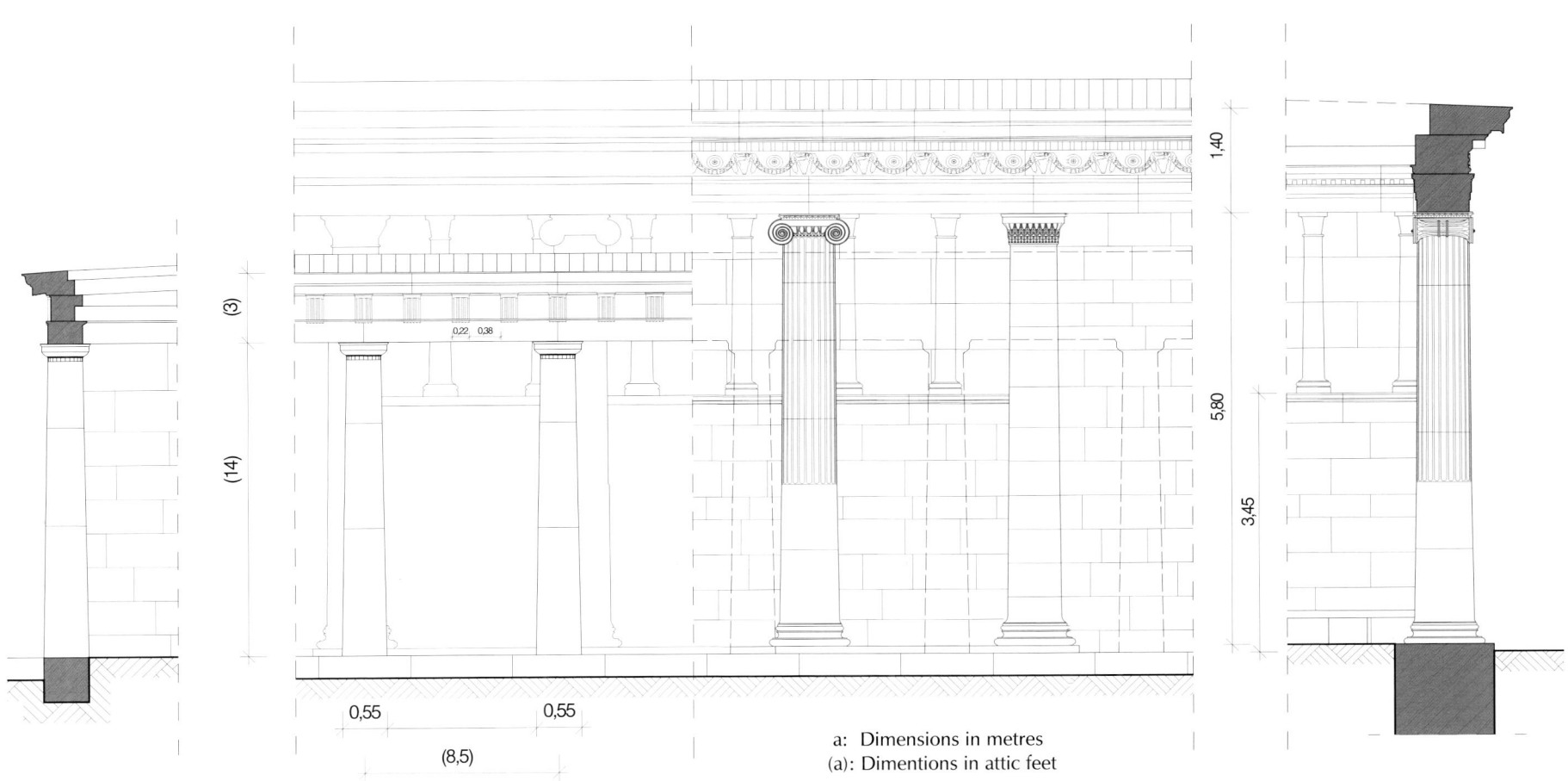

a: Dimensions in metres
(a): Dimentions in attic feet

Architectural order

The façade of the "Ephebeum" consists of two, tall marble Ionian columns standing between antae. The tori of their bases stand directly on an uninterrupted "stylobate" without any intervening plinth. Fragments of the antae, an elegant capital, several fragments of Ionic columns[3], the two capitals and several fragments of the epistyle have survived. The floor of the "Ephebeum" is of tamped earth. The marble walls, 3.35m high, conform to the isodomic system. From this point up to a height of 5.75m, estimated to be the overall height of the building, the wall is of rubble masonry containing traces of stucco. Only the lower layers of stones of the north side have survived in their original position. The upper part of the wall has a series of Corinthian half-columns and antae crowned by a cornice with dentils. These elements stood on a marble pedestal running around the wall. On the side walls four half-columns stood between the corner columns. The central, northern side contained two half-columns at the ends and four antae in the centre. At the two corners of the north side stood elaborate half-columns consisting of two quarters of a column. Seven stone bases of wooden benches have been retrieved in their initial positions along the walls.

The existence of a life-size marble statue of a man, fragments of which were found in the "Ephebeum", has already been mentioned. Schrader put together the fragments found on the floor of the hall, where no evidence of a pedestal or other support has been discovered. According to Wiegand, the statue stood in the centre of the marble northern wall between antae that supported an arch. Later, Krischen considered it more likely that the pedestal stood in front of the central column of the north side of the Palaestra. Based on the existing findings Krischen reconstructed the façades of the building. In contrast to Knackfuss and Wiegand, who believe that it was a two-storey building, Krischen claims that it only had a ground floor, a view considered today more accurate and scientifically acceptable.

The rooms on either side of the "Ephebeum" were used as dressing rooms, for bathing and body care. According to the descriptions of Vitruvius, the room west of the "Ephebeum" is the "konisterion" (7.19 x 6.78m) and the room on its east is the "elaiothesion" (7.02 x 6.6m). The space at the east end is the "korykeion" (14.08 x 6.6m).

View of Propylon

3. Unfluted elements of the lower part were found, as well as fluted elements of the upper part. According to Krischen, the overall height of "Ephebeum" is 5.75m, which is equal to 13 attic cubits (attic cubit=0.44m). Krischen, F., op. cit. p. 142.

Ephebeum as it appears today

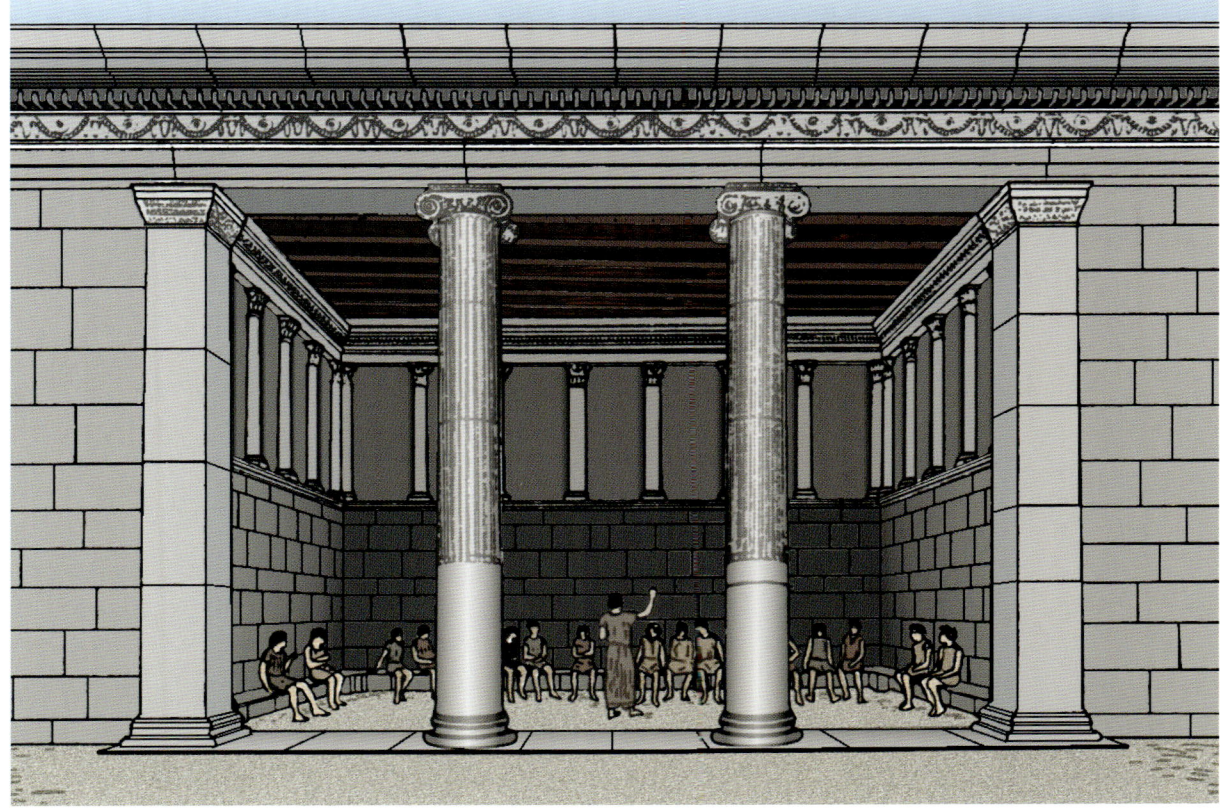
Perspective of Ephebeum (after Krischen)

LOWER GYMNASIUM

BATHS: Surviving traces prove that the first space, west of the "Ephebeum", is the Baths (6.9 x 7.48m). This is the only space besides the "Ephebeum" with a positively established function. Only conjectures can be made about the use of the other rooms, given the fact that no information about their purpose is available.

The lower parts of the Baths' walls are made of marble plinths. Above the plinth wall ran an open pipe with a gutter on its upper surface through which water was constantly channelled. Through elaborately carved lion-heads the water flowed either to the deep carved basins of the north side or directly to the floor. Six stones from this pipe with nine lion-heads have survived in situ. The pipe is at a height of 0.95m and is supported by the "orthostates", whereas the basins stand 0.2m lower. The water was diverted out of the Bath either through underground routes, by means of an aperture in a marble slab on the floor near the door, or through a pipe in the anteroom and finally flowed out in the street on the west side of the complex. Any remaining water was drained through a channel by the step of the colonnade that led to the Stadium.

The upper parts of the Baths' walls were plastered and the floor was paved with stone slabs. Two oblong marble bathtubs, 19cm deep, were near the wall of the entrance. These bathtubs, with special marble benches, served for the washing of feet. Three of the supports of these benches have been preserved in situ and a mark on the floor indicates the position of a fourth one.

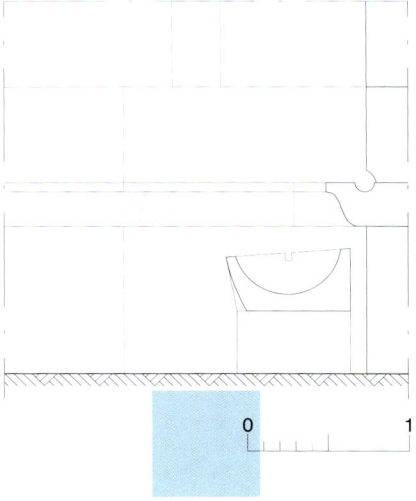

Detail of water supply

Carved basins

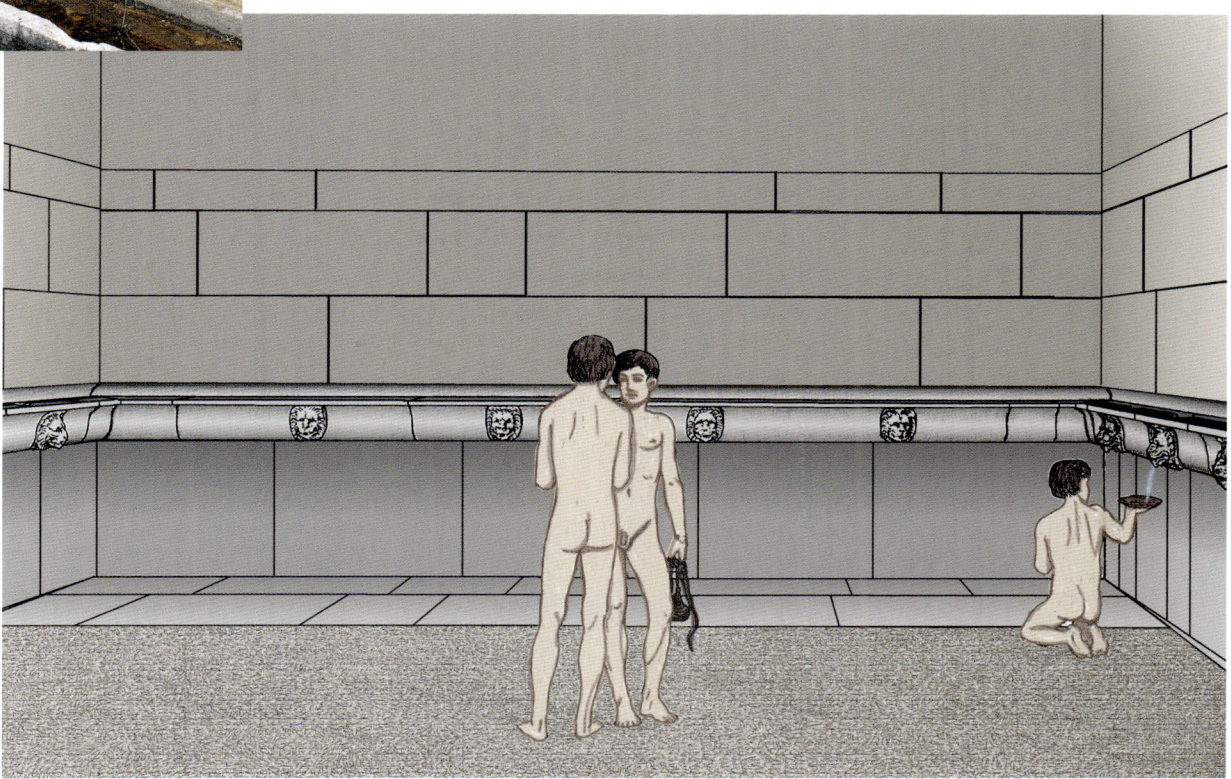
Perspective of baths
(after Krischen)

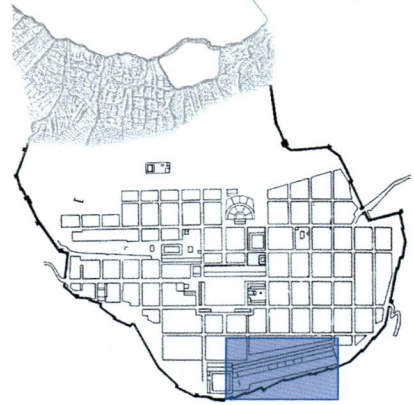

STADIUM

In order to accommodate the stadium within the city walls, a retaining wall had to be constructed, which meant that the stadium had to conform to specific dimensions. This, in turn, led to its being the only configuration that did not follow the overall rectangular grid of the city's urban planning.

DESCRIPTION: The stadium consists of a running track, the tiered seating and a stoa to the north. Entrance is through a door on the wall of the adjoining Lower Gymnasium. A staircase (3.50m wide) next to this entrance, bridges the discrepancy of 6 metres between the level of the Lower Gymnasium and that of the running track. There was a second entrance at the east end of the stoa, whose steps formed an extention of one of the descending streets of the city.

RUNNING TRACK: At the west end of the running track was a gate with partitions marking the starting line of the athletes. The distance from the gate to the boundary of the wall at the east end, is approximately 19m. Therefore, we can infer that the length of the track between the starting line and the finishing point is shorter. The likeliest length of the running track is 178m, a common length during the Graeco-Roman period, or 185m[1], a common length in the Roman period. The width of the running track is just 20m, approximately 1/3 smaller than the width of that of the track at Olympia, due undoubtedly to lack of space in Priene. The eight stones located at the west end of the track probably form the original starting line: they are pierced with holes for the placement of wooden posts, probably an older device through which the simultaneous start of the athletes could be controlled. The central space is larger, probably indicating the place of the umpire who would signal the start of the games.

During the Roman period a larger, more imposing, multiple gate with ten Corinthian pillars was constructed to the west. From surviving fragments of capitals and "epistyles" the existence of coffers is ascertained. The bases of pillars resting on foundation stones also survive. An open pipe, 23cm wide, carved on the floor of the construction runs along it from end to end, passing beneath the bases of the pillars. In the widest, central inter-columnar space the pipe bears additional vertical incisions, probably for the discharge of water. It is possible that the incisions along the long side were covered with planks. One of the preserved fragments of the sima and part of the frieze, shows a large opening that seems to correspond to the incisions of the bases.

1. Some other common lengths of ancient stadia are: 164m (Greek), 192m (Olympic) and 210m (Ptolemaic). Wiegand, Th. – Schrader, H., Priene. Ergebnisse der Ausgrabungen und Untersuchungen von der Jahren 1895-1898. Unter Mitwirkung von G. Kummer, W. Wilberg, H. Winnefeld, R. Zahn. Berlin: Königliche Museen zu Berlin, 1904, p. 260.

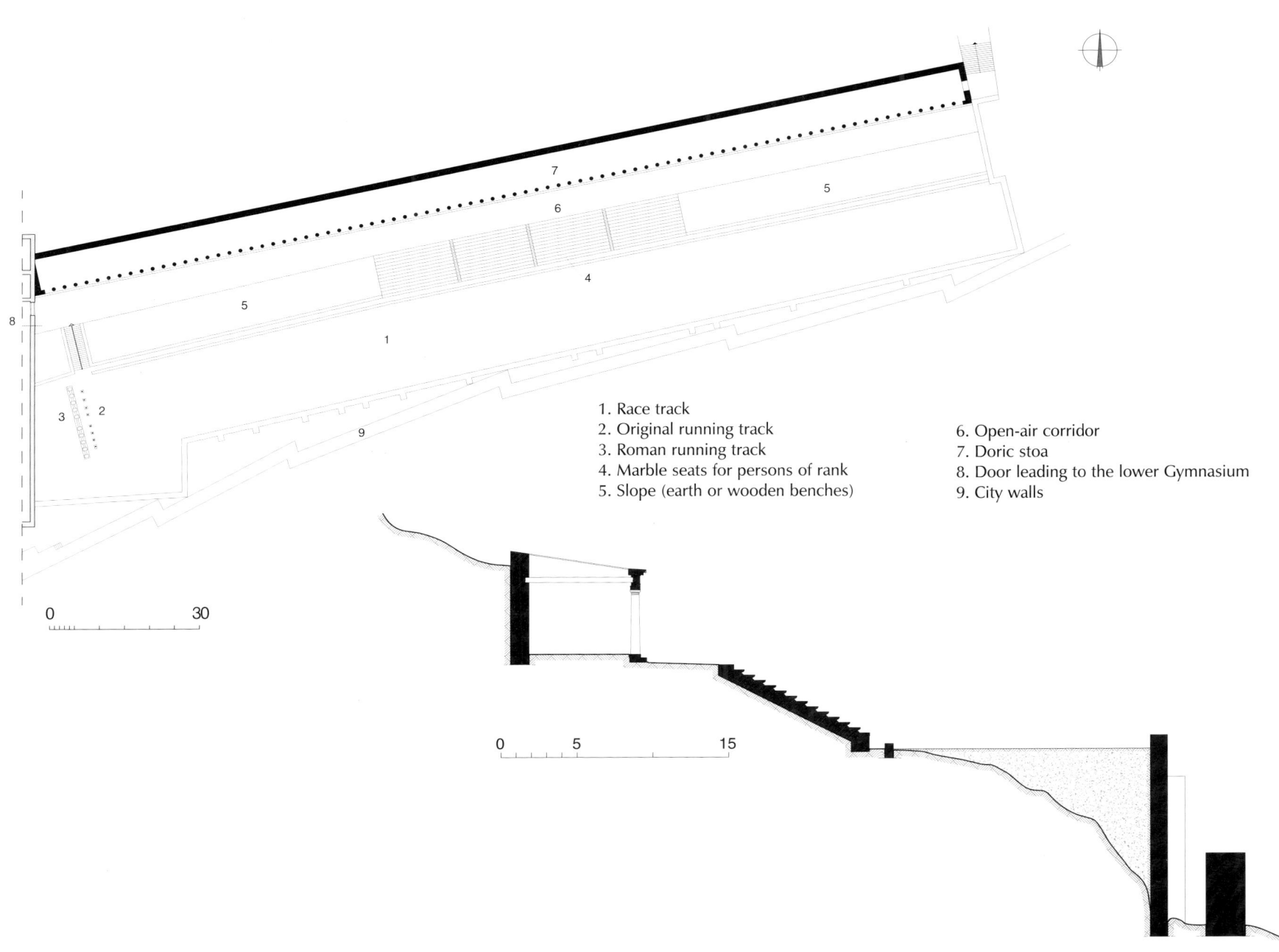

STADIUM

1. Race track
2. Original running track
3. Roman running track
4. Marble seats for persons of rank
5. Slope (earth or wooden benches)
6. Open-air corridor
7. Doric stoa
8. Door leading to the lower Gymnasium
9. City walls

Wiegand[2] claims that the incisions in question refer to a construction in which curtains were drawn at the start of the games.

Close to the staircase uniting the Stadium with the Lower Gymnasium a discharge pipe was found that was connected with the bath of the Gymnasium "Palaestra". There was probably provision for an hydraulic mechanism for the simultaneous opening of the partitions at the start of the games.

TIERED SEATING: Usually in stadia there were rows of tiered seating on either side of the track, but in Priene, due to lack of space, their construction was confined to one side only, to the north of the track. The spectator seating is divided into three sections: the central one, which includes marble seats of honour for the judges and dignitaries, and the ones on either side, formed by simple gradients with wooden benches or plain earth. The form of the marble seats of the central section is similar to that of Ekklesiasterion. In the 11th row a cylindrical stone was found with its upper surface hollow, while the external surface bears decorative half-finished ox-heads with guilloches. This is probably an unfinished altar in the centre of the Stadium. A low parapet, 1.10m high, separates the seating from the running track. The masonry of the central section is more elaborately worked, whereas its upper surface was a circulation space for the lower row of seats. In the two side sections of the spectator seating the same low parapet is made of larger, rough stones.

At a later stage along with the first row of seats and at a distance of approximately one metre, a wall 0.50m wide was constructed. Its aim was to protect the spectators in the lower row from the discharge of water and the danger of animal fighting.

STOA: At the upper level, to the north of the seating, there is an oblong Doric stoa with 85 unfluted columns, open to the south. As concluded from study of the cornices, the gradient of the monopitched roof was small. The morphology of the stoa is typical of the end of the second century BC. Between the stoa and the upper rows of seating there is an open-air corridor, 6m wide, similar to that of the Sacred Stoa. The depth of the stoa in question is 7.80m, while its floor is raised by two steps. The walls are lined with marble revetment.

2. Op. cit., p. 261.

STADIUM STOA

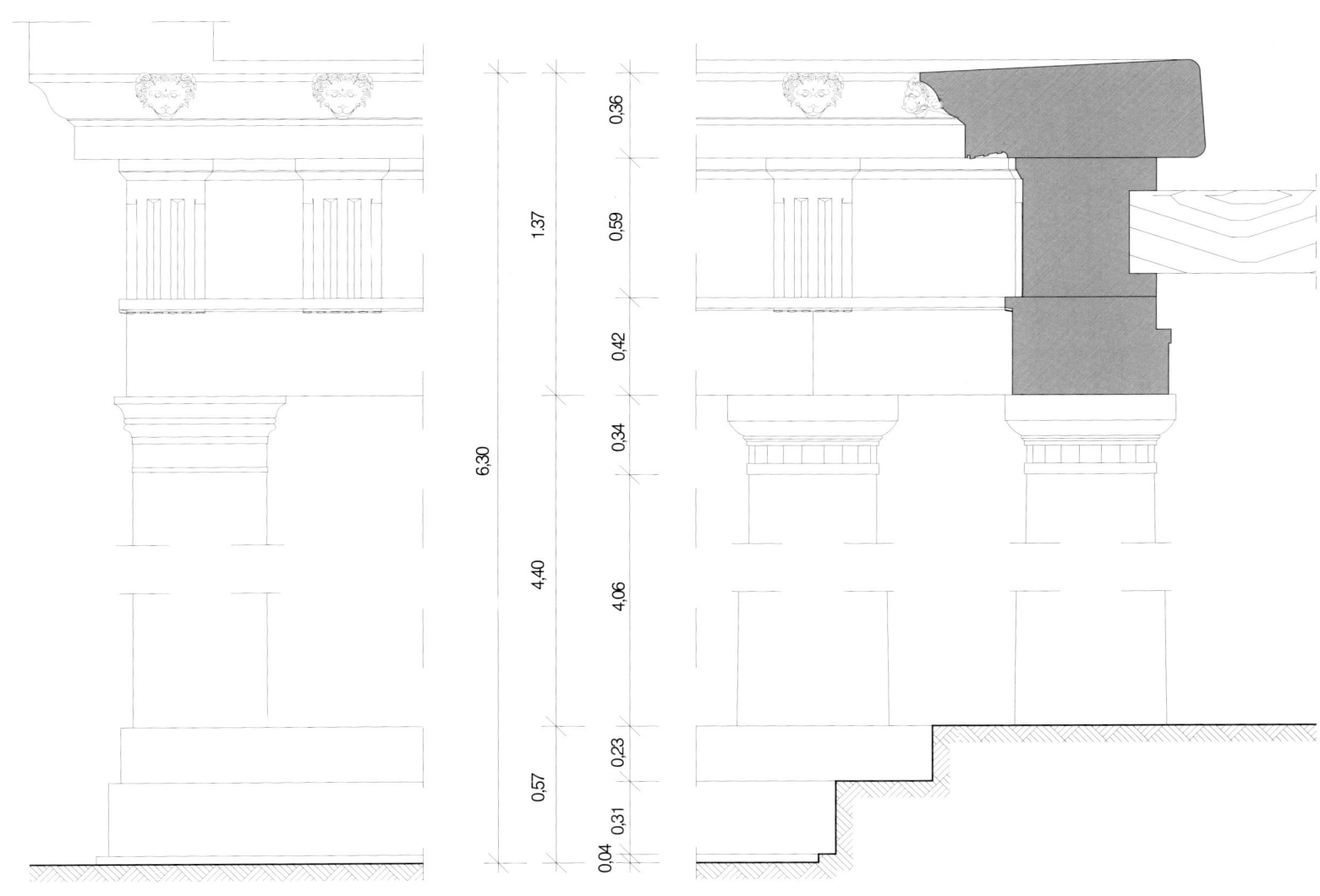

Architectural order

RESIDENTIAL AND COMMERCIAL DWELLINGS

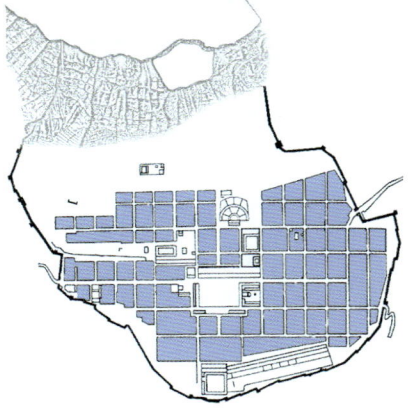

Wiegand and Schrader were the first to excavate houses (about 70 in number) dating back to the late Hellenistic period. Inevitably, early studies of Priene's housing were based on the form in which the houses were found at the time of the excavations. This form was significantly different from the original form. More recent research has brought to light new information about the first building phase of the city, which allows a reassessment of the material.

According to the initial town planning, the size of each building plot was 120 x 160 attic feet[1]. After detailed study of a considerable number of houses, it was estimated that the findings of House No. 25 could provide satisfactory answers to various questions. It was found that two stone walls divided the building plots of House No. 25 into four equal sections. The fact that the northeastern section of the block is further divided into two equal parts suggests that there were probably eight houses per block. This is confirmed by marks on the walls at the points of contact between the houses. Later, the validity of this hypothesis was confirmed by further excavations of dwellings throughout the city. The division of plots into eight private houses is evident in the area west side of the Agora and also in a smaller area on the east. Houses Nos. 8 to 12a, which are particularly well-preserved, were used by researchers as models for reconstructions.

There were two types of dividing walls: those enclosing each block on its four sides, and those defining each individual property. Several questions concerning individual properties and the unequal sizes of the divided sections remain unanswered. From observations regarding houses Nos. 32g to 32k, it is concluded that the walls dividing the properties did not actually coincide with the theoretical gridlines but were located in such a way in relation to these gridlines, that they finally divided the block into sections of equal dimensions. Inscriptions found in Pergamon mention that repairs on the dividing walls were the responsibility of the main user, i.e., the one of the two owners who used them more by supporting various auxiliary structures on them. It is conjectured that this applied to Priene as well.

---

1. An attic foot is equal to 29.46cm, therefore the dimensions of the block were 35.35 x 47.13m and its surface area 1.666 m².

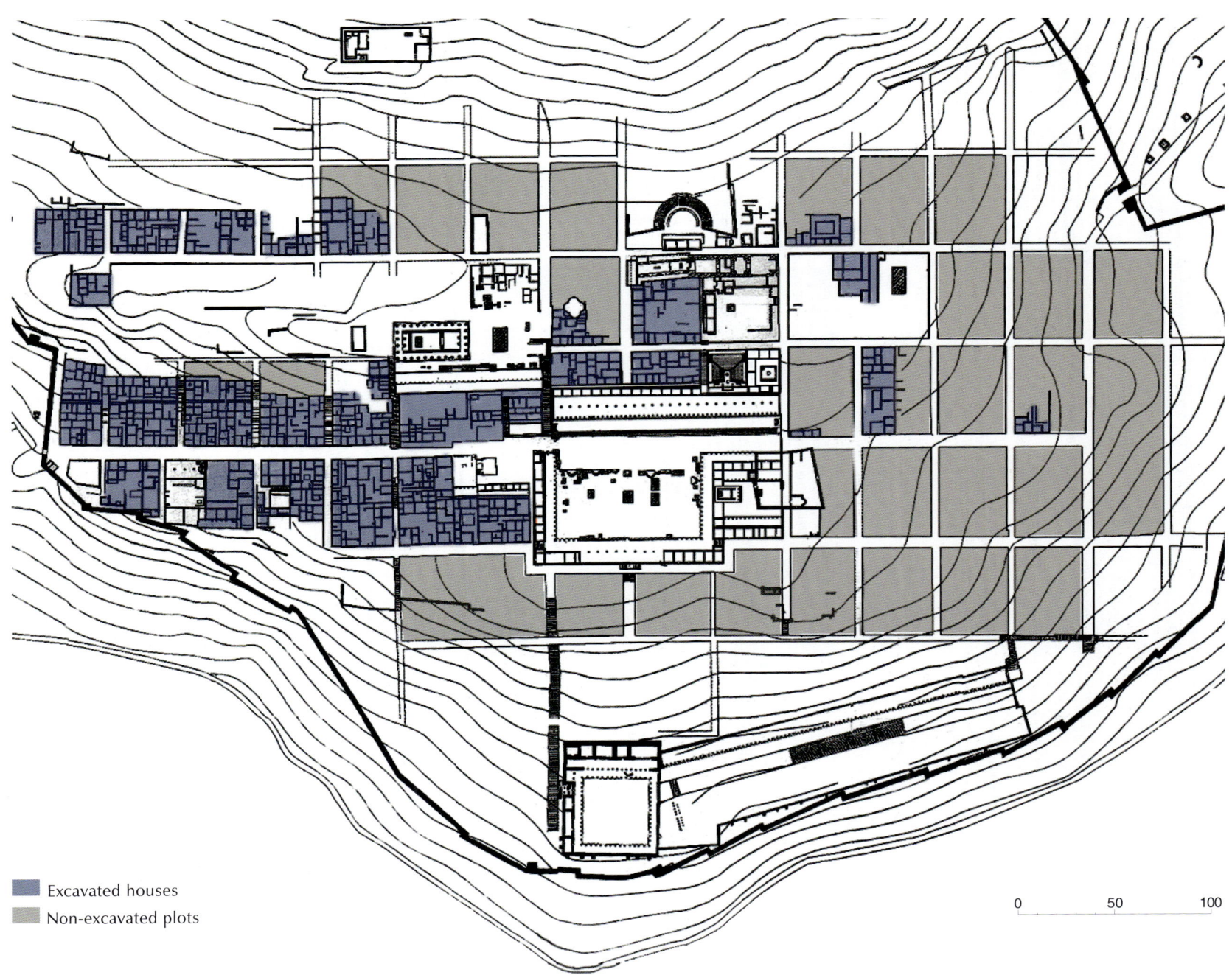

Excavated houses
Non-excavated plots

0 50 100

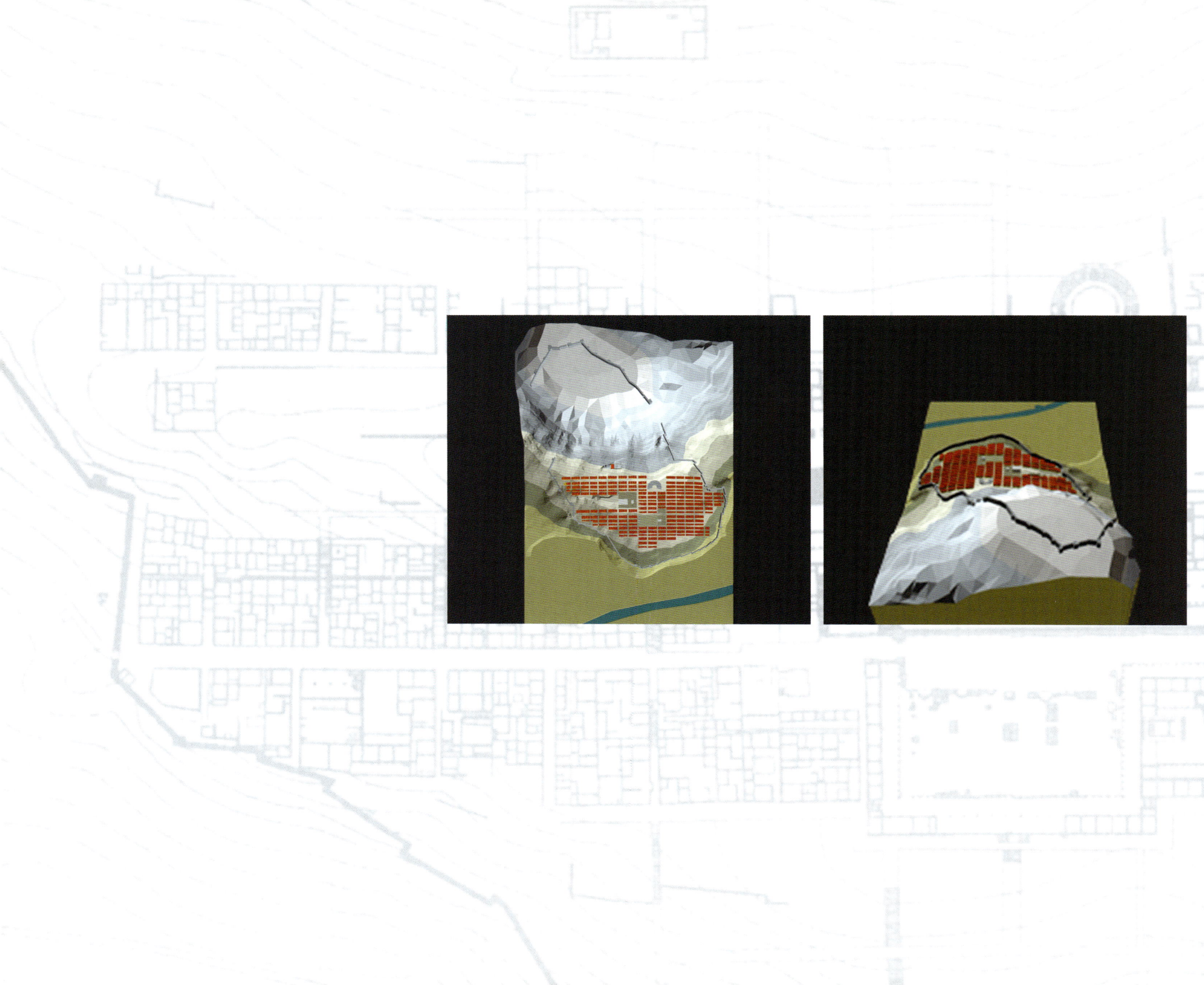

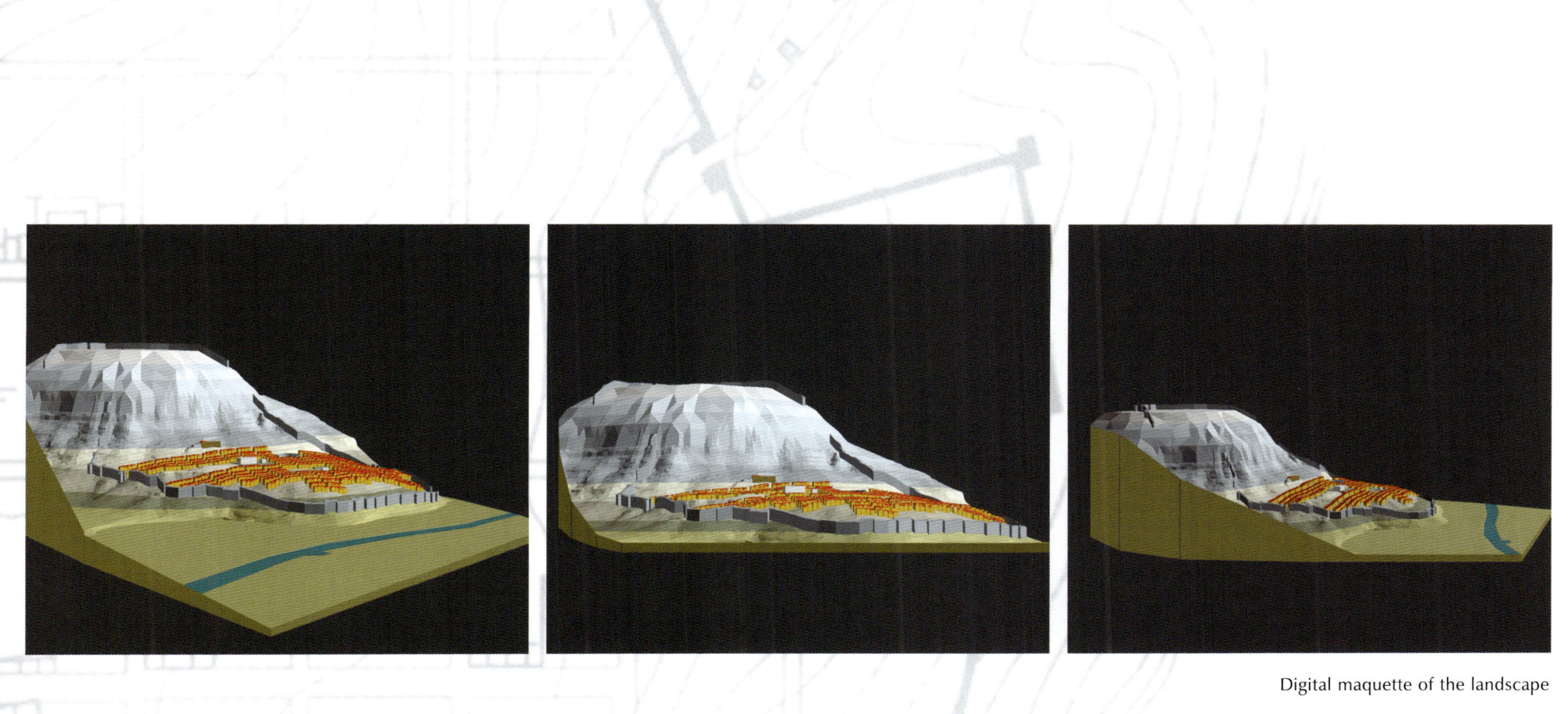

Digital maquette of the landscape

THE TYPICAL HOUSE: Closer study of the findings shows that, apart from the standard division of land according to the Hippodamian system, i.e., division into equal building plots and further subdivision into 8 equal sections, a typical house was designed to meet the multiple needs of a family. Each of the eight oblong sections of a typical plot was divided into three parts: the northern part, containing the living quarters, the central part, consisting of a square courtyard, and the southern part, containing auxiliary rooms or shops, depending on the position of the house in relation to the main commercial axes of the city. House No. 25 is probably the most typical example of this arrangement.

The northern section of each private house contained its main rooms. From evidence that will be presented later in this chapter, it is assumed that houses were two-storeyed. The ground floor contained a "prostas" (vestibule), i.e., a partially covered space facing south and opening onto the courtyard. The "prostas" was enclosed by rooms: on the east side by the "andron", and on the north side by the "oikos", which was adjacent to a second, dark room, probably a weaving workshop. The rooms were generally spacious and of considerable height. The ceiling was never lower than 2.40m in auxiliary rooms, and did not exceed 3.60m in the main living quarters. In House No. 32 one can see clearly the arrangement of two auxiliary spaces on the south side of the plot. The courtyard, defined by two built sides, is square. The same arrangement was followed in 11 other houses on the north side of the street leading to the Theatre.

In the main living quarters on the ground floor of some houses, the lower part of a staircase has survived, which indicates that there was a second floor. It is not clear whether the oikos was as high as two storeys, or if the second floor covered the whole of the ground floor. Some hearths were found in the corners, as in Olynthus, and not in the centre of the house, which may indicate that there was a fully-built second floor.

Residential Block

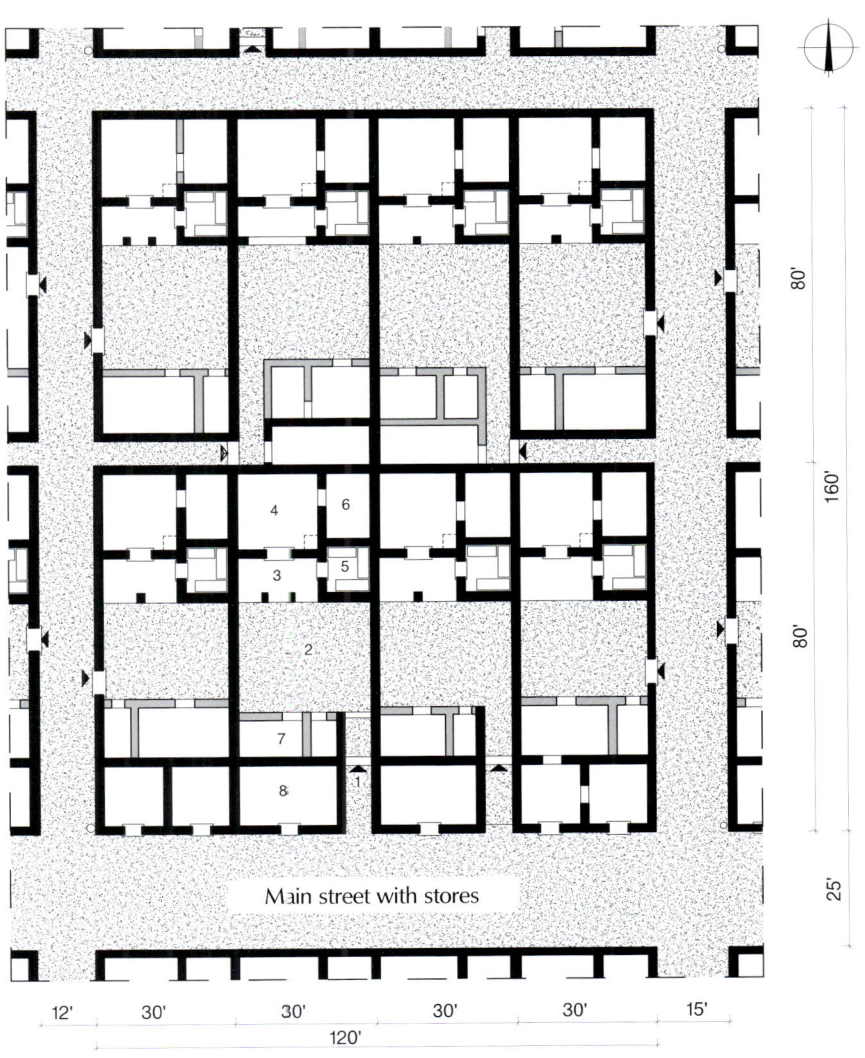

1. Entrance to house
2. Courtyard
3. Prostas
4. Oikos
5. Andron
6. Auxiliary space
7. Storeroom
8. Shop

■ 4th century BC
☐ Later annexations

RESIDENTIAL AND COMMERCIAL DWELLINGS

The structure of the houses does not suggest wealth. The walls enclosing each plot are carefully built, and it is clear that the walls built in a later period (in the middle of the 2nd century BC) are made of cheaper materials than the earlier ones, built in the 4th century BC. Mosaic floors have not survived, and the plaster floors that have been found belong to a more recent period. No traces of exterior plaster have been found, and the interior ones are very simple. The stucco on the walls of the andrones was more luxurious.

The roof frames were made of wood. The tiles that have been found are of the Corinthian type, i.e., triangular pointed tiles, but it is assumed that another type of tiles, the Laconian, was also used, i.e., tiles with a convex section, which are now called Byzantine. It is interesting to note that some tiles had circular perforations, probably to allow daylight to pass through them and illuminate rooms without openings.

The dimensions shown in the table on the right[2] are based on measurements of excavated houses. The total area of each property is 208.30m², and the total area of the covered spaces of each residence is 73.44m².

ACCESS: As a rule, one entered a house from the street through the courtyard. The question of access, therefore, can only be clearly answered for four of the houses in each block, those in which the courtyard opened directly onto the street. The doors were always double, their width ranging from 1.20 to 1.80m (usually it was 1.40m). The doors of houses on opposite sides of the street did not face each other directly.

As far as houses that occupied the "internal" part of the block were concerned, the problem of access was dealt with individually, depending on the position of each house. Thus, the two northern "internal" houses could be reached through corridors that ran between the corner residences, while the two southern residences could be reached through corridors by the sides of auxiliary spaces. In all cases the width of these corridors was equal to the opening of their doors, i.e., 1.40m on average. The doors were placed in a slight recess forming a shallow porch, apparently meant as protection from the rain.

SPACES	WIDTH	DEPTH	AREA
OIKOS	4,60	4,78	21,62
PROSTASIS	4,49	3,24	14,54
ANDRON	2,95	3,10	9,17
AUX. SPACE	2,86	4,15	11,86
COURTYARD	8,84	10	88,4
GYNAECONITIS			9,17
CHAMBER			21,62
SANITATION FACILITIES			11,86
SHOP	8,84	4,60	40,66

2. Hoepfner, W. – Schwandner, E. L., Haus und Stadt im Klassischen Griechenland. Deutsches Archäologisches Institut, Arhitekturreferat. In Zusammenarbeit mit dem Seminar für Klassische Archäologie der Freien Universität Berlin. München: Deutsche Kunstverlag, 1994, p. 215.

Street with visible channel for the drainage of rain water

LIVING QUARTERS-OIKOS: The main part of the living quarters was the "oikos". It was approximately square, occupying an area of at least 20m², with an average height of 3.60m. It could be reached directly through the "prostas", which was a kind of open-air extension of the oikos. Although the walls were plastered, the masonry was often very elaborately constructed. The floor of the oikos and the "prostas" was made of earth. The "epistyle" of the "prostas" stood on one or more supports made of stone or wood.

In several positions, mainly in the "prostas" or next to it, built-in pedestals have been found; their dimensions are 60 x 80cm, and they are almost always in corners. They were probably hearths for food preparation, which were added after the second half of the 2nd century BC, since it is known that in older times food was prepared on the ground.

Like the Prytaneion, each house had a hearth where the "Sacred Flame" burned, around which the family gathered. Only one such hearth has been found in Priene, in House No. 3. It is in a corner and not in the centre of the room, which not only facilitated the disposal of smoke but also allowed the building of a second storey. The reconstructions drawn by Hoepfner and Schwandner are based on the latter assumption, although one cannot rule out the arrangement found in excavations in Piraeus, or in the case of Orraon, a settlement near Lake Ambrakia, where the "oikos" reached the height of two storeys.

ANDRON: This was a room reserved for the banquets of the men of the family and their guests. It was reached directly from the prostas, through an opening considerably smaller than the one leading to the oikos. One can safely assume that there were openings on the side of the courtyard so that daylight could enter. Andrones were probably of limited size in Priene, not larger than 9m². As a consequence, there was room for only three "klines" (couches), but they could accommodate up to six people, as shown on scenes painted on vases. This is also confirmed by the size of the room, which could accommodate couches 2.05m long instead of the usual ones, which were only 1.80m long. The position of the wine crater depended on whether the door was in the centre or the end of the wall.

Courtyard and prostasis of a typical house (perspective after Krischen)

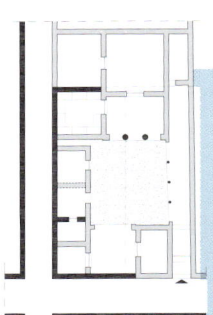

As in the case of all the other Classical Greek towns, in Priene the andrones are decorated very ornately. The absence of mosaics in Priene (in contrast to Olynthus) should not lead to conclusions about the city's prosperity: it is more likely that the practice of various techniques did not spread simultaneously all over the Hellenic world. Excavations have revealed floor coverings that cannot be dated with certainty. The orthostates of the walls are slightly protruding. The walls themselves were reveted, and in some cases they bore motifs of joints imitating masonry. The reconstruction of these rooms is not possible; therefore one can only conjecture as to their decoration. Traces of red, black, blue, and white paint have been found on the walls.

AUXILIARY ROOMS - SANITATION FACILITIES: There was a dark, therefore cool, room on the ground floor next to the oikos, the purpose of which remains obscure. On the basis of information from other excavations it is concluded that this room served mainly as a weaving workshop. However, there is also the possibility that it was a lavatory – a view supported by findings in houses of the same period in northwestern Greece. Only a built-in wash-basin has been found in Priene, in a very small room of a house of the Hellenistic period. Other probable sanitation facilities or bathrooms are the rooms exactly above the dark rooms of the ground floor; the use of the rooms on the south side of the courtyard for this purpose is ruled out because they are too far from the house. According to Georgios Velenis[3], in Classical times there were no lavatories in houses; pots were used instead.

UPPER STOREY: In some houses there are high northern walls with alcoves in positions suitable for supporting beams, probably for a mezzanine. This fact suggests that there was a second storey in the north section of the complex, a view supported by the discovery of the lower part of a staircase in House No. 16. The rest of the staircase, being wooden, has naturally not survived. There are no findings of upper storeys, but all existing evidence regarding building statics supports the hypothesis that the layout of the upper storey was identical to that of the ground floor.

---

3. Op. cit., p. 218.

View of the prostasis of House No. 33, as discovered during the German excavations in 1896
© DAI Istanbul

Above the "prostasis" was a gallery and the room above the "oikos" (the "thalamos") was mainly used for sleeping. The room next to it was probably a bathroom; above the "andron" was the women's quarters ("gynaeconitis"), used for women's beauty care.

STOREROOMS: The south section of each plot was occupied by auxiliary rooms. Although the surviving ruins probably date back to more recent times, it is almost certain that there were similar arrangements in the 4th century BC. Their function varied: they were either workshops related to the main occupation of the family, storerooms, stables, or living quarters of the slaves. In the first phase they were always used by the family.

STORES: It seems that stores existed not only within the boundaries of the two Agoras, but also along the north side of the city's main street, i.e., the street leading to the West Gate. They were probably used not only for selling but also for producing merchandise. They were, in effect, small workshops, where craftsmen lived, worked and sold their products. It is possible that these stores were included in the original planning of the city and allotted to their inhabitants. All 34 excavated stores bear so many similarities that it is safe to conclude that they were constructed according to strict specifications. They all opened directly onto the street, had two rooms, and were approximately 4.6m deep.

COURTYARD: During the early years there was a courtyard in the centre of each plot, occupying its full width. Its depth varied according to the space taken up by the auxiliary rooms of the south section. It is certain that, in its original phase, the courtyard was large enough to provide adequate sunlight and ventilation to the complex.

LATE HELLENISTIC ERA: Despite the fact that only one third of the houses of Priene have been excavated, it is possible to draw some general conclusions. As regards the changes housing underwent through the centuries, it should be noted that during the middle Hellenistic period there was no legislation about the uniformity of houses. However, the increase in population, which led to a different distribution of wealth in the city, brought about many changes in the appearance of houses: most houses were divided in order to accommodate more people, and

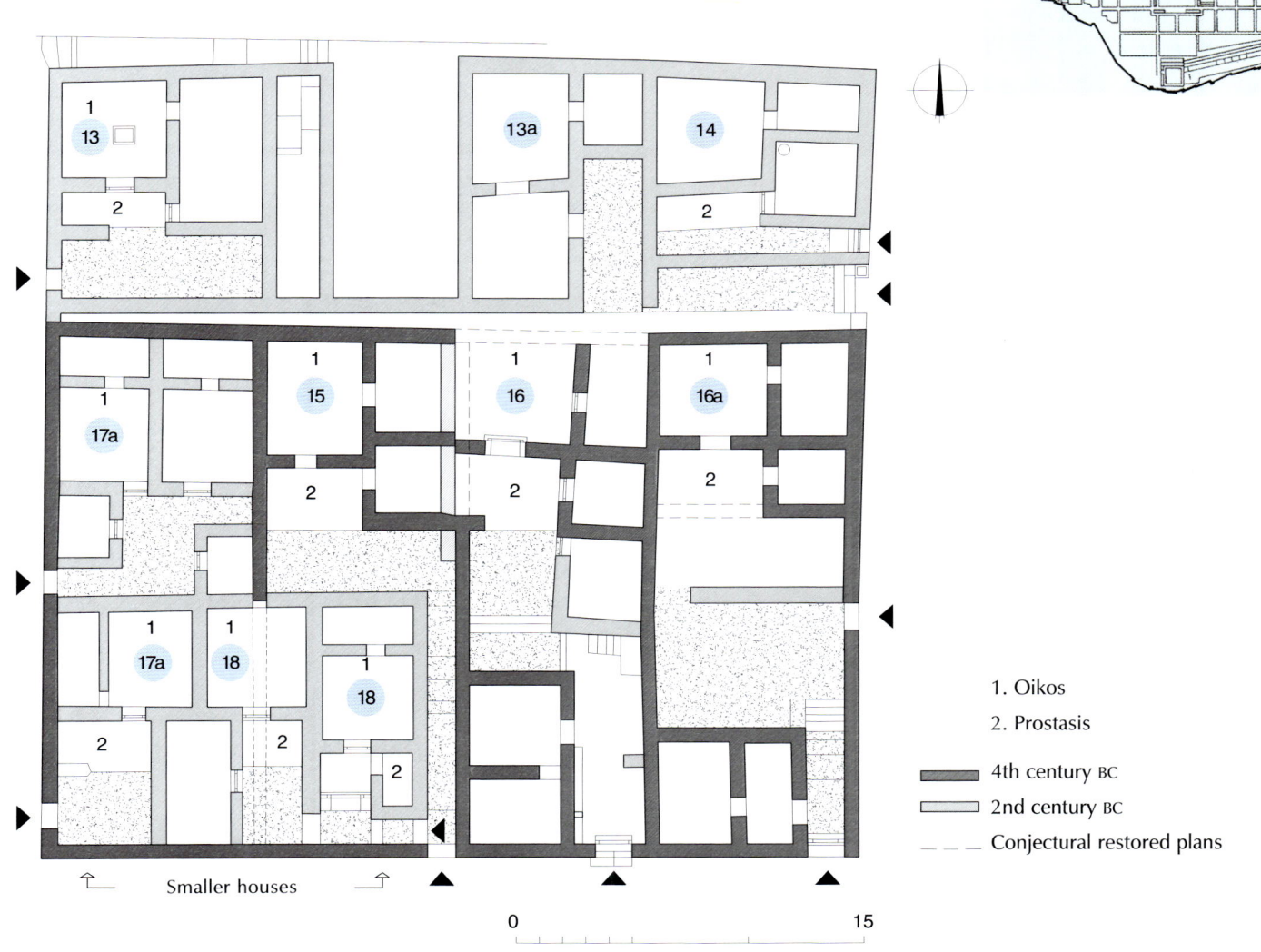

GROUND PLANS OF HOUSES 13-18

1. Oikos
2. Prostasis

▬ 4th century BC
▬ 2nd century BC
--- Conjectural restored plans

Smaller houses

0   15

those belonging to eminent citizens were extended. In many cases, apart from the division of residences, storerooms were converted into separate houses with rudimentary facilities. One can assume, not without reservation, that the poorer citizens were moved to the residences near the walls, whereas the more affluent citizens occupied the centre. The houses to the north of the Sacred Stoa are exceptionally large.

HOUSE No. 33: A typical example indicating the development of the typology of houses in Priene is House No. 33, situated at the northwest section of the city. In its final phase, dating back to the late Hellenistic or early Roman period[4], the house occupied an area more than twice as large as its original one. During the first stage of alterations the already existing rooms were extended, and during the second one, which took place in late Hellenistic times, new rooms were added.

Thus, for example, the andron included originally three couches, and later nine. Similarly, the "prostasis" and "oikos" were extended, acquiring a ritual character.

In its final phase the house takes up the full width of the building block. The rooms of the original nucleus have now become reception halls, while the added west section includes private and auxiliary rooms[5]. Because of the poor quality of these constructions and the fact that older architectural elements have been incorporated into them as previously-used material, Hoepfner and Schwandner have pointed out that the house belongs to a period of decline[6].

---

4. Op. cit., p. 225.

5. Indicative of the size of the wealthiest houses is the content of inscription No. 109, which says that the citizen Herode possessed such a large house that it could accommodate all the city's inhabitants. Op. cit., p. 225.

6. Op. cit., p. 225.

CHRISTIAN BUILDINGS

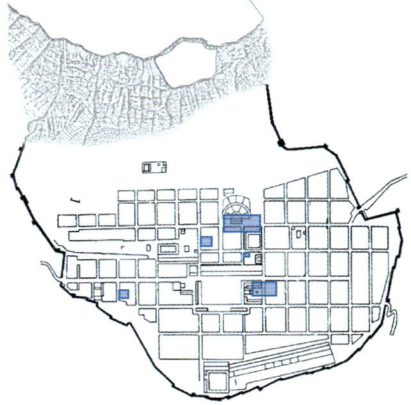

Various ruins found on the site of Hellenistic Priene date from Christian times. Their construction is characterised by irregular masonry with clay brick fragments and the use of older material. In terms of building technique and morphology, they differ very little from the Roman buildings that were slightly altered or extended during this period.

During the Christian era the walls were reinforced through a series of improvements to strengthen the city's defence system. In particular, the oldest northern section of the wall was extended by the construction of circular bastions. The water-supply system of the Hellenistic era was preserved during this period and water cleaning reservoirs were constructed to the north of the city.

Most of the buildings surviving from Priene's Christian era are churches. Some of them, however, were inevitably destroyed during lower level excavations of the Hellenistic buildings.

HOUSE No. 24 AS CHURCH: The church in West Gate street was formed by isolating the inner courtyard and some rooms of the large Hellenistic House No. 24. For the needs of the church the three rooms to the west were eliminated. The former entrance of the house was closed off and another one was opened on the new, west wall of the church. Since the sanctuary had to face towards the east, the existing parts of the house, such as the "prostas" and the oikos, could not be used. On the floor of the church there is still a series of slabs serving as the bases of two rows of columns that follow a style similar to that of a basilica. The square apse of the sanctuary, which faces east, is very small. Traces of a marble cistern have been found to the south.

CATHEDRAL: The most important of the churches is the so-called Metropolis (Cathedral) or episcopal church, which is considerably larger than the other surviving ones. It is situated to the south of the Theatre next to the Upper Gymnasium on its west side. The church consists of the narthex, the nave and an auxiliary space at the west end of the northern aisle. From the external area two doors lead to the vestibule. On the inside of the wall between the two doors there is a stone bench for catechumens. Next to it there are three doors leading to the nave, which is divided into three aisles with rows of Doric columns. The total number of columns, which probably originated form the neighbouring Upper Gymnasium[1], was 20. The middle door had a Hellenistic marble door-frame, probably taken from the Sacred Stoa.

1. The columns consist of 2 or 3 drums. The lower, unfluted part, is the largest. Above this, there are unfinished flutes, that reach to the capital. The overall height of the column including the capital is approximately 4.30m. The columns supported a wooden structure, of which no trace whatsoever has survived. Wiegand, Th. – Schrader, H., Priene. Ergebnisse der Ausgrabungen und Untersuchungen von den Jahren 1895-1898. Unter Mitwirkung von G. Kummer, W. Wilberg, H. Winnefeld, R. Zahn. Berlin: Königliche Museen zu Berlin, 1904, p. 482.

HOUSE No. 24 AS CHURCH

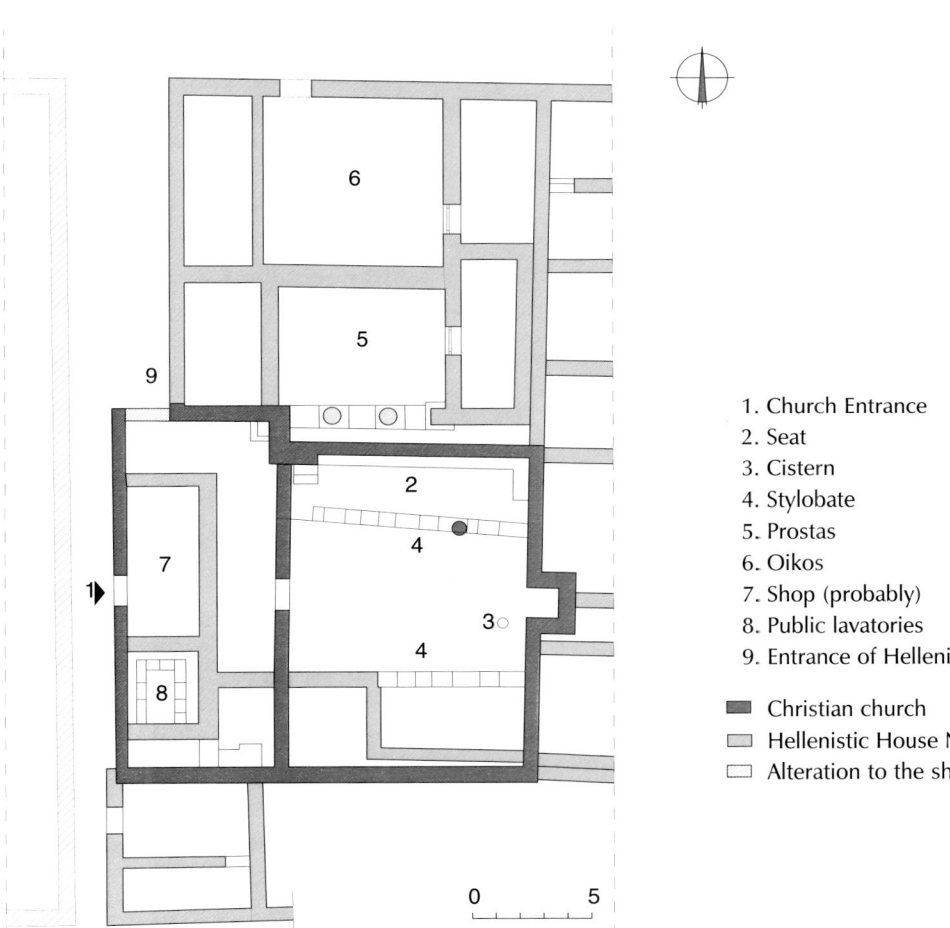

1. Church Entrance
2. Seat
3. Cistern
4. Stylobate
5. Prostas
6. Oikos
7. Shop (probably)
8. Public lavatories
9. Entrance of Hellenistic house

■ Christian church
▢ Hellenistic House No. 24
▢ Alteration to the shell

The Metropolis as it appears today

In the central aisle there was a hexagonal pulpit, probably wooden, whose base has been found. In front of the pulpit there was a marble staircase with four steps, richly decorated on three of its sides with sculptures depicting grapevines and peacocks. There were also three alcoves. A marble parapet resembling a metal railing, of which only two of the corner slabs have survived, separated the presbytery (i.e. the area restricted to clerics) from the nave. The altar was shaped like a tomb. The foundations and the surrounding parapets have survived, and are decorated with a series of white, black, red and blue stars. When the shrine was abandoned, people removed the martyr's bones. At the east end of the church there is the apse and the synthronon, containing the seats of the bishop and the priests. Apart from the episcopal throne, which must have occupied the centre of the synthronon, there was enough space to accommodate 12 to 15 clergymen.

Slabs bearing inscriptions from the Temple of Athena were embedded into the floor of the church. Under these slabs were tombs. Initially the church was covered by a level roof. Later a vaulted masonry was constructed and ten irregular pilasters made of bricks were added between the columns. They have only survived up to a height of 1.5 - 1.8m, which makes it difficult to determine the form of the roof. The walls of the church were finished to resemble marble slabs. The neighbouring buildings on the south and northeast sides of the church were probably the living quarters of the clergymen.

SINGLE-HALL CHURCH: The small church in the area of the Upper Gymnasium consisted of a single hall and was in use at the same time as the Cathedral, probably as its chapel. It could be entered through a door on the south aisle of the Metropolis.

THEATRE CHAPEL: The chapel in the eastern passageway of the Theatre was demolished in the winter of 1896 to facilitate excavations in the orchestra. Its floor was approximately 1 m higher that of the ancient passageway. The Altar, built of rubble masonry, has survived almost intact. The "iconostasis" was also found in its original position and has been preserved intact up to a height of 0.8m. The walls were painted brick-red. In front of the chapel stood two unfluted marble columns with crude capitals, which probably supported a shelter.

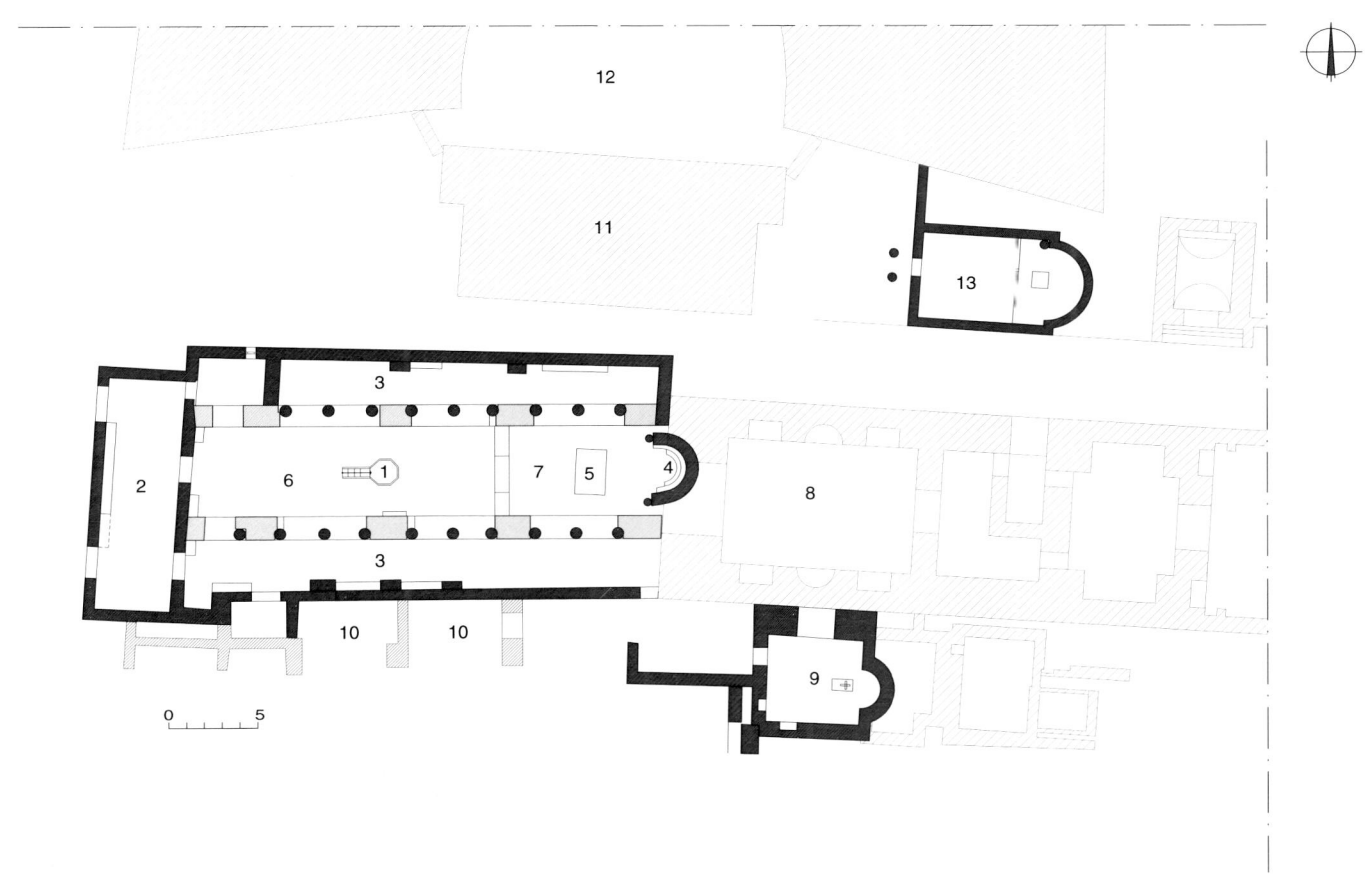

CHRISTIAN STRUCTURES

1. Ambo
2. Narthex
3. Lateral naves
4. Synthronon
5. Altar
6. Central nave
7. Presbytery
8. Roman baths
9. Chapel
10. Probable dwellings of the priesthood
11. Stage of the theatre
12. Theatre
13. Theatre Chapel

■ First phase
□ Second phase

CHRISTIAN BUILDINGS

EKKLESIASTERION CHAPEL: A single hall chapel, discovered in the area of the Ekklesiasterion, was demolished after having been recorded and documented. All that has survived is a marble slab with a cross and traces of revetment imitating marble, similar to that of the Cathedral.

BAPTISTERY: A building with alcoves to the east of the Temple of Athena was probably the Baptistery of the Cathedral. It has survived in very bad condition.

FORTRESS: One of the most imposing Christian buildings is the fortress standing in the area of the Temple of Asclepius. This fortress includes the chapel on the east side of the street leading to the Agora Gate. It is the most recent of the large buildings of Priene, the last bastion before the invasion of the Seljuks.

CHRISTIAN STRUCTURES

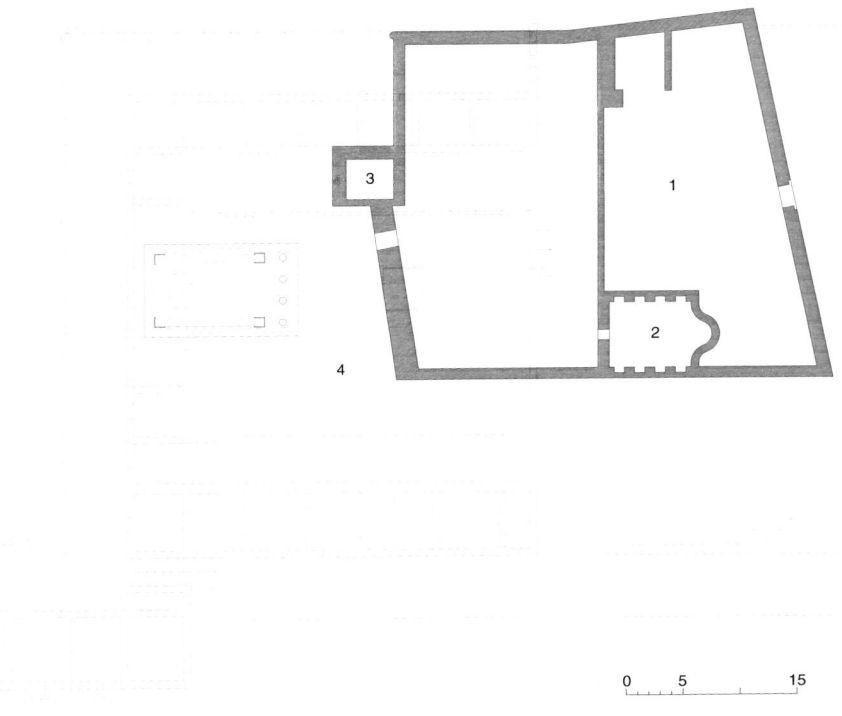

Plan

1. Byzantine fortress 2. Small church on the fortress
3. Tower 4. Temple of Asclepius

☐ Hellenistic period
■ Christian era

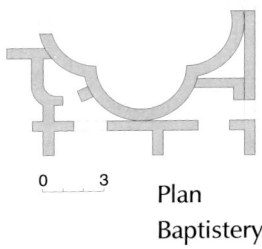

Plan
Baptistery

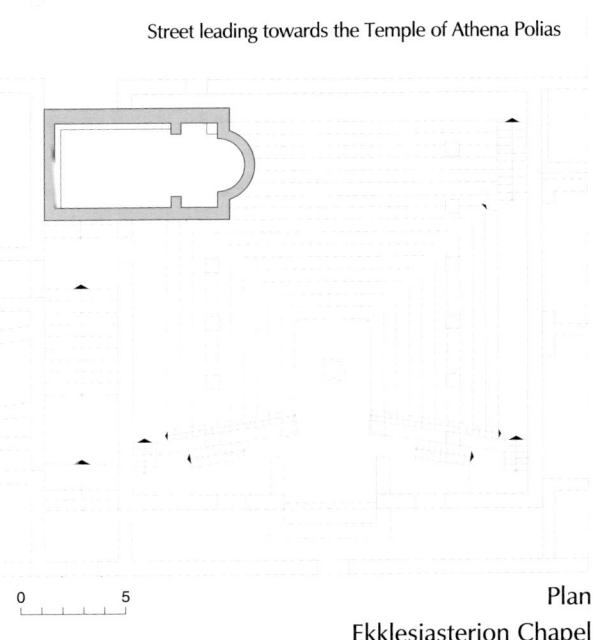

Plan
Ekklesiasterion Chapel

SCULPTURE – POTTERY
by Eleni Zymi

SCULPTURE: In Priene, as in other towns of Asia Minor, sanctuaries and temples were the primary venues for the display of sculpture. Excavations in Priene reveal a considerable number of sculptures and sculpture fragments from sanctuaries (such as the sanctuary of Athena, Demeter and Cybele, in the Ephebeum of the Lower Gymnasium, in the interior of the Sacred House), as well as sculptures from private houses. These finds, dating from the second half of the 4th century BC to the 2nd century AD, are today in the Berlin State Museums, the British Museum of London, the Archaeological Museum of Constantinople and the Balat Museum of Miletus. The discovery of numerous statue bases in the Agora area indicates that a large number of offerings and statues existed there. Since these statues were usually made of copper, they have not survived. Finally, bases of statues have been found in the Theatre, and part of the base of a copper statue originating from the Temple of Asclepius or Zeus, east of the Agora.

THE SCULPTURAL DECORATION OF THE TEMPLE OF ATHENA POLIAS: The canopies of the panels added to the temple during its last construction phase (i.e. just before the construction of its roof), had relief decorations[1]. There were 26 panels with relief decoration depicting the Gigantomachy, with the participation of Amazons in certain scenes. The subject of the Gigantomachy was from the second half of the 6th century BC, already closely linked to the worship of Athena Polias and the festival of Panathenaea, which had been adopted by Priene.

The dating of the sculptural decoration is very important since it is related to the completion date of the temple. According to Carter, as the panels were ready to be installed in temple during the 3rd quarter of the 4th century BC, the relief decorations were part of the initial decoration plan. The anatomy of the figures and the depiction of clothes are similar to those found in the Mausoleum of Halicarnassus[2].

The relief decorations have only partially survived and their surface is severely damaged. The composition of a panel canopy has the following arrangement: two or three relief figures (the third figure is usually an animal) are arranged on diagonal axes creating a pyramidal composition. Although it is impossible to reconstruct the sequence of the relief canopies on

---

[1]. Carter, J. C., *The Sculpture of the Sanctuary of Athena Polias at Priene. Reports of the Research Committee of the Society of Antiquaries of London,* XLII, London, 1983, pp. 44-56.

[2]. *Op. cit.,* pp. 63-70, 99-103.

Relief from a panel canopy of the Temple of Athena Polias in Priene. Cybele is depicted on a lion and the giant Keneas rises from the ground

Carter, J. C., op. cit. Pl. XI.

the panels of the roof, Carter claims that the most important figures of the Gigantomachy were placed on the east side. More specifically, the central position was probably occupied by Zeus with Athena on his right, while the chariot of the Sun was placed at one end[3].

THE SCULPTURE OF THE ALTAR OF ATHENA: Very few of the reliefs that decorated the alcoves between the columns on the three sides of the altar have survived. One of them is a sitted female figure, resembling the Muse Urania (Archaeological Museum of Constantinople) and three others are standing female figures (Balat Museum of Miletus and Berlin State Museums). A piece of relief decoration depicting Apollo playing the kithara survives only in a photograph taken during the first excavations in Priene conducted by Pullan. Carter's view about the dating of the relief decoration is the most widely accepted. On the basis of a stylistic study of the figures, Carter suggested that they were created in the last quarter of the 3rd century BC[4]. The construction of the altar probably began earlier, in the second half of the 4th century BC, following the plans of Pythius, but was completed with the sponsorship of the Ptolemies during the 3rd century BC[5]. The subject of this relief was Apollo and the Muses and was probably specially requested by the sponsors, since this kind of decoration was not common in monuments dedicated to Athena.

The colossal statue of Athena, of which only a few marble fragments have survived, is a typical acrolith, i.e., a statue with marble members (hands, feet, head) and a wooden torso.

VOTIVE OFFERINGS IN THE SANCTUARY OF ATHENA POLIAS: According to inscribed bases of statues found in the sanctuary, among the honorific statues of the Hellenistic period was a copper statue of Megabyzos, who had sponsored the building of the Temple of Athena. In the Roman period, the Emperor Tiberius and Julia, daughter of Augustus, were also honoured by statues in the sanctuary. Statues of emperors were also discovered in other areas of the town. The statue of Domitianus, founder of the city, was found near a small shrine next to the Gymnasium. Apart from emperors, other Roman officials were also honoured by copper statues which were finally destroyed.

Of special interest are certain statues found inside the cella of the Temple of Athena, such as the statue of Ada, the adopted mother of Alexander and Claudius. The existence of this statue can be explained by the fact that the temple was dedicated, during Roman times, to the cult of Augustus and also served as a museum of sculptures of various periods, as did the Temple of Hera at Olympia[6].

---

3. Op. cit., pp. 88-90.

4. Op. cit., pp. 192-198. Cf. Linfert, A., Kunstzentren Hellenistischer Zeit. Studien an weiblichen Gewandfiguren, Wiesbaden 1976, pp. 167-168, for the dating of the altar and the reliefs around 180 BC.

5. Op.cit., pp. 199-201.

6. Op. cit., pp. 262-266.

Sanctuary of Athena Polias: high relief of the Sanctuary of Athena Polias that, according to Carter, probably depicts the goddess Athena and dates from the Roman period

© DAI Istanbul

The marble statue of Nikesso originated from the Temple of Demeter and Persephone. Apart from its artistic value, its importance lies in the inscription found on its base. This not only provides information about the name of the person depicted, her father's and husband's names and status, but also dates the statue, almost with certainty, to the first half of the 3rd century BC (300-250 BC). This makes it one of the few points of reference for the dating of Hellenistic sculpture, and its stylistic comparison with other sculptures can lead to their approximate dating. As to the identity of the figure, it is unclear whether it depicted Nikesso, a priestess of Athena, or an offering by the priestess to Demeter depicting the goddess herself[7].

Recently there has been some dispute as to whether or not the fragmented marble statue of a young male figure from the Sacred House depicted Alexander[8]. This male figure is stylistically similar to a statue from Magnesia dating from the second half of the 2nd century BC, depicting the Sun or Apollo, according to some researchers, or, according to others, Alexander.

The assumption that it was a statue of Alexander supported the theory that the Sacred House was dedicated to him. However, the discovery of bases of other large statues there has challenged the view that Alexander was the dominant cult figure, although it cannot be doubted that his contribution to the completion of the temple of Athena was decisive and it is likely that he was worshiped in the city of Priene.

Marble statues, mainly with Dionysian subjects or depictions of Aphrodite, also decorated the mens' quarters of houses belonging to wealthy citizens of Priene[9]. In a late Hellenistic house, where pieces of 10 statues were found, there was probably a sculpture collection, a common occurence in other Hellenistic cities, such as Delos or Pompey.

Finally, Priene was the home of famous sculptors. One such was Archelaus, creator of the famous relief from the second half of the 2nd century BC, which depicted the apotheosis of Homer and which was found in Italy (Bovillae). Another form of plastic art that flourished in Priene in Hellenistic times was the production of terracottas, i.e. clay statuettes. Numerous statuettes have been found in houses and in the Sanctuary of Demeter[10].

---

7. Ridgeway, B. S., Hellenistic Sculpture I. The Styles of ca. 331-200 BC, Bristol, 1990, p. 210.

8. Op. cit., pp. 122-123.

9. Wiegand, Th. – Schrader, H., Priene. Ergebnisse der Ausgrabungen und Untersuchungen von den Jahren 1895-1898. Unter Mitwirkung von G. Kummer, W. Wilberg, H. Winnefeld, R. Zahn. Berlin: Königliche Museen zu Berlin, 1904, pp. 366-375.

10. Raeder, J., Priene. Funde aus einer griechischen Stadt im Berliner Antikenmuseum, Berlin, 1984, pp. 22-29, 33-39, 72-85 (cf. also bibliography).

A female figure decorating one of the external alcoves of the altar of Athena Polias

© DAI Istanbul

POTTERY: The pieces of pottery discovered during excavations in Priene include vases produced in local workshops or imported from other areas of Asia Minor, the islands of the Aegean Sea, and mainland Greece[11].

Numerous clay vases were found in the kitchens and warehouses of the Hellenistic houses of Priene. Vases for everyday use, most of them produced locally, were usually undecorated or simply had a fine external surface. They include "pyrauna" (i.e., jars for storing various goods, e.g., cereals), "amphorae", "oinochoai", "lagenoi", plates, "skyphidia", spindle-shaped perfume vases, and oil lamps. Oil lamps, in particular, fall into two categories: wheel-thrown lamps, similar to the type found in the Agora of Athens during the late Classical and early Hellenistic periods (last quarter of 4th and early 3rd century BC), and moulded lamps (3rd century BC and in the Roman period) with relief decoration on the upper part.

An interesting category of vases for everyday use includes the small pointed-base "oinochoai" and "skyphoi" of natural clay. They bear a stamped name and the seal of the city (Priene) with the head of Athena under their rim or along their shoulder. These pots obviously contained goods that had to be approved by the city authorities and stamped by the official in charge, whose name was inscribed on the surface. According to accounts of ancient writers, various manufactured products, such as textiles, were subject to commercial control in Priene.

Pointed-base "amphorae" found in Priene and used for the transport of goods were brought mainly from Cos and Rhodes, while a few of them came from Italy. Their origin is indicative of the commercial relations of the city with the rest of the Hellenistic world.

Apart from pottery discovered in houses, high quality pieces of pottery have also been found in other parts of the city, such as the Agora, the Sanctuaries, the Theatre and the Gymnasia. There are specimens of black-figure vases with impressed decoration of the 5th century BC, red-figure sherds of the second half of the 4th century BC, and black-figure "kantharoi" and "omphalos" plates of the 4th century BC. In the 4th and 3rd centuries BC, workshops in Priene produced local imitations of Attic black-figure pottery: they are made of local gray clay and the lower quality glaze is hazy and peels off easily. In the 3rd century BC, imitations of Attic vases with "West Clitys" decoration were produced. In the 2nd century Priene produced "lagynoi" with an off-white slip and a brown-reddish decoration, and relief "skyphoi" mainly

---

11. Wiegand, Th., – Schrader, H., op. cit., pp. 394-465. Raeder, J., Priene. Funde aus einer griechischen Stadt im Berliner Antikenmuseum, Berlin 1984, pp. 16, 18, 40-59, 67, 68, 71.

Vases for every day use from Priene: stamped skyphoi and oinochoai with a pointed base

© Bildarchiv Preussischer Kulturbesitz, Berlin 2000

with motifs of plants, imitating those of other Ionic workshops. Imported pottery probably included the so-called "Pergamene" skyphoi, decorated with ivy-leaves bunched together with ivy buds. These skyphoi were widely used during the 2nd half of the 2nd century BC.

In Priene there are numerous examples of the vases of red-glaze pottery, for which the name terra sigillatta has been adopted, that appeared in the middle of the 2nd century BC in the Eastern Mediterranean, and which by the end of the first century BC had replaced black-figure pottery. Towards the end of the 2nd century BC this pottery was adopted in Italy and from there spread all over the Roman dominions. This class of pottery is characterised a brownish-red, even orange, colour, and by a very glossy internal and external glaze, angular outlines, and during the Roman period, relief or impressed decorations.

It is evident from this brief presentation of the pottery of Priene that all types of late Classical and Hellenistic pottery are represented in Priene, and that, to a considerable extent, the production of local workshops was able to supply the needs of the city.

From top left: red-figure sherd, black-glaze sherd, fragment of "Pergamene" ware skyphos, sherd of relief skyphos (bowl), sherd of lagynos (squat, long-necked jug) with off-white slip and fragment of red-glaze vase (terra sigillata)

© Bildarchiv Preussischer Kulturbesitz, Berlin 2000

APPENDIX I

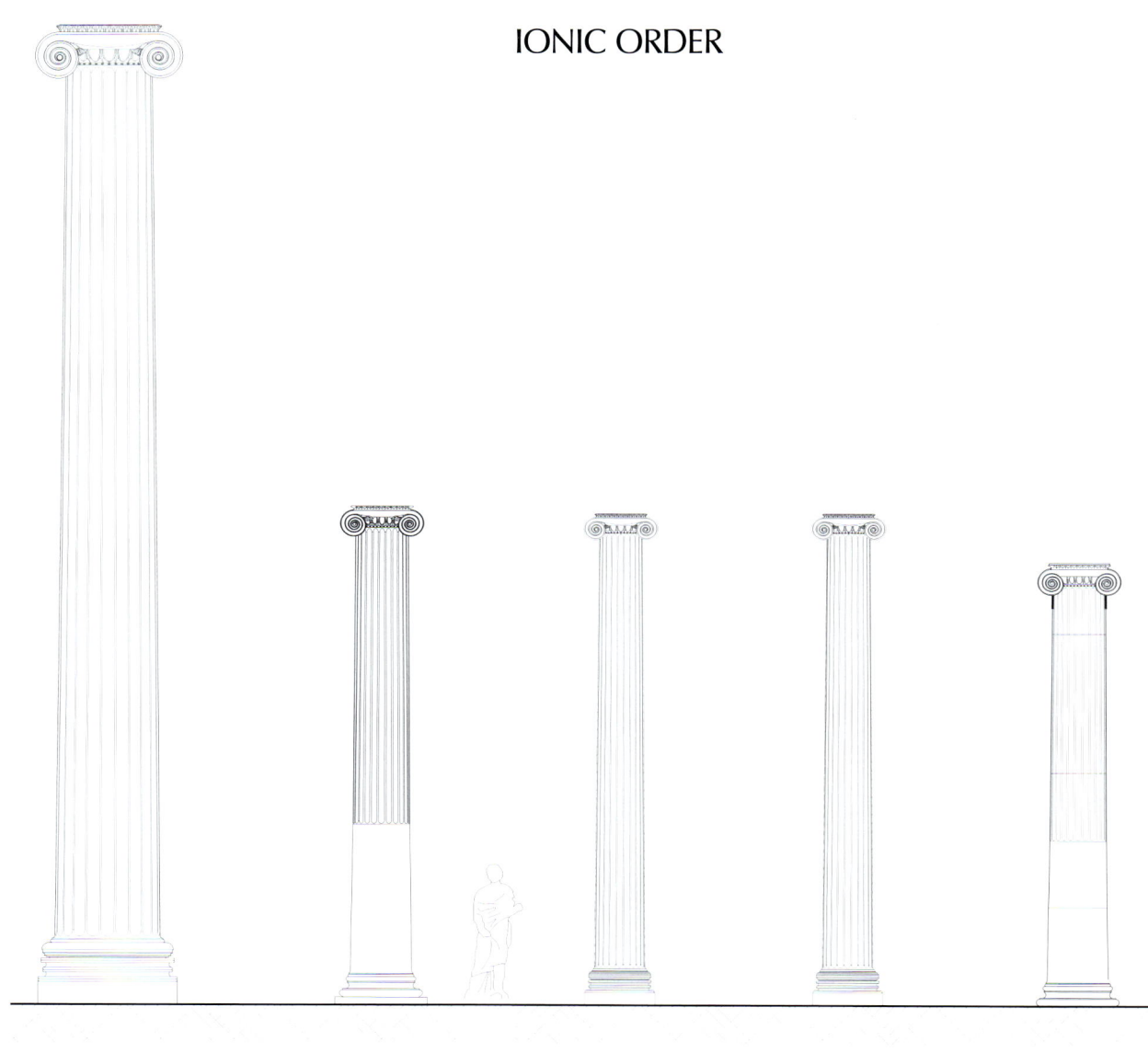

IONIC ORDER

Athena Polias · Sacred Stoa · Asclepieion or Temple of Olympian Zeus · Altar of the Sanctuary of Athena Polias · Lower Gymnasium

0 — 5

DORIC ORDER

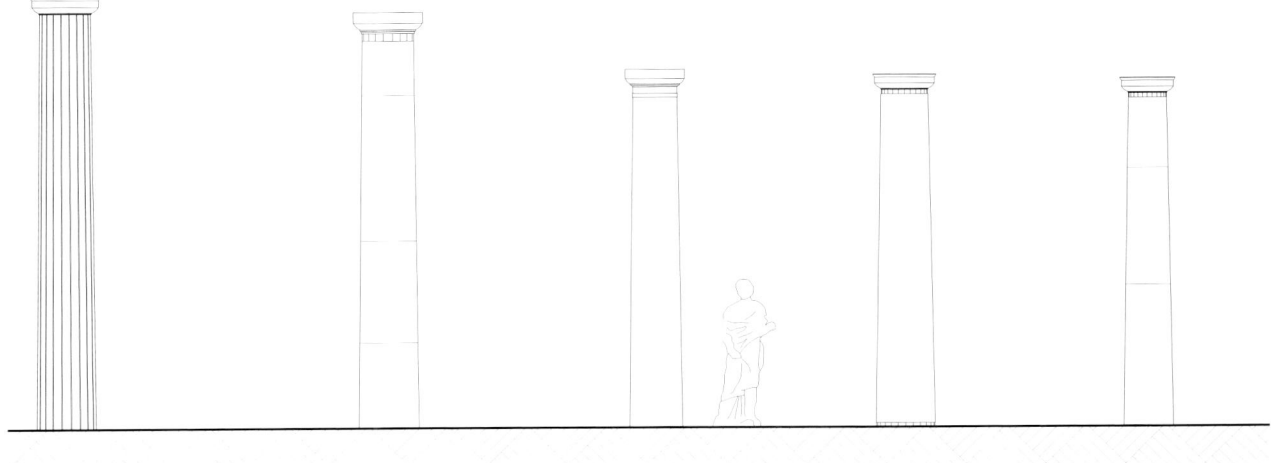

Sacred Stoa | Lower Gymnasium – Propylon | Stadium | South Stoa | Lower Gymnasium

0   5

DORIC ORDER

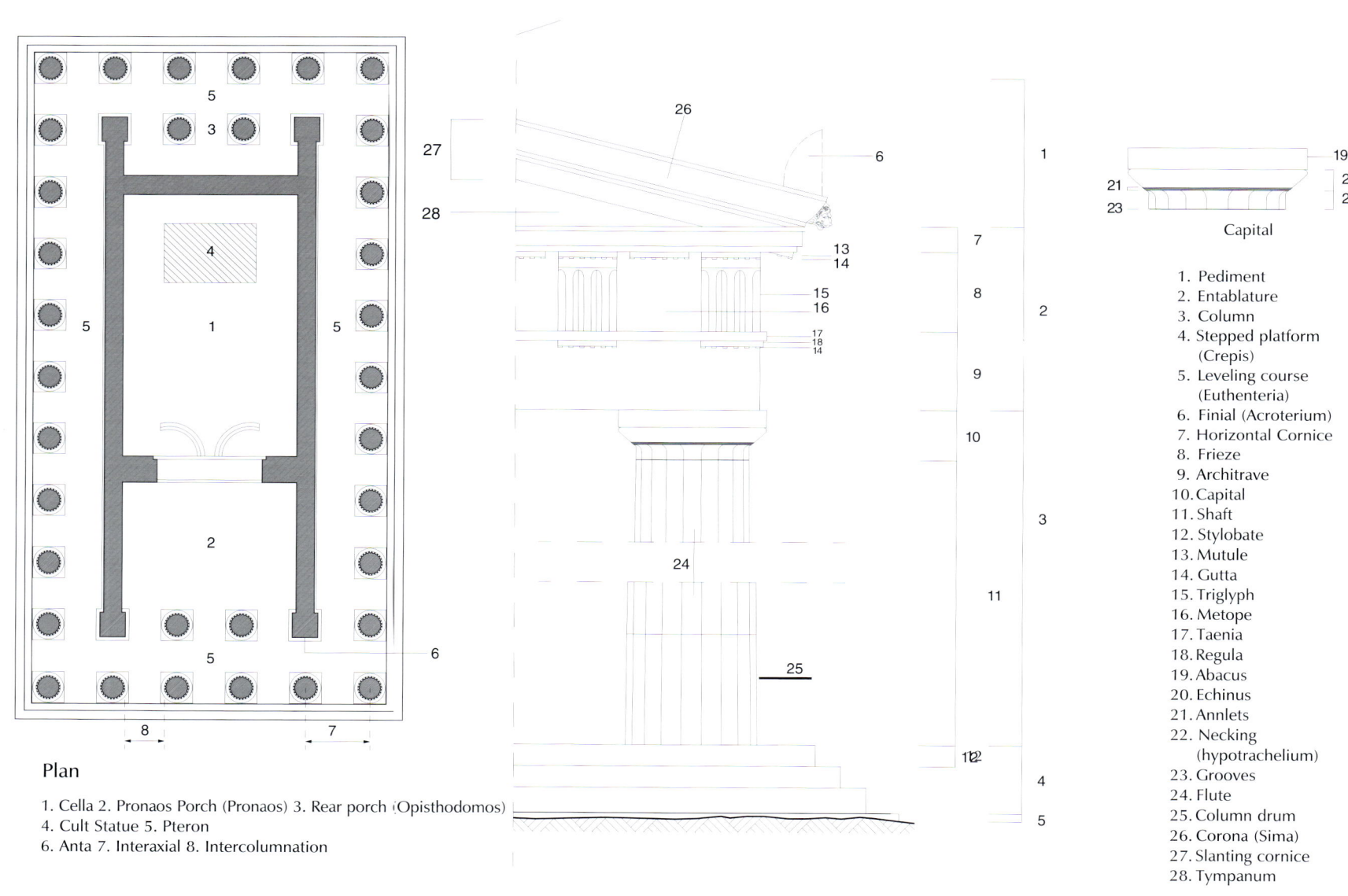

Plan

1. Cella 2. Pronaos Porch (Pronaos) 3. Rear porch (Opisthodomos)
4. Cult Statue 5. Pteron
6. Anta 7. Interaxial 8. Intercolumnation

Capital

1. Pediment
2. Entablature
3. Column
4. Stepped platform (Crepis)
5. Leveling course (Euthenteria)
6. Finial (Acroterium)
7. Horizontal Cornice
8. Frieze
9. Architrave
10. Capital
11. Shaft
12. Stylobate
13. Mutule
14. Gutta
15. Triglyph
16. Metope
17. Taenia
18. Regula
19. Abacus
20. Echinus
21. Annlets
22. Necking (hypotrachelium)
23. Grooves
24. Flute
25. Column drum
26. Corona (Sima)
27. Slanting cornice
28. Tympanum

IONIC ORDER

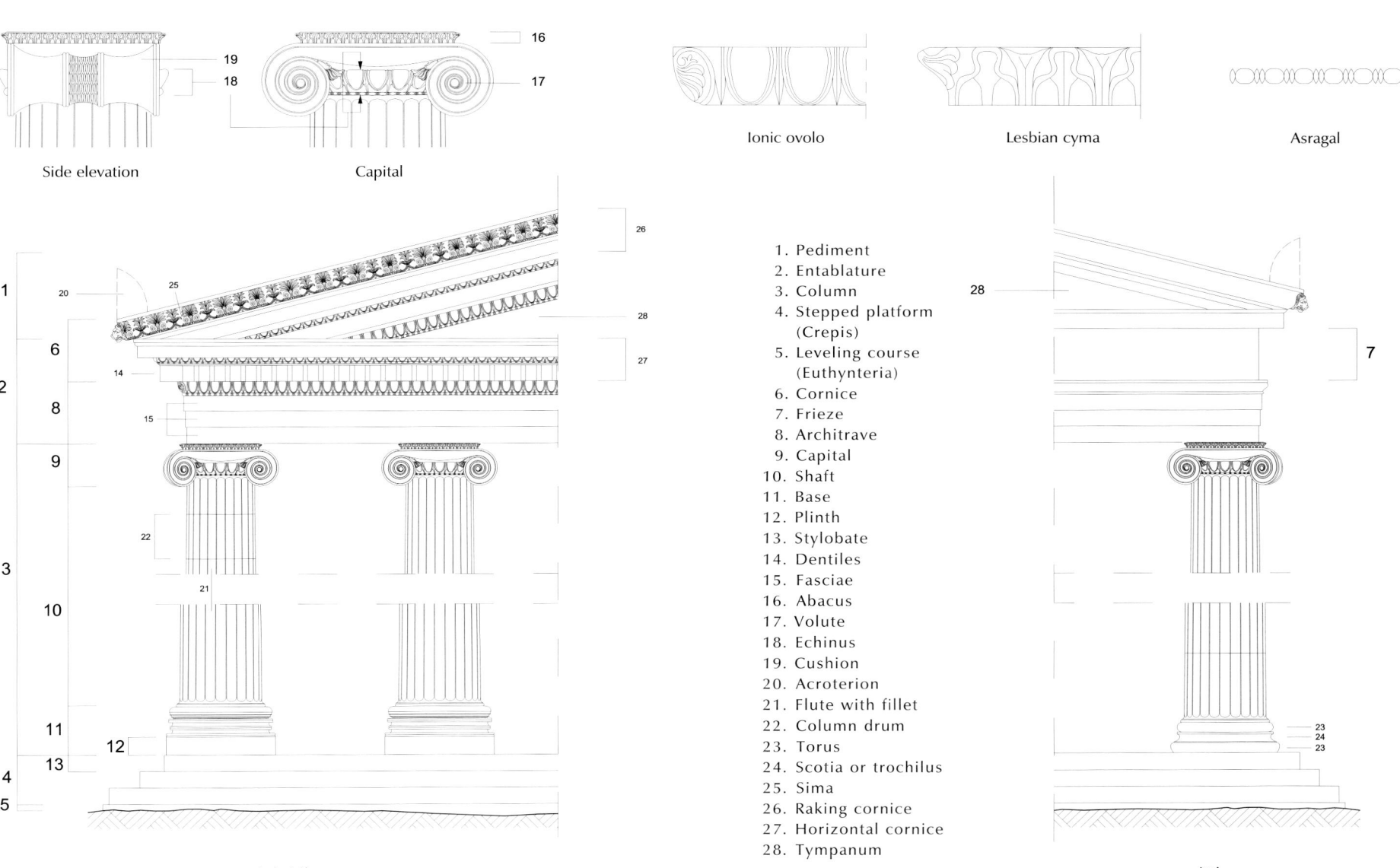

GLOSSARY

Abacus: a square plaque on the top of a column capital. See also page 214, number 19, page 215, number 16.

Acrolith: a statue whose extremities are of stone, the trunk being generally of wood.

Alexandreion: a building or shrine dedicated to the worship of Alexander the Great.

Alindisis: wrestling on the ground.

Amphiprostyle: a building (usually a temple) with a single or multiple rows of columns (a portico) at its front and back.

Amphora (pl. amphorae): the main container used for transporting and storing wine and oil, ovoid or biconical in shape, with a narrow neck and two vertical handles.

Anathyrosis: a labour-saving practice used when laying two stone blocks next to each other. Instead of finishing and smoothing the entire surface of those areas of the blocks in contact with each other, only a narrow border around the edges of the block is finished, while the remaining contact area is made slightly concave and left unfinished.

Andron: reception and banqueting room, frequently the most decorated room in the house, used predominantly for entertaining male guests (lit. "room reserved for men").

Anta (pl. antae), in antis: pilaster; the projections or extremities of the lateral walls of a building. 'In antis' designates the existence of columns between these walls. See also **Pronaos** and page 214, number 6.

Anthemion (pl. anthemia): a floral decorative motif in the form of a palmette, very widespread in the Greek art and architecture.

Apodyterion (pl. apodyteria): a changing room, next to the entrance of a bathhouse, a gymnasium, or a palaestra.

Apse: a domed or vaulted recess or projection of a building, often of arc-shaped plan, especially the east end of a church.

Architrave: See **Epistyle** and also page 214, number 9, page 215, number 8.

Archon: "ruler." The general Greek term for office-holders in a polis. In the late 5th and 4th century BC the archon was responsible for a number of religious festivals and for lawsuits concerning family matters.

Bothros: pit or trench, especially one used for ritual purposes, including sacrifice.

Boule: The council which had day-to-day responsibility for the affairs of state. Its membership and powers varied according to the type of regime.

Bouleuterion: see **Ekklesiasterion**

Bucranion: an ornament in the form of a bull's skull. It was usually applied to a frieze and it was in vogue mostly during the Hellenistic and Roman periods.

Catechumen: convert (neophyte) to Christianity under the instruction of a catechist.

Cella: The main temple chamber usually containing the cult statue and sometimes one or more altars and offering tables. See also page 214, number 1.

Cornice: the upper part of the entablature of a building, protecting the lower parts from rain. It appears in three forms: horizontal, lateral, sloping or slanting. See also page 214, numbers 7, 27, page 215, numbers 6, 26, 27.

Crepidoma or **Crepis**: a stepped platform constituting the normal substructure of a Greek temple, treasury or other building. The number of steps varies from building to building. See also page 214, number 4, page 215, number 4.

Demos: originally means "district" land, the place where 'the people' live. The word then came to mean "the people" themselves and especially the people as the sovereign element in the polis.

Dentil: projecting parallelepipedic volumes underneath the horizontal **Cornice** of an Ionic order building. See also page 215, number 14.

Diaulos: measure equivalent to two **Stadia** (approximately 385 m).

Diazoma (pl. diazomata): a horizontal passage dividing the auditorium of a theatre into an upper and lower landing or level.

Ekklesiasterion: the assembly house, the place where the ekklesia of the **demos** took place.

Ekklesia: the assembly of adult males, which had the ultimate decision-making power in a Greek state. The membership, the frequency of its meetings, and the extent and freedom of discussion varied according to the type of regime.

Elaiothesion: a room in which oil was stored and possibly the room where athletes anointed themselves before or after the exercise.

Embates: dimensional module in ancient Greek architecture equal to half the diameter of the column.

Embolium: independent sculpted architectural decoration fixed on a stone or marble surface. Eventually came to mean any relief decoration added to any material.

Ephebeum (Gr. Ephebeion): meeting hall, associated with the gymnasium complex, for ephebes.

Ephebe (Gr. ephebos, pl. epheboi): male adolescent, teenager.

Epistates: "chairman" or foreman of the **prytaneis**, elected daily by lot to serve a 24-hour term. He held the state seal and keys and in the Classical Period presided with his fellow prytaneis over the council (boule) and the assembly (ekklesia).

Epistyle: the **architrave**; horizontal slabs resting on the top of independent supporting elements such as columns, pillars or pilasters. See also page 214, number 9, page 215, number 8.

Euthynteria: the leveling course on which the building is constructed. See also page 214, number 5, page 215, number 5.

Exedra (pl. exedrai): a particular form of the **Ephebeion** with benches along the walls and a wide entrance with columns or pillars **in antis**.

Gigantomachy: "The Battle of the Giants". One of the most popular myths in Greece, the details and participants of which vary from writer to writer and from representation to representation. Zeus, Heracles, Poseidon and later Athena are the protagonists. The myth originally seems to represent a variation of the popular motif of the tribe that attempts to dethrone the gods; the myth was later interpreted as the fight of civilization against barbarism.

Guilloche: a decorative pattern consisting of two or more multiple intercrossed lines. It was usually engraved on architectural elements, on jewelry and other metal artifacts.

Gynaikonitis: the women's quarters.

Hekatompedos: a temple measuring one hundred feet in length. Hekatompedoi are the most important Archaic Greek temples.

Heroon: any building or monument destined to serve as the grave of a hero. The term refers to the function of the structure, not the architectural type, which may vary from a simple funerary enclosure to a monumental grave.

Hypocaust: a furnace connected with a series of small chambers and flues made of tiles or other masonry through which the heat of a fire was distributed to rooms above. This contrivance was first used in antiquity in baths, while later it was also adopted in private houses.

Hypotrachelium: "necking" or lowest part of the capital block, carved in the form and the circumference of the upper column drum and measuring a few inches high. See also page 214, number 22.

Iconostasis: (picture screen) the principal and most distinctive feature in all Greek churches. It consists of a great screen or partition running from side to side of the apse or across the entire end of the church, which divides the sanctuary from the body of the church. It is usually built of stone, marble or wood.

In antis: See **Anta**

Kantharos: a drinking vessel with greater height than width, usually with two vertical handles and a base or a high foot. A frequent attribute of Dionysos in representations from the Archaic and Classical periods.

Klepsydra: a system of two vessels placed at different heights. Water from the upper vessel dripped slowly into the lower, serving as a means to measure the time elapsed. The system was used to time the length of speeches in assemblies and courts.

Kline (pl. klinai): 1. Couch, in symposium context. 2. Bed.

Konisterion: building where athletes covered their bodies with fine sand and practiced wrestling on the ground.

Konistra: deep sandpit in the **konisterion**, filled with fine sand.

Korykeion: building used for training in ball games or for boxing training with a punching bag.

Koryx (pl. korykes): punching bag; leather bag full of sand for boxing training.

Lagynos: squat, long necked jug for wine, popular in the Hellenistic period.

Logeion: speaking place used by performers on the roof of the **proscenium**.

Metic: freeborn foreigner having the right of residency in a community but not citizenship.

Metope: rectangular element separating the **triglyphs** on a Doric frieze. Metopes often have figurative relief representations. See also page 214, number 16.

Monopitched: roof with only one inclined surface (when composed of two the roof is called double-pitched).

Mutules: rectangular plackets underneath the **cornice** of a Doric-style building, usually decorated with pegs (guttae). See also page 214, number 13 & 14.

Narthex: a portico or a transversal room at the west end of an early Christian basilica or church. See also page 199, number 2.

Nave: main aisle; part of a room or a temple between two rows of columns. Lateral naves are sometimes also called aisles. See also page 199, number 6.

Necropolis: graveyard, cemetery or funerary enclosure, which was usually situated at the city limits or next to a road leading to the city.

Neopoios: civil or religious officer charged with the management of the construction of a temple.

Oecus maior: the main room of the house, sometimes serving as a reception or a banquet hall.

Oikos: 1. Household: the fundamental social, political and economic unit of ancient Greece. It included members of the household but also their property, land and animals. 2. The main part of the living quarters of a house.

Oinochoe (pl. oinochoai): wine jug found in a wide variety of shapes.

Omphalos plate: a phiale or shallow cup with a central protuberance inside, usually without handles or base, used for libations.

Opisthodomos: Rear porch or back chamber of a temple similar in construction to the **pronaos** (wall with door, columns in antis or prostyle) See also page 214, number 3.

Orthostate: a slab positioned on one of its narrow faces, usually in the lower course of a wall while the upper courses are made of smaller slabs or bricks.

Palaestra (Gr. palaistra): a building in which young people and athletes practised combat sports, usually simply a part of the gymnasium; a rectangular court surrounded by porticoes, often of monumental size, and comprising auxiliary rooms such as vestibules and halls.

Paradromia (pl. paradromiai): open air track where athletes trained, when the weather was good, usually situated in front of and alongside the **xystos**.

Parodos (pl. parodoi): passage by which the chorus entered the orchestra and by which spectators gained access to the lower seats of the theater. Sometimes, as in Priene, it was closed by doors.

Pentalitha: A game in which five pebbles or postherds or dice were tossed from the back of the hand and caught in the palm.

Peplos: a garment worn by women in ancient Greece; cloth caught at the shoulders and draped in folds to the waist.

Peripteral: a temple (or occasionally other building) entirely surrounded by a single or double colonnade. See also **peristasis** and page 88.

Peristyle: range of columns surrounding the entire building.

Phratria: in Greek states, group with hereditary membership and normally associated with specific loyalties.

Phyle (pl. phylai): is used in the Greek world to denote the principal components or divisions ('tribes') of the citizen body.

Proedria (pl. proedriai): The front tiers in the auditorium of a theatre, often provided with more elaborate and comfortable seating for priests and officials.

Pronaos: Space before the main temple chamber (**cella**), on the same axis and having the same width. The front may be open or closed by a wall with one or more doors. When columns are erected between the lateral wall projections, called **antae** or pilasters, the pronaos is called "**in antis**" (in the case of two columns, "distyle in antis", in the case of three, "tristyle in antis", six "hexastyle in antis" etc.). When the columns are simply placed in front of, rather than between, the antae, this arrangement is called prostylos or prostyle. See also page 214, number 2

Propylon: gate-building, monumental entrance, most often to a temple.

Proscenium (Gr. proskenion): A row of columns in front of the stage building (skene) supporting a high platform. This came to be used as a raised stage.

Prostas house: a house with a front chamber open to the courtyard and with two columns (or pillars) between the lateral walls reproducing the scheme pronaos-cella.

Prostasis: a porch or a particular form of the **pronaos**, when the pronaos projects beyond the main temple's ground plan.

Prytaneion: the council house, a building where the prytaneis (state officials) held meetings and were accommodated.

Prytanis (pl. Prytaneis): Title of a state official, often with responsibility for presiding over a city council.

Pseudo-isodomic (pseudisodomic): masonry consisting of alternate courses of stones of two markedly different heights. Pseudisodomic masonry was in great vogue in the 2nd century BC, especially in Asia Minor.

Pteron: a portico or aisle; the colonnade and the corridor it creates around a temple. See also page 214, number 5.

Pulvinus (pl. pulvini): baluster end; the lateral, often concave, surface of the volutes of the Ionic capital. See also page 215, number 19.

Pyraunos (pl. pyraunoi) or **pyraunon, (pl. pyrauna)**: brazier.

Sima or corona: the tiles at the extremities of the roof, with much higher and very often decorated border, serving to retain rain water (for this reason lateral sima is interrupted by rain spouts). See also page 215, number 25, page 214, number 26.

Skyphidion: a small **skyphos**, often without handles.

Skyphos: a cup or drinking vessel with height greater than width, usually with two horizontal handles and a base or a high foot. Very popular throughout antiquity and found in many varieties.

Sphairomachia: training with boxing balls or playing ball games.

Stadion (pl. stadia): (stade) measure of length. Originally the distance covered by a single draught of the plough, it was the equivalent of about 600 feet (app. 192 meter).

Stephanephoros: "wreathbearer", official, mainly responsible for carrying out large sacrifices. He was also charged with the expenses for the meals of the citizens involved in the rites.

Stoa: a portico, a long building with a colonnade on one side along its length. A stoa is simultaneously open and covered, thus offering protection from sun and rain. Used as a place for meetings near the agora or next to an important sanctuary, sometimes including small shops and serving a commercial purpose.

Strobilos: 1. playing with a whirligig, 2. an ancient Greek dance called also "ballismos".

Stylobate: row of stone slabs of the **crepis** supporting a colonnade. See also page 214, number 12, page 215, number 13.

Synthronon: the seats of the bishop and the priests usually situated in the **apse** of a church. See also page 199, number 4.

Terra sigillata: earthenware with bright reddish glaze and in its finest forms with stamped or relief decoration. Invented in Asia Minor in the middle of the 2nd century BC, it quickly became very popular all around the Mediterranean.

Tetraktys: the symbol of Pythagoreans; an equilateral triangle composed of ten dots and expressing the ratios 2:1, 3:2 and 4:3, which were applied to musical consonances and occasionally in town planning. See also figure on page 34.

Thalamos: bedroom.

Theologeion: 'The god's speaking place'. The roof of the skene (stage building) was occasionally used by performers, usually for the appearance of gods. See also **Logeion**.

Thermae: bath complex, made up of various rooms and pools, often connected to a gymnasium.

Thesaurus: "treasury". Thesauri were built in panhellenic sanctuaries by individual cities or confederations to house dedications to the divinity and also to serve as offerings themselves.

Thiasos (pl. thiasoi): Associations centered on the worship of a particular god or hero.

Tholaria: small vaulted funerary chambers, usually with three funerary couches.

Toichobates: a row of slabs integrated in the **crepis** and supporting a wall.

Torus (pl. tori): concave part of column base. See also page 215, number 23.

Triclinium (pl. triclinia): in the Roman house the chamber corresponding to the Greek **andron** (dining room). It contained three beds or couches along the walls.

Triglyph: a rectangular plaque on the Doric frieze with two entire and two half sculpted vertical channels (making thus in total three channels or glyphs). Triglyphs on the Doric frieze alternate with **metopes**. See also page 214, number 15.

Trochilus or scotia: the convex part of the column base. See also page 215, number 24.

Tympanum: the recessed triangular wall enclosed by the cornices of a pediment. See also pages 214, number 28, page 215, number 28.

Xystos: a covered running track allowing training even under bad wheather conditions.

GENERAL BIBLIOGRAPHY

Ager, S. L., *Interstate Arbitrations in the Greek World, 337-90 BC*, Hellenistic Culture and Society 18, Los Angeles/Berkeley/London: Californian University Press, 1996.

Akurgal, E., *Ancient Civilizations and Ruins of Turkey from Prehistoric Times until the End of the Roman Empire*, 4th ed., Istanbul: Turk Tarih Kurumu Basimevi, 1978.

Ameling, W., Bringmann, K., Schmidt-Dounas, B., *Schenkungen hellenistischer Herrscher an griechische Städte und Heiligtümer 1: Zeugnisse und Kommentare*, Berlin: Akademie, 1995.

Asbock, A., *Das Staatswesen von Priene in hellenistischer Zeit: Inauguraldissertation*, München: F. X. Seitz, 1913.

Bean, G. E., Cook, J. M., "The Halikarnassus Peninsula", *BSA* 50, 1955, pp. 85-171.

Beloch, J., *Die Bevölkerung der griechisch-römischen Welt*, Historische Beiträge zur Bevölkerungslehre, Leipzig: Duncker & Humbolt, 1886.

Berchem, D. van, "Alexandre et la restauration de Priène", *MusHelv* 70, 1972, pp. 198-205.

Botermann, H., "Wer baute das Neue Priene? Zur Interpretation der Inschriften von Priene Nr. 1 und 156", *Hermes* 122, 1994, pp. 162-187.

Bouras, Ch., *Μαθήματα Ιστορίας της Αρχιτεκτονικής*, 1, 1st ed. 1968, 2nd ed. 1980, 3rd ed., Athens: Symmetria, 1991.

Buraselis, K., *Das hellenistische Makedonien und die Ägäis: Forschungen zur Politik des Kassandros und der drei ersten Antigoniden (Antigonos Monophthalmos, Demetrios Poliorketes und Antigonos Gonatas) im Ägäischen Meer und in Westkleinasien*, Münchener Beiträge zur Papyrusforschung und antiken Rechtsgeschichte 73, München: C.H. Beck, 1982.

Carter, J. C., "Pytheos", in *Akten des 13. Internationalen Kongresses für Klassische Archäologie, Berlin 1988*, Mainz am Rhein: P. von Zabern, 1990, pp. 129-136.

Cohen, G. M., *The Hellenistic Settlements in Europe, the Islands and Asia Minor*, Hellenistic Culture and Society 18, Los Angeles/Berkeley/London: Californian University Press, 1995.

Coulton, J. J., *Greek Architects at Work – Problems of Structure and Design*, London: Elek, 1977.

Crowther, C. V., "Priene 8 and the History of Priene in the Early Hellenistic Period", *Chiron* 26, 1996, pp. 195-239.

Demand, N. H., "The Relocation of Priene Reconsidered", *Phoenix* 40, 1986, pp. 35-44.

Demand, N. H., *Urban Relocation in Archaic and Classical Greece: Flight and Consolidation*, Bristol: Bristol Classical Press, 1990.

Dräger, M., *Die Städte der Provinz Asia in der Flavierzeit (69-96 n. Chr.): Studien zur Kleinasiatischen Stadt- und Regionalgeschichte*, Europäische Hochschulschriften 3: Geschichte und ihre Hilfswissenschaften 576, Frankfurt am Main/Berlin/Bern: P. Lang, 1993.

Fehr, B., "Kosmos und Chreia", *Hephaistos* 2, 1980, pp. 155-185.

Fletcher, B. Sir, *A History of Architecture*, 1st ed. 1896, 20th ed. London: Architectural Press, 1996.

Foss, C., *History and Archaeology of Byzantine Asia Minor*, Aldershot/Hampshire: Variorum, 1990.

Frank, T., Broughton, T.R.S., et al., eds, *An Economic Survey of Ancient Rome*, Baltimore: Johns Hopkins Press, 1933-1940.

Gauthier, Ph., "Les cités hellénistiques", in Hansen, M. H., ed., *The Ancient Greek City State: Symposium on the Occasion of the 250th Anniversary of the Royal Danish Academy of Sciences and Letters, July 1-4 1992*, Historisk - filosofiske Meddelelser 67, Copenhagen: Koneglige Danske Videnskabernes Selskab, 1993.

Gauthier, Ph., "Ατέλεια σώματος", *Chiron* 21,1991, pp. 49-68.

Gruben, G., *Die Tempel der Griechen*, München: Hirmer, 1986.

Habicht, Ch., *Gottmenschentum und Griechische Städte*, 2nd ed. München: C.H. Beck, 1970.

Hansen, E. V., *The Attalids of Pergamon*, 1st ed. 1946, 2nd ed. revised and expanded, Ithaca/London: Cornell University Press, 1971.

Hiller von Gaertringen, F., ed., *Inschriften von Priene*, Berlin: G. Reimer, 1906.

Hoepfner, W., Schwander, E.L., *Haus und Stadt im klassischen Griechenland*, Wohnen in der klassischen Polis 1, München: Deutsche Kunstverlag, 1994.

Hoepfner, W., ed., *Geschichte des Wohnens,1: 5000 v.Ch – 500 n.Chr.: Vorgeschichte, Frühgeschichte, Antike*, Stuttgart: Deutsche Verlagsanstalt, 1999.

Hornblower, S., *Mausolus*, Oxford: Clarendon Press/ New York: Oxford University Press, 1982.

Hotz, W., *Die Mittelmeerküsten Anatoliens: Handbuch der Kunstdenkmäler*, Darmstadt: Wissenschaftliche Buchgesellschaft, 1989.

Hubbe, R. O., *Public Service in Miletus and Priene in Hellenistic and Roman Imperial Times*, Ann Arbor: UMI, 1989.

Jerphanion, G. de, "Σαμψών et Αμισός: une ville à déplacer de neuf cents kilomètres", *Orientalia Christiana Periodica* 1, 1935, pp. 256-267.

Jones, A. H. M., *The Cities of the Eastern Roman Provinces*, 1st ed. 1937, 2nd ed. revised by M. Avi-Yonah, G. Bean, *et al.*, Oxford: Clarendon Press, 1971.

Kleine, J., (ed.), *Führer durch die Ruinen von Milet, Didyma, Priene*, Ludwigsburg: Karawaneverlag, 1980.

Kleiner, G., "Priene", in *RE* Suppl. 9, 1962, col. 1181-1221.

Kobes, J., *Kleine Könige: Untersuchungen zu den Lokaldynasten im hellenistischen Kleinasien (323-188 v. Chr.)*, Pharos Studien zur griechisch - römischen Antike 8, St. Katharinen: Scripta Mercatura Verlag, 1996.

Konstandinidis, D., *Παραδόσεις Ιστορίας της Αρχιτεκτονικής, 2.2: Ιστορική Ελλάς: Αρχαία Εποχή*, Athens: NTUA, 1973.

Krischen, F., *Die griechische Stadt*, Berlin: Gebr. Mann, 1938.

Lund, H. S., *Lysimachus: A Study in Early Hellenistic Kingship*, London/New York: Routledge, 1992.

Magie, D., *Roman Rule in Asia Minor: to the End of the Third Century after Christ*, Princeton: Princeton University Press, 1950.

Marchese, R. T., *The Lower Maeander Flood Plain: a Regional Settlement Study*, BAR-IS 292, Oxford: British Archaeological Reports, 1986.

Marchese, R. T., *The Historical Archaeology of Northern Caria: a Study in Cultural Adaptations*, BAR-IS 536, Oxford: British Archaeological Reports, 1989.

Martiensen, R. D., *The Idea of Space in Greek Architecture: with Special Reference to the Doric temple and its Setting*, Johannesburg: Witwakisrand University Press, 1958.

Mastrocinque, A., *La Caria e la Ionia Meridionale in epoca hellenistica (323-188 a.C.)*, Problemi e ricerce di storia antica 6, Roma: Erma di Bretschneider, 1979.

McCabe, D. F., Ehrman, B. D., Elliott, R. N., *Priene, Inscriptions: Texts and List*, Princeton: The Institute for Advanced Study, 1987.

McNicoll, A. W., Milner, N.P., *Hellenistic Fortifications from the Aegean to the Euphrates*, Oxford Monographs on Classical Archaeology, Oxford: Clarendon Press, 1997.

Mellor, R., *Θεά Ρώμη: the Worship of the Goddess Roma in the Greek World*, Hypnomnemata 42, Göttingen: Vandenhoeck & Ruprecht, 1975.

Meyer, E., *Die Grenzen der hellenistischen Staaten in Kleinasien*, Zürich/Leipzig: Orell Füssli, 1925.

Momigliano, A., Pace, B., "Priene", in *Enciclopedia Italiana di Scienze, Lettere ed Arti* 28, Roma: 1935, pp. 236-238.

Müller, D., *Topografischer Bildkommentar zu den Historien Herodots: Kleinasien und angegrenzte Gebiete mit Südostthrakien und Zypern*, Tübingen/Berlin: Wasmuth, 1997.

Müller-Wiener, W., *Griechisches Bauwesen in der Antike*, München 1988

Orgels, P., "Sabas Asidenos", *Byzantion* 10, 1935, pp. 67-80.

Orth, W., *Königlicher Machtanspruch und Städtische Freiheit: Untersuchungen zu den politischen Beziehungen zwischen den ersten Seleukidenherrschern (Seleukos I, Antiochos I, Antiochos II) und den Städten des westlichen Kleinasien*, Münchener Beiträge zur Papyrusforschung und antiken Rechtsgeschichte 71, München: C. H. Beck, 1977.

Otto, W., "Hieron", in *RE* 8.2, 1913, col., 1513-1515, no. 17.

Pick, B., Rez., "Regling, Die Münzen von Priene", *Gnomon* 5, 1929, pp. 113-121.

Price, S. R. F., *Rituals and Power: the Roman Imperial Cult in Asia Minor*, Cambridge/New York: Cambridge University Press, 1984.

Raeder, J., *Priene: Funde aus einer griechischen Stadt im Berliner Antikenmuseum*, Bildheft der Staatlichen Museen Preußischer Kulturbesitz 45/46, Berlin: Gebr. Mann, 1984.

Ratté, Ch., "Priene", in Meyers, E.M., ed., *The Oxford Encyclopedia of Archaeology in the Near East* 4, Oxford/New York: Oxford University Press, 1997, pp. 351-352.

Robuck, C., *Ionian Trade and Colonization*, Monographs on Archaeology and Fine Arts, New York: Archaeological Institute of America, 1959.

Rostovtzeff, M. I., *The Social and Economic History of the Hellenistic World*, Oxford: Clarendon Press, 1941.

Schede, M., *Die Ruinen von Priene: kurze Beschreibung*, 1st ed. 1934, 2nd ed. revised and expanded by G. Kleiner und W. Kleiss, Berlin: W. de Gruyter, 1964.

Schipporeit, S., "Das alte und das neue Priene: das Heiligtum der Demeter und Gründungen Prienes", *IstMitt* 48, 1988, pp. 193-236.

Sherwin-White, S. M., "Ancient Archives: the Edict of Alexander to Priene: a Reappraisal", *JHS* 105, 1985, pp. 69-89.

Theophaneides, B.D., "Πριήνη", in *Μεγάλη Ελληνική Εγκυκλοπαιδεία* 20, Athens: Pyrsos 1929, pp. 674-678.

Tietze, Ch., "Priene: Rekonstruktion einer antiken Stadtplanung", *Altertum* 34, 1988, pp. 217-223.

Tomlinson, R., *From Mycenae to Constantinople: the Evolution of the Ancient City*, London/New York: Routledge, 1992.

Wiegand, Th., Schrader, H., *Priene: Ergebnisse der Ausgrabungen und Untersuchungen von den Jahren 1895-1898*, Berlin: G. Reimer, 1904.

Wiegand, Th., *Ein Begleitwort zur Rekonstruktion von A. Zippelius*, Leipzig/Berlin: B. G. Teubner, 1910.

AGORA

General Bibliography

Koenigs, W., "Planung und Ausbau der Agora von Priene", *IstMitt* 43, 1993, pp. 381-396.

Sacred Stoa

Dinsmoor, W. B., "The Repair of the Athena Parthenos", *AJA* 38, 1934, pp. 93-106.

Gerkan, A. von, *Griechische Städteanlagen: Untersuchungen zur Entwicklung des Städtebaus im Altertum*, Berlin/Leipzig: W. de Gruyter, 1924.

Koenigs, W., "Planung und Ausbau der Agora von Priene", *IstMitt* 43, 1993, pp. 381-396.

Krischen, F., "Orophernes Halle", *JdI* 31, 1916, pp. 306-309.

Miller, S. G., *The Prytaneion: its Function and Architectural form*, Los Angeles/Berkeley/London: Californian University Press, 1978.

Regling, K. L., *Die Münzen von Priene*, Berlin: H. Schoetz & Co., 1927.

Robert, L., *Noms indigènes dans l'Asie Mineure Gréco-romaine*, Bibliothèque Archéologique et historique de l'Institut Français d'Archéologie de Beyrouth 13, Paris: A. Maisonneuve, 1963.

Schede, M., "Heiligtümer von Priene", *JdI* 49, 1934, pp. 97-108.

Thiersch, H., *Pharos, Antike Islam und Occident: ein Beitrag zur Architekturgeschichte*, Leipzig/Berlin: B. G. Teubner, 1909.

Walbank, F. W., *A Historical Commentary on Polybius* 3, Oxford: Clarendon Press, 1979.

South Stoa

Schede, M., "Heiligtümer von Priene", *JdI* 49, 1934, pp. 97-108.

BOULEUTERION OR EKKLESIASTERION

Gneisz, D., *Das Antike Rathaus: das griechische Bouleuterion und die frührömische Curia*, Dissertationen der Universität Wien 205, Wien: VWGOE 1990.

Hansen, M. H., Fischer-Hansen, T., "Monumental Political Architecture in Archaic and Classical Greek Poleis: Evidence and Historical Significance", in Whitehead, D., ed., *From Political Architecture to Stephanus Byzantius: Sources for the Ancient Greek Polis*, Historia Einzelschriften 87, Stuttgart: F. Steiner, 1994, pp. 23-90.

Koenigs, W., "Planung und Ausbau der Agora von Priene", *IstMitt* 43, 1993, pp. 381-396.

Kolb, F., *Agora und Theater, Volks - und Festversammlung*, Archäologische Forschungen 9, Berlin: Mann, 1981.

Krischen, F., *Antike Rathäuser*, Studien zur Bauforschung 4, Berlin: Gebr. Mann, 1941.

McDonald, W. A., *The Political Meeting Places of the Greeks*, John Hopkins University Studies in Archaeology 34, Baltimore: John Hopkins Press, 1943.

PRYTANEION

MacDowell, D. M., Hornblower, S., "Prytaneis", in Hornblower, S., Spawforth A., eds, *Oxford Classical Dictionary*, Oxford/New York: Oxford University Press, 1996, p. 1269.

Miller, S. G., *The Prytaneion: its Function and Architectural Form*, Los Angeles/Berkeley/London: Californian University Press, 1978.

Regling, K., *Die Münzen von Priene*, Berlin: H. Schoetz & Co., 1927.

SANCTUARY OF ATHENA POLIAS

Temple of Athena

Bauer, O., "Vorläufiger Bericht über die Neubearbeitung des Athenatempels zu Priene in den Jahren 1965-66", *IstMitt* 18, 1968, pp. 212-220.

Bauer, O., "Beobachtungen am Athenatempel bei Priene bei den Bestandsaufnahmen 1965 und 1966", *BJb* 169, 1969, pp. 117-129.

Carter, J. C., *The Sculpture of the Sanctuary of Athena Polias at Priene*, Reports of the Research Committee of the Society of Antiquaries of London 42, London: Thames and Hucson, 1983.

Gerkan, A. von, "Zum Gebälk des Athenatempels in Priene", *AM* 42, 1918, pp. 165-176.

Koenigs, W., "Der Athenatempel von Priene: Bericht über die 1977-82 durchgeführten Untersuchungen", *IstMitt* 33, 1983, pp. 134-176.

Rumscheid, F., *Untersuchungen zur kleinasiatischen Bauornamentik des Hellenismus*, Beiträge zur Erschließung hellenistischer und kaiserlicher Skulptur und Architektur 14, Mainz am Rhein: P. von Zabern, 1994.

Schede, M., "Heiligtümer von Priene", *JdI* 49, 1934, pp. 97-103.

SEG 30, 1980, no. 1362.

Stevens, G. P., "The Volute of the Capital of the Temple of Athena at Priene", *MAAR* 9, 1931, pp. 135-144.

Wilberg, W., "Zum Athenatempel in Priene", *AM* 39, 1914, pp. 72-82.

Cult Statue of the Goddess

Carter, J. C., *The Sculpture of the Sanctuary of Athena Polias at Priene*, Reports of the Research Committee of the Society of Antiquaries of London 42, London: Thames and Hudson, 1983.

Damaskos, D., *Untersuchungen zu hellenistischen Kultbildern*, Stuttgart: F. Steiner, 1999.

Regling, K., *Die Münzen von Priene*, Berlin: H. Schoetz & Co., 1927.

Simonetta, B., "Notes on the Coinage of the Cappadocian Kings", *NC* 1, 1961, pp. 9-50.

Altar

Gerkan, A. von, Der Altar des Athenatempels in Priene, *BJb* 129, 1924, pp. 15-35.

Linfert A., *Kunstzentren hellenistischer Zeit: Studien an weiblichen Gewandfiguren*, Wiesbaden: Steiner 1976, pp. 167-170.

ASCLEPIEION or SANCTUARY OF ZEUS

Bankel, H., "Jahresbericht 1988 des Deutschen Archäologischen Instituts: Abteilung Istanbul, Ausgrabungen und Untersuchungen", *AA* 1989, pp. 683-685.

Damaskos, D., *Untersuchungen zu hellenistischen Kultbildern*, Stuttgart: F. Steiner, 1999.

Schede, M., "Heiligtümer von Priene", *JdI* 49, 1934, pp. 97-108.

SANCTUARY OF DEMETER AND KORE

CIG 2907.

SACRED HOUSE

SEG 15, 1958, no. 687.

Sokolowski, F., *Lois sacrées de l'Asie Mineure*, Travaux et mémoires des anciens membres étrangers de l'École Française d'Athènes et de divers savants 9, Paris: E. de Boccard, 1955.

SANCTUARY OF EGYPTIAN GODS

Vidman, L., *Sylloge inscriptionum religionis Isiaca et Satrapiaca*, Religionsgeschichtliche Versuche und Vorarbeiten 28, Berlin: W. de Gruyter, 1969.

SANCTUARY OF NAULOCHOS

CIG 2907.

THEATRE

Ciancio Rossetto, P., Pisani Sartorio, G., (eds), *Teatri greci e romani: alle origini del linguaggio rappresentato*, Roma: SEAT, 1994.

Doerpfeld, W., "Das Theater von Priene und die griechische Bühne", *AM* 49, 1924, pp. 50-101.

Gerkan, A. von, *Das Theater von Priene: als Einzelanlage und in seiner Bedeutung für das hellenistische Bühnenwesen*, München/Berlin: F. Schmidt, 1921.

Gerkan, A. von, "Die Datierung der Statuenbasen vor dem Proskenion in Priene", *IstMitt* 49, 1924, pp. 225-230.

Gerkan, A. von, "Zum Skenengebäude des Theaters von Priene", *IstMitt* 9-10, 1959-60, pp. 97-108.

Gerkan, A. von, "Nochmals die Skene des Theaters von Priene", *IstMitt* 13-14, 1963-4, pp. 67-72.

Hansen, M.H., Fischer-Hansen, T., "Monumental Political Architecture in Archaic and Classical Greek Poleis: Evidence and Historical Significance", in Whitehead, D., ed., *From Political Architecture to Stephanus Byzantius: Sources for the Ancient Greek Polis*, Historia Einzelschriften 87, Stuttgart: F. Steiner, 1994, pp. 23-90.

Izenour, G., *Theatre Design*, New York: McGraw Hill, 1977.

Izenour, G., *Roofed Theatres of Classical Antiquity*, New Haven/London: Yale University Press, 1992.

Kern, O., *Die Inschriften von Magnesia am Mäander*, Berlin: W. de Gruyter, 1900.

Bosnakis, D., Gangtzis, D., Lange, J., Stefossi, M., *Αρχαία Θέατρα... θέατρα θέας άξια...*, Athens: Itanos, 1996.

Neppi Modona, A., *Gli edifici teatrali greci e roman: teatri, odei, anfiteatri, airchi*, Firenze: L. S. Olschki, 1961.

GYMNASIA

Delorme, J., *Gymnasion: études sur les monuments consacrés à l'éducation en Grèce, des origines à l'Empire romain*, BEFAR 196, Paris: E. de Boccard, 1960.

Dragatsis, Iak. Ch., "Γυμνάσιο", in *Μεγάλη Ελληνική Εγκυκλοπαίδεια* 8, Athens: Pyrsos 1929, p. 763.

Gauthier, Ph., Les cités grecques et leurs bienfaiteurs, *BCH* Suppl. 12, 1985, pp. 7-74.

Habicht, Chr., "Makedonen in Larisa?", *Chriron* 13, 1983, pp. 21- 32.

Krischen, F., "Das hellenistische Gymnasion von Priene", *JdI* 38-9, 1923-24, pp. 133-150.

Migeotte, L., *L'emprunt public dans les cités grecques: recueil des documents et analyse critique*, Collection d'études anciennes, Québec : Editions du Sphinx / Paris: Belles Lettres, 1984.

Robert, L., *Études anatoliennes: recherches sur les inscriptions grecques de l'Asie Mineure*, Études orientales 5, Paris: E. de Boccard, 1937.

Yegül, F., *Baths and Bathing in Classical Antiquity*, Cambridge Mass./London: MIT Press, 1992.